FROM DARK

TO

LIGHT

The Mysteries of The Gospel

in Romans Revealed

by Ray Roberts

THE FUNNY FARM BOOKS

All Bible quotes are from the King James Bible.

Book cover design by: @aimasterdesign on Fiverr

Please feel free to send any comments you have to;
Thefunnyfarmbooks@gmail.com

First addition 2023

DEDICATION

To my Wife for challenging all that I know to be true. She by doing so pushed me into deeper understandings of the truth. Without her this book would have come out looking a lot different in the grammar department (LOL). You are a piece of me and you always will be.

My friend, and brother in spirit, Galvin; thank you for all the years of being there for me, even when I was not there for myself.

To my children, Ameir Roberts and Summer Roberts, along with my Grandchildren Zayne and Melak Roberts. You are who this book was written for. All those years you knew me when I was trying to figure out who God was. Well, this is what I found out.

Also, a special thank you to John and Julie Ringgold. For reading my book before it came out. Plus, Ray and all our extended family, Mary and I love dearly.

To my dad and mom along with my sisters. Thank you for the experience in my youth. That made me the man I am today.

Bill Swannie Swanson my brother from another mother.

CONTENTS

ABOUT THE AUTHOR

If I go into my mind's eye and pull down a book from the shelf, I can remember the day I died. Whether we recognize it or not, we have all died at some point. I am not talking about a fleshly death, but a spiritual one from an early age in my childhood. I can remember questioning things about nature and life. Mostly it was about nature, I loved bugs.

My Mother introduced my sisters and me to a couple of different religions in those early years. First, there was the Catholic religion and then the Jehovah's witness.

Right from the start, I can remember those questions shifting from nature to questions about God. I did not talk with people about the many questions I had. But I had many conversations with myself within that little head of mine.

I spent most of my days outside chasing butterflies and bugs. I would stand still with my arms stretched wide, and butterflies would land on my arms. I would stand there and look at them, how beautiful they were. It seemed like those days would last forever. But they did not; they would end sooner than I could imagine.

One Sunday, we were at the Kingdom Hall of Jehovah's Witnesses. We sat in our seats, and they had a sermon on imperfection. I remember the man preaching that no man is perfect; all are sinners in God's eyes. I remember a soft voice within me telling me that was untrue. That voice said," all God's creations are perfect." I thought within myself for a long time about what that man said. And also, what that voice was saying within me. Later, I talked with my mother about perfection. I asked her if it was possible to be perfect. Because the man at a meeting earlier said it was impossible to be perfect. My Mother told me the man was right, that nothing was perfect in God's eyes. And There it was; I had my answer, my mother confirmed it.

Looking back, I don't blame my mother for the answer she gave me. She was passing on the same deceptions that were passed down to her. I have also come to understand something about that old deceiver Satan. He has worked at his fraud job longer than my mother and I have been around. For the record, he is very good at his job.

All my memories are books on a shelf in my mind. I pull them down and read from them when I need information from my past. But, when I am done reading that particular book, I put it back on the shelf, so I do not get lost in any one story. I can become lost in a story that belongs in the past. That said, I will take you to one of my books from my mind's library and tell you one of the stories from my past.

One afternoon I remember enjoying my favorite pastime, playing with those bugs, the ones I loved so much. I remember seeing some butterflies flying around me. So, as always, I stretched out my arms like an airplane's wings. I still remember it so clearly, and I will never forget that day as long as I live.

I can see this little concrete pond with a little waterfall that we had in the backyard. It made the beautiful sound of running water. It was a lovely California day, the kind they sing about in songs. My eyes were barely open; they are light blue and have always been sensitive to the sunlight. I can still see the butterfly that landed on my arm that day so long ago. It was brown with yellow and black spots at the bottom of the wings. It looked like the butterfly had an eyeball on each wing. I always call them bullseye butterflies because of the little bullseye on the rear bottom part of the wing. I looked at it for what seemed forever; both the bullseyes were the same size. It had very intricate patterns on the wings. The wings were perfectly the same size. The eyes and antennas were the exact same sizes. I looked so hard for that imperfection my mother and preacher said existed in God's Creation. I wonder if any butterfly has ever had a more thorough inspection. But the more I looked, the more I could find no imperfection. I could hear that calm voice from within me telling me it was perfect.

Mostly, people do not remember the day they die. But I do. The following words I would speak that day would send me to my grave and cause my soul to sink into the abyss of my flesh. I spoke. "My mother would never lie to me. The imperfection must be on the inside of the butterfly." At that moment, the butterfly flew off my arm. That calm voice that I heard speaking within me. It stopped talking with me until years later. That was the day I became a dead man walking. The weird part is that butterflies would not land on me until years later. I have missed that more than I realized. Years later, I had a butterfly land on me when I was 50 or so years old. It stayed with me for about an hour. I was out with a friend; he laughed because it was on me for so long. But I knew that butterfly was telling me everything would be alright.

I grew up in a loving household in the early years of my life. I had my dad and mom, along with three sisters.

Vietnam came along and changed all that happiness in our family. As I am sure, it did for many families back then. My dad was never the same when he returned from that terrible war. It never ceases to amaze me what man will do in the name of God and country. My dad and my mom split apart when he returned home. He wanted to have nothing to do with the family. I could not understand why my dad had changed so much at the time. It was not until years later that my spiritual Father explained that my dad had killed many people during that war, and it was hard on his mind, heart, and soul. That is what affected him when he came home. He did not feel he deserved a family after taking the loved ones of so many other families. My dad and I remained estranged for most of our lives. My dad reached out to me through my sisters a couple of months before he passed away. He wanted to tell me he was sorry and that he loved me. He did not need to tell me that. I have kids of my own now, and I cannot see how it is possible for a dad not to love his children. If God had not explained to me what had happened with that war. And if I had not had my son and daughter, which I love with a deep heart. I could not have forgiven my dad, mom, and the Vietnam war and myself for all those years of pain that it caused me. For so long, I blamed that war on my mom and my dad for all the pain and loneliness I felt throughout much of my life. I thank God for giving me the understanding that he gave me.

I had a conversation with my dad a few days before he passed. I told him he lived his life the way he had created it and had nothing to apologize for. Suppose I did not have a Father (God) that gave me understanding about my dad. I don't know what I would have said to him, to be honest. As a child, I did not have all the information about my dad that I have today. All I knew, as a kid, was that it was killing me inside. I have lost both my mom and dad now. They both passed within a few months of each other. I pray they will find peace in their next go-around in life.

When I was a teenager, I became very self-destructive. If it was self-destructive in any way, I was doing it. I wouldn't say I liked school and I did not enjoy life.

My friend Rob was the only thing that kept me going through my early teens. He and his family were my angels sent from God that helped me make it through my younger years and early teens. Rob was my best friend, compadre, and brother. We were like two peas in a pod. Where you see one, you see both of us. And that was the way it was with Rob and me.

Much later in my life, I received a call from my sister. She told me that Rob had taken his own life. I wish I had been there for Rob to talk with him. I wish I could have told him; I knew how he felt. I wish I could have told him what I had found out about life's journey and the "Father". Well, it is time to put that book back on the shelf. I will not find any happiness in reading this part of the book. There are so many pages; I like reading about Rob and me. When looking back on our incredible journey in this life.

I think I was 16 or 17 when the voice of the Spirit came back to me and started talking to me again. I was at the house of a person I knew that was in a motorcycle club. I was just about to take a hit off a joint. That calm voice was back within me telling me; if I took one hit from that joint, I would drop dead where I sat. I did not think much about it at the time; I mean, it was just a voice. Until that moment, I started to put my hand to my mouth. The closer I got to my mouth with that joint, I could feel my soul leaving my body. When I put my arm back down, I could feel my soul entering back into my body. I put my hand up and down two or three more times. I could feel each time, my soul leaving and reentering my body. I will tell you now; I put that joint down. It scared me that much. I understand what my mom meant when she would say to me as a child, "Boy, I am going to put the fear of God in you" God had other plans for me, and he was not messing around.

When I returned home, the voice within would tell me to go to the Mountain. We lived at the foothills of some mountains at the time. So, I would get on my motorcycle and go to the mountains. When I had gotten to the mountains, I would go into these areas called turnouts. I began to pray out loud to God, asking what he wanted me to do. Now the funny thing is small clouds would come and hover over me when I prayed. When I stopped praying, they would float away. If I started praying again, they would return again. It was as if they were listening to me pray. That will always have a place in my heart. While I was up on the Mountain, that voice within would say, go to the Mountain. I went from the city back to the Mountain. From the Mountain to the town again. I can't tell you how many times I went back and forth. At more than one point, I thought I was losing my mind. Most of my friends had already thought I had lost my mind. When I would explain to them what I was going through. It was not until later that I understood what going to the Mountain meant. And yes, I will keep you on the edge of your seat and explain it later in the book.

While riding my motorcycle home one day, I ran out of gas. I was about 15 miles from the house. I was happy only because it was all downhill to my house. If you have ever had a motorcycle run out of gas, you will know it is still a challenging push going downhill. Cell phones did not exist at that period. So, I started pushing the bike home because no one would be coming for me. I went to an intersection at a place called Shannon hills. When I arrived at the corner, that calm voice spoke with me. It told me to push my bike up this steep hill to my right. Now, the way home was all downhill, even though it was long. I decided to listen to the voice and did as it asked. I pushed the bike up three short blocks. Then faintly I heard, go to the right. Going in that direction takes me uphill and opposite my home. But I needed to find out if there was something to this voice. Or if I was going crazy. Half the way up the road on the left, I found my answer.

There was a guy I knew, from where I can't tell you now; I don't remember. He was in his driveway washing his car. He asked me what I had been up to. I told him I was on the way home, and I ran out of gas. So, I was pushing my bike back to the house. He told me to hang on for a second, then went to his garage, got a gas can, and filled up the tank on my bike. I thanked him and God, and after the visit with him, I headed home. I started believing in that voice more than ever. Amazing things have happened to me ever since.

The calm voice within me started talking more and more. The more I listened, the more it would speak. The biggest problem I had at that point was; I did not understand what that voice was saying half the time. God has a language, and I did not understand the interpretation of his language. But for truth, he was going to make sure I did. That calm voice was telling me I needed to leave town. I did not understand why I needed to leave the city I grew up in. But now I know I could never rise as a new spiritual being in that place where I grew up. I knew too many people and had not overcome too many temptations and distractions from my old life. When that calm voice would tell me to leave town, I remember saying; I only have a motorcycle; it offers no protection from the weather. I need a car, so I can have something to sleep in. Now, this would be the next miracle that I remember.

I visited a friend's house, and he worked on his car in the garage. He had a 911 Porsche, white in color. The car's transmission was on the ground because he had just had it rebuilt. I had a Yamaha 500 Enduro; it was a nice bike. We were talking, and my friend said. "I love your bike; would you like to trade it for my car?" He said I would have to put the transmission back into the car. I could not believe it, a 911 Porsche for a bike; I was all in. I returned the transmission to the vehicle, which ran like a champ.

Now that calm voice was back within me saying you have a car it's time to go. At this point, I was a teenager with a 911 Porsche and was not going anywhere. Enter the gas station; I remember going around the corner, hitting some loose gravel, and losing all control of the car. I had a friend with me in the car. I remember looking up and seeing a gas station attendant sitting at his desk. We are heading right at him through a sizeable L-shaped corner glass window. I suppose if it was not for the bricks between the bottom of the glass window and the ground on the building. I don't know if that gas station attendant would be alive today. But I can still see the expression on his face. He looked more afraid than I did. And I was the one getting ready to hit the building. I was not wearing a seat belt, but I remember the feeling of a hand pushing my body back against the seat. I should have gone through the window of that car, but I didn't. They say I exited the car, walked to the other side, and pulled my friend to safety. I cannot tell you if that is true. I don't remember a thing after the gas station attendant. I regained consciousness in a hospital with a doctor sewing my nose back on. FYI they can't use anything to numb the nose cartilage. I felt it all, every time that needle went through the skin on my nose every stitch. The side of my face was caved in, and the doctor had to put it back into place. My jaw was broken, they had to sew it shut. The doctor sewing my nose back on, seemed to enjoy my pain. In the middle of getting my nose sewed back on, that voice was back, and in a calm, soft voice, I told you to leave. Just like the joint, I could tell God was not playing around any longer, and I should have left town.

After being released from the hospital, I went to my mom's house for a few days. The voice was so strong within me, telling me to leave town. I felt an urgent need to go, like sand was running out of an hourglass. And there was not much sand left in the bottle. It was that kind of urgency. But I had all this metal in my mouth from where they wired my broken jaw together. The voice was relentless, telling me to go. I spoke within myself, saying I had to wait until my jaw was better to remove the metal.

Then the voice spoke, telling me my jaw was healed and would be fine and for me to cut the metal out of my mouth, that I would be fine, and then leave town. Without a second thought, that is just what I did. I went to the garage, picked up a pair of wire cutters, and cut that metal out one piece at a time. I was carefully pulling each wire through my teeth and gums. I have not had any problems with my jaw since God is great and wonderful. That was 30 some odd years ago.

I left that town with $5 in my pocket, wearing an orange and white striped Tank top T-shirt and a pair of blue jeans. My hair was down to the middle of my back. So, I used the $5 for a haircut. I was starting a new life one of faith. And after spending that $5 faith is all I had left.

I Suppose If I wrote about all of my experiences and miracles which happened to me while I was living on the road. It would take me another book, but maybe I will someday. But it is essential for whoever reads this book to know a little about me and where my knowledge about God comes from.

You see, I am not a well-educated man by any means. When I read books on spiritualism, I have to read them two to three times before I can understand what the writer is trying to say. I go to the "Father" and he breaks them down for me. What knowledge to keep and what knowledge to lay down. You won't find any big words in this book. And I don't want there to be any, either. I hope that any person on any level can pick this book up and understand the things that God has shown me in his love and mercy, without having to run to a dictionary to look up every third word. I wish to share with you a couple more stories about my travels. To lay a foundation for where my knowledge about God comes from. I hope you find it an exciting read as I have found it an interesting life.

Enter the desert: I left my hometown, family, and friends. I did not know where I was going, and it did not matter. Or what I was going to do when I got there. I was walking alongside the highway. A man stopped and gave me a ride to the outskirts of Las Vegas, Nevada. I did not stop in Las Vegas but my ride did. When I had gotten dropped off, I just kept walking. I did not believe it was a place to be for me and what I was trying to find. So, I found myself walking again away from the glitter of Las Vegas.

A few hours later, I was getting hungry and ready for food and water. I had no money and I was in the middle of nowhere. I prayed to God, who I did not know. But I knew that God knew me. I knew God had a plan for me. Though I did not know what it was. I remember the big miracles as well as the small ones. But to be honest, when you are living on the streets, they are all big. You also seem to appreciate them more when you have nothing. I prayed for food and water and that I might understand him better and know who he was. You might think it was a coincidence, but when I prayed and thanked God, I found an unopened pack of lifesavers, multi-flavored, and a beautiful puddle of water beside the highway. I bent down and drank that water and was thankful for it. I did not care who had seen me drinking from it. I knew God had put them there for me. As I write this in this book, my eyes are tearing up, and I am smiling with joy in my heart, remembering this gift from God. Well, it was getting late, I was tired and cold, and all I had on was that tank top. I had my thumb out, desperately trying to get someone to pick me up. The sun was going down for the day. I did not want to spend the night in the middle of the desert. Nobody was going to pick me up that night. I had a date to meet someone else who lived inside me later that night. And it was not the calm voice that I grew to know. I was going to meet with God's adversary and mine. It had become so dark and so cold, so fast.

I found myself between Las Vegas and Utah in the dark of night. I do not remember any moonlight that night, and I could see nothing except headlights coming and going. Nobody was picking up a guy in the middle of the desert wearing a Tank top T-shirt, and I don't blame them. I would have done the same thing if I was driving. I went about thirty feet off the road, so I would not get run over by a passing car. I lay down and tried to get some sleep. It had been a long day and I was tired. But there would be little sleep that night, and it was cold, I mean bitterly cold. I tried covering myself with sand; it was so cold.

In the middle of the night, I met the other voice that lives in man, The adversary and deceiver (Satan); he was in me. His voice is not calm but rather loud. I always thought he was some guy running around in the world. Whether you know it or not, Satan lives in us, just as God does. He wanders to and fro, up and down in this life. He told me, "There is no God. If a God existed, why would he bring you here to die"? I started to find myself that night, and I started believing in something more than myself. I spoke up and said God called me here; he will not let me die. Satan said, "If there is a God, why does he let you suffer if he exists? Why did no one pick you up when you needed it most? If God was real surely, he could have put it in someone's heart to pick you up. But here you are freezing". All I could think to do was to quote bible verses, things that I had read. Like "now faith is the substance of things hoped for." Then I would pray to my God that I did not know, but that I was looking for, as he surely knew me. The war went on all night, and all night it grew colder. I am surprised I did not lose a tooth that night from shivering.

In the morning, I saw a Highway Patrol officer standing over me. He looked down and said, "are you ok?" "I just called the coroner for you. How are you alive? It got well below freezing last night". He said, "I do not see how you are alive. Did not bother even checking on you before calling him." He was amazed I was alive But, I knew why I was alive. I had found my faith in something higher than myself that night, God my Father. I also found something else in me that night: I have spent years waging war against that old adversary. He is hiding in the shadows of the depths of humanity's souls and whispering in the ears of all people, telling them to do his bidding.

The officer put me in his patrol car and took me to his highway patrol station. On the way, he asked me why I was out in the desert at night. I said, "I am looking for God." When we arrived at the station, he gave me some coffee and asked me to wait because he had to run an errand. I was in no hurry because I did not know where I was going. I was still freezing and wanted more coffee to warm up. You could hear my teeth rattling a block away. I was not looking forward to getting back out into the cold. When that officer returned to the station, he had a jacket and some tuna sandwiches with him, which he gave me. He had gone home to get me some of his things.

Now, I don't care what some people say about the police. They are people just like you and me. Some do God's work some do Satan's. If you want to know anyone, you must look at their deeds. After that, he took me to an onramp, gave me $20, and told me to go to Salt Lake City, Utah that I might find my answers about God there. He never told me to look at any particular religion. I thought he might be talking about the Mormons. I do not remember this officer's name, but if for any reason, he reads this book; thank you, I ask God to bless you for all you did for me. But I know in my heart God has already blessed you for what you did that day.

So, I thought the Mormons had the answers I sought. I went to the Mormon temple and libraries to study the religion. I found some truth in what the Mormons had to offer. However, the voice inside me was saying there was something more.

I began living at the park and in shelters in Salt Lake City. There was a church that came by on either Saturdays or Sundays to feed the homeless people, which was a blessing. A church building also allowed homeless people to come in and watch tv during the day. I happened to be there one day, not watching the tv, but praying to God, asking if he would allow me to understand who he was. It was a place that was inside out of the elements. Now this place always had a lot of people because it was out of the weather. I remember the day he (my brother) walked in. He looked right at me, with all the people in that place. He walked right up to me and sat next to me. He was a black man, his face glowed, and he had an afro. His eyes peered into the depth of my soul. He said with a voice as if he already knew. "Are you the one looking for God? who has questions that need to be answered? God told me to talk with you and give them to you; come with me." He spoke with the voice of power and conviction.

The first thing he said when we had gotten outside was, "do you believe it is possible to be perfect?" I said, "I don't know". He opened up the Bible to:

Matthew 5:48

48 Be ye therefore perfect, even as your Father which is in heaven is perfect.

He began to explain to me a new law, a spiritual law, born of Spirit, not flesh. I told him God would ask me to go to the Mountain when he talks with me. "What Mountain is he talking about?" Here is the answer to the question I kept you in suspense about. He told me that the Mountain God wanted me to go to was within me, a spiritual mountain.

That is when I started to understand the language of God. Now, off and on, I have spent years with my brother living together in the streets, in apartments, or hotel rooms. In the years to come, I met more brothers. Some knew they were my brother, and some did not know yet. But I know, and I wait for God to wake them up while I watch over them and keep that old serpent at bay.

The fleshly man does not know God's language; only those in Spirit can understand it. I started climbing that spiritual Mountain that day so long ago. I have been climbing that Mountain ever since. It has heights, depths, and many valleys. But I will never stop climbing that, Mountain. I have always been satisfied with the journey.

I know our world and learned early on that I preferred to avoid hitchhiking. Don't get me wrong; I found many good people on the road. But there are many more which are ungodly. I found trains to be an excellent means of transportation. The libraries show you all the tracks and where they are going. I spent a few years riding around studying in different libraries all over this country of ours.

Ultimately, I wound up in Las Vegas, NV., after all that distance of travel. I came up out of the streets there. I became a painter, painting foreman, Superintendent, and Coordinator for the Union painting apprenticeship. I've had a 19-year failed marriage, a son and daughter, and two grandchildren; worth all of it. I hope my children and grandchildren will one day read this book. Learn from it and know the All of All things. That which they are part of and are. Today, I live in Oklahoma, on 40 acres the "Father" gave me with my loving wife Mary, of 14 years. After all that, I can say God is good; God is good.

This book's information is what I have learned over years of seeking and knocking on God's door, sometimes pounding, sometimes scratching, and sometimes crying at that door. I hope you find something in this book that you can cling to in your time of need. God is real, and he is inside you. You are inside him, and you are one. With much love and peace.

INTRODUCTION

The book of Romans is by far one of the most essential books of the bible. Paul's writing to the gentiles, is a letter to every soul, dead in sin, living in the flesh today. Most of the world's population is dead in sin and is in a Gentile state of mind. But all can become true Jews (of the heart). The ones calling themselves Jews today are not faithful Jews. But they are of the synagogue of Satan.

Revelation 2:9

9 I know thy works, and tribulation, and poverty, (but thou art rich) and I know the blasphemy of them which say they are Jews, and are not, but are the synagogue of Satan.

Revelation 3:9

9 Behold, I will make them of the synagogue of Satan, which say they are Jews, and are not, but do lie; behold, I will make them to come and worship before thy feet, and to know that I have loved thee.

Those that call themselves Jews today live by and after the flesh. God has nothing to do with those that live after the flesh.

Galatians 5:17

17 For the flesh lusteth against the Spirit, and the Spirit against the flesh: and these are contrary the one to the other: so that ye cannot do the things that ye would.

Those living in the flesh, war against their true self, which are spiritual beings. It is easier to understand the battle if you can tell the difference between flesh, soul, and Spirit.

Romans 2:29

29 But he is a Jew, which is one inwardly; and circumcision is that of the heart, in the Spirit, and not in the letter; whose praise is not of

men, but of God.

A person that, is spiritual in nature, is a faithful and true Jew. That can be anyone that has gone through the process of being reborn in and of Spirit. That soul is resurrected from the death of sin. Anyone living in sin and under the law of the fleshly man is a Gentile. And the book of Romans was written for you. The book of Romans is a blueprint and a book of instructions on how to put off the Gentile man of the flesh and put on the spirit man of God. It is a book that shows you the distance you need to travel between the two.

John 3:3

3 Jesus answered and said unto him, verily, verily I say unto thee, except a man be born again, he cannot see the kingdom of God.

This birth Jesus was talking about is that of the soul in the flesh, which is dead in sin. It must be born as well as resurrected into a spiritually quickened being. Into a spiritual being; as Christ was in Jesus.

John 3:4

4 Nicodemus saith unto him, how can a man be born when he is old? Can he enter the second time into his mother's womb and be born?

People that live after the flesh have always only seen the limitations of fleshly man. They do not see the soul (seed) that dwells within them. It is understandable when you see that it is just as hard for a shell to understand the nut that lives within it. The shell cannot realize the nut's potential to grow into a tree. And the vast DNA seeds hold. And that is mankind's same dilemma, the fleshly man trying to understand the soul that dwells within them. But I have learned all things are possible through God.

Isaiah 61:9

9 And their seed shall be known among the Gentiles, and their offspring among the people: all that see them shall acknowledge them, that they are the seed which the Lord hath blessed.

The soul is the seed that holds the DNA of a spiritual being which has the potential to quicken into a god. This is what God is talking about in this verse.

John 3:5

5 Jesus answered, verily, verily, I say unto thee, except a man be born of water and of the Spirit, he cannot enter into the kingdom of God.

Christ has that living water, his words are that water. They show you how to put off the old man of the flesh and put on the new man of the Spirit. By awakening the soul (seed) that dwells within you. This enables you to enter the Spirit and God's true kingdom. This allows you to manifest eternal life within yourself. Right here and now on earth while you live, not after you die.

You see, there is a war in the world today with governments, school systems, businesses, and our everyday life in general. Most of the population does not even know that we are at war. It is an old war that has been going on since the days of Adam and Eve. It is a challenging war to see with the eyes. Because it can only be seen in the deeds of the people. That war I am talking about is a Spiritual war. It is fought in the flesh of men, with Spiritually wicked souls with very high understanding on how this world works.

Ephesians 6:12

12 For we wrestle not against flesh and blood, but against principalities, against powers, against the rulers of the darkness of this world, against spiritual wickedness in high places.

Yes, this war is happening now. And has been happening for a very long time.

We have been lied to about our history on many more levels than can be counted. So much, so if I told you what I knew and believed to be true; you might think I had lost my mind. As Paul was supposed to have lost his mind in his day.

Acts 26:24

24 And as he thus spake for himself, Festus said with a loud voice, Paul, thou art beside thyself; much learning doth make thee mad.

While people are going about their ordinary lives. Trying to make money to feed their families and pay for their houses, cars, and video games. Everyone is being programmed to be slaves and serfs to this system without even knowing it. A system designed to keep you distracted. Distractions keep you from knowing who you indeed are. Because if you found out who and what you were, the system would collapse. So, this system of theirs was designed to keep you numb and dumb.

A good example would be a friend who worked for a large banking firm. He had his mortgage for his house with the same bank he worked for. His car loan was with the same bank. His checking and savings accounts were with the same bank. His retirement was with that same bank. His life had become nothing but that bank. So, he went to work like he was always programmed to do. He received his paycheck from the bank like all good serfs do, then he would turn around and cut a check back to his handler, the bank. All for a few necessities that he needed to be able to go to work for that bank. He needed his car; otherwise, he would not be able to get to his job to work for the beast. But we are all told cars are a luxury and not a necessity. So, they make you feel good about this arrangement. By allowing you to pick the car, the make, and color. Sometimes, you might even think you have gotten a good deal on this car from the beast. Truly that never happens because the game is rigged. They know everything about you, exactly how much you make and can afford, based on the credit score they assign to you. That score shows just how reliable of a serf you are to the system. Make no mistake, they will squeeze you for every penny they can. They know how much you can afford and will keep you in their choke hold. They know the more debt you owe to the system the more you put stock in that 3-number score. The more controlled and well-behaved of a serf you are to the system. All of this is for the honor of driving that new car of debt every day to a place to work for them. They must keep the serfs happy; otherwise, they might wake up to their game. My friend also needed a house to live in. So, he could get ready to work, sleep, and rest from his labors. But that house is something he will never pay off. They give you that allusion that you can pay your home off after working for 30 years. But if you miss paying your taxes, they will take it back. And sell it to the next serf waiting in line. Even now, they have passed new laws to make that so-called house and property of yours harder to leave to your children. You must pay taxes to the beast to be born, live, and die in this world. It is essential so you can fund the beast and demon's lifestyles.

My friend worked for this bank for nineteen years, receiving numerous awards for service. He was to be given the golden carrot at the twenty-year mark. He was to receive a guaranteed package of benefits that could not be taken away if he ever did lose his job. They dangled that carrot in front of him for 19-plus years. But right when he was ready to get to that twenty-year mark. He was no longer the great employee he once was. So, they came up with a charge and fired him. It was never more than a carrot on a string. My friend had seen the same thing happen to many others in the belly of the beast. While he was working for that company. Even if my friend had reached the end of the road after working his fingers to the bone and paying off his house. The demons can and do change the rules of the rigged game at their pleasure. They raise your taxes at any time they want to. Where people can no longer afford them after retirement. Then houses are taken away after working all those years in a rigged system. The beast will let you work right up to the point of retirement. But that is unlikely to happen for most. You see that carrot they dangle gets further and further away from you. Just like my friend, they can fire you for any reason they want at any time. They devise very clever ways to get the serfs to do their bidding.

A perfect example of that would be the Right to Work Law. The corporations went from State to State, pushing this tool of the beast into law. Making it look like the people were the ones pushing for the bill. And the masses went along with it and passed it into law. After all, everyone believes they have the right to work. This is what they were saying in all the commercials. Telling everyone, "You have the right to work; vote for the right to work law". It was a very clever and deceitful campaign. It was not about the right to work at all. It was about the right to fire you at will for any reason. The corporations, the beast, pulled a fast one on the people, and they fell for it, hook, line, and sinker. They also gave the allusion to people that their votes counted for something. It's always nice when you control the machines and counters. It is no different from people using a computerized slot machine. Whoever is writing the program is the winner, not you.

The beast has also put judges and laws into place to protect themselves from the evil they do to the masses. This beast knows everything about your life and every detail of my friend's life. Because all are serfs in their system. Just like they never planned on paying my friend all those benefits. And why would they when they could hire a younger and more naive college grad to replace him or you and save all that money for the corpses in the corps. Thanks to the right-to-work law that they put into place. All thanks to the deception of the beast. But make no mistake, the demons will always have balloon packages guaranteed never to go away. You know, the ones where if they lose their jobs, they make millions. It is a rigged system, and everyone is afraid to say anything because they do not want to lose what little they have. Almost all are serfs in the land of demons. And no one in the land of flesh cares about you and me and our problems. And no man on this earth and of the flesh is coming to save you. Expecting a man of sin to fix your problems. It is like seeing through a drinking glass full of oil.

The Government, courts, and schools have become a playground for demons. I am not saying everyone in these lines of work is a demon. But you must remember a third of the host of heaven was sent to earth with Satan. They are spiritual beings living in the flesh, as you are. The difference is the demons have been awake this whole time. While all of God's children have been sleeping in sin. Have you never wondered what happened to the demons? We are talking about 1 out of 3 hosts of heaven who were sent to earth to rule. Did you think it was over, that they went somewhere else? They are still around as they have always been around. They are the elite ones that are at the very top of power. The ones that decide what curriculum to teach our children at schools. Or the ones that make the unrighteous laws you and I must follow. These are the same laws that they do not have to adhere to themselves. While raking in millions and billions of our dollars to fund their own lifestyles.

The ones that sit in the judge's seats and let killers out of jails to run wild in the streets etc. While they live in guarded communities. These are the demons playing in Satan's playground. The problem is you cannot see them. Just as people could not see Christ alive in Jesus. The only way you can tell one from another is in their manifest deeds. Also, become awakened souls as they are, but in light. It is the same problem today as they had back then. People are too busy looking and working in the flesh to be able to see the Spirit within them.

John 14:11

11 Believe me that I am in the "Father," and the "Father" in me: or

else believe me for the very works' sake.

The works are the deeds the "Father" did through Christ that were done through Jesus. The "Father" in Christ is that perfect knowledge, wisdom, and understanding at conception. Christ is that perfect knowledge, wisdom, and understanding at expression through Jesus.

Matthew 7:16

16 Ye shall know them by their fruits. Do men gather grapes of thorns or figs of thistles?

Fruits are the deeds of the people

Matthew 7:17

17 Even so, every good tree bringeth forth good fruit; but a corrupt tree bringeth forth evil fruit.

A righteous person does good deeds (good fruit). A unrighteous person does terrible deeds (evil fruit).

Matthew 7:18

18 A good tree cannot bring forth evil fruit, neither can a corrupt tree bring forth good fruit.

An actual righteous person will not do evil deeds. A terrible person will not do any righteous deeds.

Matthew 7:19

19 Every tree that bringeth not forth good fruit is hewn down and cast into the fire.

Any person that does not do righteous deeds is cast into the fire. The realm of the torment of the mind, the constant and never-ending Tree of Good and Evil. Never seeing the realm of Spirit, but only living in the realm of chaos, matter, and flesh.

Matthew 7:20

20 Wherefore by their fruits ye shall know them.

The fruit is the deeds of mankind, but it is so much deeper than that. Because in doing so, it is the deeds of the souls of men. Whereby we know those of Satan and we know them of God. There are a lot that serve Satan and are unaware that they are doing so. But the deeds of people tell the whole story of that individual. It is the ones that portray themselves as sheep on the outside that you have to worry about. But in the Spirit, they are ravening wolves, seeking to devour you.

Matthew 7:15

7 Beware of false prophets, which come to you in sheep's clothing, but inwardly they are ravening wolves.

They are everywhere and can be so lovely to you. But inside, they want to take all you have, even your soul. They want your soul while it is asleep or dead in sin. Because when it wakes up, it is too late to control it. Notice that movie stars and musicians always say they sold their souls. They never say, I sold my Spirit to Devil; a spirit is an awakened soul. By selling their soul, it awakens in spiritual wickedness. And they do their fathers bidding, for the riches while in the flesh. But if they truly knew what they were doing, I don't know if they would.

Matthew 10:28

28 And fear not them which kill the body, but are not able to kill the soul: but rather fear him which is able to destroy both soul and body in hell.

The words of God are not written in vain. You can dance to the piper, but you have to pay him sooner or later.

Matthew 7:21

21 Not everyone that saith unto me, Lord, Lord, shall enter into the

kingdom of heaven; but he that doeth the will of my "Father" which is in heaven.

You must do the commandments to enter into the kingdom of heaven. There are no 'ifs' 'ands' or 'buts' about it. Christ did not do away with the commandments. Christ just made them easier to understand.

Matthew 5:28

28 But I say unto you, that whosoever looketh on a woman to lust after her that committed adultery with her already in his heart.

In the eyes and mind is where sin starts for all. Desire begins in the eyes, then the heart. And desire needs to be brought under control with reason. But the question is, where did Christ say it was ok to continue in sin?

Matthew 7:22

22 Many will say to me in that day, Lord, Lord, have we not prophesied in thy name? and in thy name have cast out devils? And in thy name done many wonderful works?

These are the ones living in sin and teaching other men it is ok to be sinners and live in sin. Telling you it is impossible to do the will of God. The ones that say do your best and God will forgive you. Even though Christ commanded you to do the law. They preach what Satan sat up a long time ago in churches. God has nothing to do with any of them. Because they have nothing to do with the true Spirit of God and the law. Which is the actual life of the soul that dwells in man.

Matthew 7:23

23 And then will I profess unto them, I never knew you: depart from me, ye that work iniquity.

Those that are dead in sin never please God or Christ. For those that sin, Christ will say to them, "I never knew you". Just like it stated above for all to see. It could also say, "depart from me, ye that sin".

According to **<u>Bing's word search</u>**, the meaning of the word iniquity is:

"<u>Iniquity</u>"

"Immoral or grossly unfair behavior".

In other words, a man of sin.

Revelation 3:16

16 So then because thou art lukewarm, and neither cold nor hot, I will spue thee out of my mouth.

There is no middle ground with God. There is living in the flesh or living in the Spirit. And we need to know what the difference is between the two of them.

That said, Satan and his demons started a long time ago. It started out slow, with the husband needing to go to work to provide a decent living for his family. Then we needed the most precious gift to the family, the wife and Mother of our children. The Mother taught our children to respect us as parents. And to love God and put God into their lives. She needed to go to work to help make ends meet for the family. As well as the new toys they dangled in front of us. They taught her to be independent of their husband and God. Now we had a problem, the children needed to be watched. Not to worry, Satan had plans for them in daycares and schools. While both parents were at work. Satan had plenty of time to corrupt their little minds. He would teach them his beliefs and doctrine. Satan was the one now raising our children with his values. He had corrupted children's minds in the entire world in one or two generations.

To get away with this plan, Satan and his Demons must pit the husband against the wife. And the wife against the husband. Women against men and men against women. The parents are against the children. And the children against the parents. One race against another race, you get the point, etc. Come on now, it is not like Satan got away with it, did he? It has always been one distraction after another distraction. The plan had and has worked perfectly for the beast. That is because he has been doing this for a long time. It is always something; today, it is pronouns, boys being girls and girls being boys. The people do not understand that Baal, their God is a Transgender god. Boys playing on girls' teams pretending to be girls. All this is just offerings to the god they worship. Anything and everything to distract you from one thing, who and what you indeed are. A seed that is a soul with the potential to become a god. A god in the image of your "Father", a creator creating a creation in love. It was all predicted; there is nothing new here. Why do you think our children want to be far from wisdom? Because this is what they have been taught to do by demons in the school system. Now, are all teachers' demons? Of course, not. They are only teaching a curriculum written by demons. Most not even knowing what is truly happening. But some know in their heart of hearts that something is very wrong today. But most are afraid of losing their jobs. So, they go along with Satan, knowingly or unknowingly.

Because all true hope and faith in God have been lost. It is the same with doctors and hospitals today. Administering whatever drugs, they are told to dole out at Med. School. They get so many kickbacks for pushing certain drugs. Not too often do they truly help cure anyone of anything. They treat the symptoms and relieve the pain. But to go in and come out healed, we would need Christ back in our world for that. Or to manifest Christ within ourselves as Jesus did. Doctors, in general, keep people drugged up on so many pills. That we have a numb and dumb population.

My Mother, for example, when she was alive. Had two shoeboxes of pills she took. She did not know what half of them were for, but she took them. I cannot believe that any doctor would know all the interactions that were possible with all those pills taken together. My Mother was a zombie half the time. She had a hard time concentrating when talking to her. But she did what the Doctors told her to do and took them all. I find it hard to believe my mother had a pill to wake her up in the morning. And another medication to help her sleep at night. It is like senior citizens competing to take the most pills and who has the bigger problem with themselves. But that is all part of the program that all go through. Doctors will make a follow-up appointment with you before you leave their office. Even if you don't need one. They have to pay for that lifestyle that they are accustomed to. What little savings you have left at the end of the day. They do not want you to give to your children or grandchildren. God, forbid you enjoy your money yourself by living life. If you were able to leave all your money to your relatives. They may not need to become serfs, and they can't have that. Then what would they do to keep the children distracted from the truth?

But it is always the same for the people. We have been through so many resets in our civilization. Even the bible tells us this if people would believe in what they read. But don't take my word for it. Listen to the Preacher, the son of David, king in Jerusalem, the wisest man to ever live.

Ecclesiastes 1:9

9 The thing that hath been, it is that which shall be, and that which is done is that which shall be done: and there is no new thing under the sun.

All that is here has already been in this world. Do a search for helicopters and submarines on the Egyptian pyramids. You will find hieroglyph drawings of them on the pyramids. And yes, even you have been here many times. I am talking about the true you, a seed (soul) in human flesh.

The war we are in is old, and most souls are sleeping right through the war. That is to say, they are dead in sin while living in mortal bodies. This is the same war Paul was talking about in Ephesians 6:12 earlier. This is the actual war that we are in today.

The people in high positions in control of governments and schools, for the most, part are wicked people. Not just wicked but spiritually wicked, living in the bodies of mortal people.

It is hard to believe that many people could be of this world, not God. But nonetheless, you may be one of these people yourself, unaware that you are. Doing what you feel is right when in actuality, it is all wrong. You see, there are three kinds of people in life. People of Spiritual righteousness, those that are asleep or dead in sin, and those that are spiritually wicked. All three are living in the flesh of humans. Or, as God called it in Genesis, "Coats of Skin" There is no in-between or lukewarm as it is called.

Revelation 3:17

17 Because thou sayest, I am rich, and increased with goods, and have need of nothing; and knowest not that thou art wretched, and

miserable, and poor, and blind and naked.

People may have riches in this world and an abundance of worldly things. This does not mean they are happy in this life. They may be miserable, knowingly or unknowingly. If a person does not have God and his knowledge, wisdom, and understanding. They are naked or dead in sin, and in this life, they have nothing. Most of humanity does not understand that they have been blinded to the truth about God on purpose. Many people know that they are unhappy and miserable with this life. They do not like how the governments control things and keep them poor in this life while telling them that they are free. You are not free in this world; you are serfs to this world. And that's just how the beast likes it to be. The problem is that they also keep you poor in Spirit by design. They know if you wake up in the Spirit, it is over for them. To be naked is to be living in sin before God. God sees all things and knows just how naked everyone is. But God is patient and loving to us all.

God is Spirit, Spirit at a compelling energy, with very high vibration and frequency dancing to a perfect rhythm. God and God's children have a language all their own. Just as the children of darkness have their own language. The children of light can understand both languages. While the children of darkness cannot. They have scales on their eyes to keep them from seeing the truth. They have wax in their ears, so they cannot hear the truth. Even if they were to read God's words in plain print, they could not understand them. And even if they did understand God's Word. They could not manifest the truth, because it must be done in perfection, love, truth, and Spirit.

Isaiah 44:18

18 They have not known nor understood: for he hath shut their eyes, that they cannot see; and their hearts, that they cannot understand.

Romans 11:8

8 (According as it is written, God hath given them the Spirit of slumber, eyes that they should not see, and ears that they should not hear;) unto this day.

And even unto this day as well; nothing new under the sun to see here.

1 Corinthians 15:23

23 But every man in his own order: Christ the first fruits; afterward they that are Christ's at his coming.

Every person comes in their own order when waking up in the Spirit. No one can speed it up or slow it down. God's will, has been done in the past, as it is done now, and as it will always be done in the future.

My prayer is that God might use this book to help those waking up now. I have seen many starting to wake up in the last few years. But I see some of them being led back into this world with its distractions. Also, people put their trust in men to solve the problems of this world. We are not of this world; Satan is the god of this world. Our God is the God of Spirit, which we are. God called me over 30 years ago. And has been waking me up ever since. It is the "Father" that I thank for all things. The information in this book will be a comfort in your awakening process. And help with the language of the "Father", the All in All of the All. He that hath ears to hear, let him hear what the Spirit has to say.

Revelations 3:18

18 I counsel thee to buy of me gold tried in the fire, that thou mayest be rich; and white raiment, that thou mayest be clothed, and that the shame of thy nakedness does not appear; and anoint thine eyes with eye salve, that thou mayest see.

The gold tried in the fire is you changing from a carnally minded person to a spiritually minded person. Through the changing of our thoughts and deeds. When our old ways of sin (our nakedness) are taken away. We put on clean raiment (spirit-the sins are covered) and become holy before God. The nakedness we cover is the sins we have committed throughout our lives. To anoint thine eyes with eye salve, that thou may see. It is to pray to the "Father" within you, ask for forgiveness, and for God to lead you. That he may overcome the fleshly man (carnal) for you.

You are either of God and his world of Spirit. Or Satan and his world of flesh. You cannot serve both heaven and earth. I will cover how all this works a little later in the book.

Matthew 6:24

24 No man can serve two masters: for either he will hate the one, and love the other; or else he will hold to the one, and despise the other. Ye cannot serve God and mammon.

This is simply saying that you cannot simultaneously serve the fleshly man and spiritual man. Now, what do we do? It would seem we cannot live in this world and do that.

1 Corinthians 5:9-10

9 I wrote unto you in an epistle not to company with fornicators

10 Yet not altogether with the fornicators of this world, or with the covetous, or extortioners, or with idolaters; for then must ye needs go out of the world.

We are being told not to keep company with the wicked. But since there are so many wicked. We would have to leave earth all together. And I have felt this way more than once over the years. It is hard in this day in age while we work in this world. To separate yourself from the world, I know. But I have learned all things are possible through <u>**faith**</u> in God.

2 Corinthians 6:14

14 Be ye not unequally yoked together with unbelievers: for what fellowship hath righteousness with unrighteousness? And what communion hath light with darkness?

This is pointing out if you are a child of light. Why would you want to keep company with children of darkness? Someone that wants to keep you down in a low state of vibration. Someone wishing to entrap you in the first place, they know what they are doing and how to play the game. They have been doing it for a long time now. It could be cutting you off in traffic with their car. If you get out of tune and upset, they win, and you lose. You have to always stay in love, which is problematic. Until you learn the perfect law, how to truly love, and why you should.

2 Corinthians 6:15

15 And what concord hath Christ with Belial? Or what part hath he that believeth with an infidel?

People of the flesh are of their father, Satan. Children of light are of their "Father", God (Spirit). Light and darkness cannot exist in the same room. If your room within you is dim, how great is that dimness?

2 Corinthians 6:16

16 And what agreement hath the temple of God with idols? For ye are the temple of the living God; as God hath said, I will dwell in them, and walk in them; and I will be their God, and they shall be my people.

You as a spiritual being are the temple of the living God. Why would you set up idols in your mind (false beliefs)? Come out of the world, and God will dwell in you, and walk in you, the key word being in. God will walk in his people. Then and only then will he be your God and you a member of his body. Remember, there is only one body, as well as one Spirit, with many members

2 Corinthians 6:17

17 Wherefore come out from among them, and be ye separate, saith the Lord, and touch not the unclean thing; and I will receive you.

So, God will raise us above that worldly state of conscious. And put on the body of God, or the spiritual man. That is when we come out of this world, and God receives us.

2 Corinthians 6:18

18 And will be a "Father" unto you, and ye shall be my sons and daughters, saith the Lord Almighty.

All mankind has been here before, whether they know it, remember it, or believe it, to be so or not. I shall show this a little later. We come back over and over because we, as dead souls living in humans, have not followed the commandments of God. We have all sinned and our souls have died in those sins. That does not mean you must let your soul stay dead in sin. There is a way out of this life that I call hell. You must be resurrected from the tombs of the fleshly bodies and minds. We must be reborn into the Spirit. And it is pretty simple if you want to call it simple. Here we go; this is all we have to do.

Matthew 5:48

48 Be ye therefore perfect, even as your Father which is in heaven is perfect.

Ok, it may not be as simple as I lead on. But have no fear; this book will be all about this.

Paul, in the book of Romans, shows us how to put off the old man of the flesh and put on the new man of Spirit. And that shall enable us to fulfill the first and second commandments.

Matthew 22:37

37 Jesus said unto him, thou shalt love the Lord thy God with all they heart, and with all thy soul, and with all thy mind.

Jesus did not say to love God with 10, 20, 50, or 90% of who we are but, 100% of our heart, soul, and mind. Notice he did not say the flesh of man. The flesh in its lowest vibration cannot now nor never will please God. It must be raised to a higher vibration of light. Where it can also be redeemed, as Christ did with Jesus, and also as Elijah had done. When it is raised to a higher vibration of Spirit it is no longer lower vibrations of flesh. But it becomes a little lower than the angels, or a being of light. Thereby being able to enter into heaven.

Romans 8:8

8 So, then they that are in the flesh cannot please God.

If you are trying to please God with the man you see in the mirror every morning. It is never going to happen because that is not who you are. That person that you see in the mirror is of the lower vibration.

When a cat looks into a mirror, it tries to attack the reflection that it sees. Because that cat knows that the image it sees is not himself. That cat sees the illusion of it all.

Matthew 22:38

38 This is the first and great commandment.

This is not the first and great suggestion, but the first and great commandment. A commandment is a rule to be observed.

Matthew 22:39

39 And the second is like unto it, thou shalt love thy neighbor as thyself.

Now, this is a very hard commandment to keep in this life. Most people do not know how to love themselves or their neighbors. The only way to love yourself or anyone else is to first love God. God gives you knowledge, wisdom, and understanding of all things. Enabling you to properly love all things with a clear eye. Of what is right or wrong or who is a friend (lost) or a foe (awakened spiritual wicked ones).

Matthew 22:40

40 On these two commandments hang all the law and the prophets.

Now on these two suggestions, I am sorry, I mean commandments. Hang all the laws that are in existence. God the All, has built into the construct a perfect law. And this law runs on auto-pilot. It exists in the background doing its job. And it is essential to truly understand this law. And most people do not see it, or they do not believe it to be true. But this law is as fundamental as the words on this paper. It is called the Law of Cause and Effect, and no one, good or evil, escapes it. Christ, Buda, and all the wise men of old told us about it. No person ever needs to judge another person in this life. Once they understand that this law is accurate and does exist.

Galatians 6:7

7 Be not deceived; God is not mocked: for whatsoever a man soweth, that shall he also reap.

It has always been there for all to see. Plant the seeds of love. Receive a harvest of love from the perfect law. Plant hatred in the construct of your mind. And receive a big old basket of hate coming your way. Fear for fear, hope for hope, and so on.

The reason everything that has ever happened to you in your life. It is not because of God or his judgment or other people judging you. It is because of you, and I know it is hard to hear. But it is you, through your lack of faith, doubts, fears, unbelief, or whatever it was, that Satan fooled you into believing at the time.

But you can't blame Satan for all your woes in life. To do that would be to say you had, or have, no power over him, which is invalid. We are children of light lost in a world of children of darkness. We are of our "Father" as they are of their father. But have no fear; there is a way out of this darkness. There is a light that has been overlooked, and we will dive into this light.

PAUL THE MINI-CHRIST

I have read many books. And seen videos talking about Paul's works in the bible being a forgery. Well, I am going to be writing about how that is impossible. As well as show how, the bible could never be possible without Paul and his writings. There would never be any hope for humanity if it were not for Paul's writings in the book of Romans. He explained to the Gentiles how to put off the old man or sinful man of the flesh. And the putting on the new man of the Spirit. I believe Satan has messed with many Bible books in one form or another. But Paul is what I like to call a mini–Christ. Many believe that God would not allow the bible to be tampered with in any way.

But as you can see below, there was a warning to those who would do just that, which means it was a concern back then. It also shows that it was possible to happen if there was a penalty for it. But God has hidden his message for those of a Spiritual mind to see in plain sight.

Revelation 22:19

19 And if any man shall take away from the words of the book of this prophecy, God shall take away his part out of the book of life, and out of the holy city, and from the things which are written in this book.

One thing all should know about the Apostles is they did not start as Apostles. They started just as you and I did, not knowing much about God. They were Disciples of Christ far before they were Apostles. Some might think it is the same, but it is untrue. And it is essential to know the difference when reading the bible. A disciple is someone new to the faith and uneducated in the mysteries of God and his language. An Apostle is a teacher of Christ in their own right. Also, able to explain all the mysteries of God and the body of Christ. They could go out independently, heal the sick, and raise the dead. To raise the dead is to take someone from a Gentile (carnal) state of mind into a Jewish (Spiritual) state. They could also feed the poor (those without knowledge, wisdom, and understanding). In addition, they were working all the miracles of God.

In the beginning, the Disciples did not understand or comprehend who Christ was. All they could see, touch, or feel was the man they called Jesus. They could not see Christ, the Son of God. Christ is Spirit and is not visible except in deeds. It is crucial to understand the difference between Christ (higher vibration) and Jesus (lower vibration). The reason for this is that many people are anti-Christ and do not realize that they are. Christ is the blessed Son of God, the Spirit that came forth from God. Jesus is a man of the flesh and is God's creation in this world. The fleshly man, made from Atoms, is for the Sons of God (Spirit) to manifest themselves within to express Spirit in the matter world.

When you put the Fleshly man before the Spiritual man, you are putting the creation of God before the Creator. For example: When someone is praying, they say, "...through Jesus Christ, Amen". They unknowingly put God's creation before Christ, the Son of God. They unknowingly worship a false idol, becoming an anti-creator and pro-creation. When this happens, people fall into a trap by the god of this world. And have become pro-flesh (lower vibration) and anti-Christ (Spirit or higher vibration). God was plain when he said put no other gods before me.

Exodus 20:3

3 Thou shalt have no other gods before me.

Notice the small 'g'; it will be important later. Also, note that there were not any other gods. They were not to be put before the "Father".

Exodus 20:4

4 Thou shalt not make unto thee any graven image or any likeness of anything that is in heaven above, or that is in the earth beneath, or that is in the water under the earth.

A picture has been made of Jesus today that is all over the world. Yet it says not to have a likeness of anything in heaven. This Jesus image is of a man with long, flowing blondish hair and blue eyes.

Romans 1:23

23 And changed the glory of the uncorruptible God into an image

made like to corruptible man, and to birds, and four-footed beasts, and creeping things.

The human being is, at best, a reflection of the Spirit man. It is a creation of God for the lower vibration earth. God is Spirit and is at the highest vibration of heaven, which we cannot imagine in our mortal minds. A car is to a human being what the human body is to a soul or Spirit man—so, putting the fleshly man before the Spirit man is like putting the car before the man that designed it. Man can enter into corruption while in the flesh. God is not in any way able to be corrupted in Spirit.

So, when someone prays in the name of Jesus Christ, that person is putting the creation before the "Father". That is putting the fleshly person in front of God. Those doing so enter the category of worshiping a false idol, an image of God. Because they are praying through a man of flesh to get to the "Father" of Spirit. This is how Christ taught people how to pray.

Matthew 6:9-13

9 After this manner, therefore, pray ye: Our "Father" which art in heaven, hallowed be thy name.

10 Thy kingdom come, thy will be done in earth, as it is in heaven.

11 Give us this day our daily bread.

12 And forgive us our debts, as we forgive our debtors.

13 And lead us not into temptation, but deliver us from evil: For thine is the kingdom, and the power, and the glory, forever. Amen

Where is the name Jesus or Christ in this prayer? But you must pray in the name, and everyone knows that. Yes, in the name (Word) or living within the law. Living it, not saying it, pray in the Word of God by living the Word every day of your life.

John 14:13

13 And whatsoever ye shall ask in my name, that will I do, that the

"Father" may be glorified in the Son.

Christ's name is the Word of God, and to ask in his name means manifesting and living in the Word of God. Notice the word in my name and not through my name.

Romans 1:24-25

24 Wherefore God also gave them up to uncleanness through the lusts of their own hearts, to dishonour their own bodies and themselves.

25 Who changed the truth of God into a lie, and worshipped and served the creature more than the Creator, who is blessed forever. Amen.

When you worship a god of the flesh, you are not of God. God is Spirit and must be worshiped by the Spirit that dwells within the flesh. When you put flesh before Spirit, you become lost in a world of imagination and false beliefs. You have changed the truth about God, the Almighty being pure and perfect, into a fleshly man that can enter into sin. And still, men worship Jesus and put him before the Creator today. And all other means of idols of brass or other men of the flesh. And do not give all glory to the beloved "Father" of Christ the Son (Sun-Bright one of God), which came forth from the Almighty God.

Romans 8:8

8 So, then they that are in the flesh cannot please God.

Christ said, "That there would be those greater than himself". He never put himself above anyone. What is said to us also applies to Jesus. The flesh cannot please God, no matter who's flesh it is. As long as it is vibrating in the realm of matter. It must be raised into a light being or it will return to the dust in which it came.

Romans 2:11

11 For there is no respect of persons with God.

God has no respect for persons, no matter who that person is.

Christ never said to worship him. What he did tell the people was the only way to the "Father" was through and in the son. And that is a true statement from Christ. But that is also misinterpreted by people. Because of the deceptions of Satan.

Revelation 19:13

13 And he was clothed with a vesture dipped in blood: and his name is called The Word of God.

Christ is the Word of God, and the only way to the "Father" is in the Son (the Word). So, to get to the "Father", you must understand who the "Word" is. Once you know who the Word is. You will realize that he laid down a new set of laws to follow. Christ never spoke his own words while on earth. But what the "Father" gave him to tell the people is what Christ said.

John 12:49

49 For I have not spoken of myself: but the "Father" which sent me, he gave me a commandment, what I should say, and what I should speak.

Christ and God are one with each other. As the words that we speak are one with our bodies and minds. Christ is the voice for the mind of the Almighty. My understanding from the "Father" is that "Christ" is perfect knowledge, wisdom, and understanding <u>at expression</u>. And that The Almighty is perfect knowledge, wisdom, and understanding <u>at conception</u>". Christ is truly the Word of God proceeding forth from the body of God.

John 12:50

50 And I know that his commandment is life everlasting: whatsoever I speak therefore, even as the "Father" said unto me, so I speak.

As the Mind (God) thinks, the Word (Christ) speaks. Christ came to show the souls on earth the New Kingdom and the Tree of Life. He talked to the people about God's new commandments. Because the old commandments were done away with in Christ (The Word), he was moving away from the fleshly deeds of humankind. To the new ideas of the mind, the inside of the cup. Notice he gave us God's new commandments and not new suggestions. So, to do away with the old commandments, you must keep the new Commandments. Or you must manifest the new commandments (Word of God). That is the only way to confess Christ's name. To confess the Word of God is to manifest the new law.

Christ has appointed some as teachers (apostles) to show us how to put off this old way of thinking. And put on a new man of Spirit altogether. That new man is what we are; that new man is a Spirit being. It is not the old being of the fleshly man. This is the true resurrection from the dead. The soul raises from the grave of your flesh while raising the vibration of the flesh. Satan has deceived the religions into thinking it is after death. After people die, it is too late to be resurrected. Right now, who knows anyone that is not already dead in sin? This is the death you are resurrected from.

Ephesians 3

3 For this cause I, Paul, the prisoner of Jesus Christ, for you Gentiles.

Paul was given the Apostleship over the Gentiles. Even though Paul made himself a servant to them in deeds. Now, a Gentile is a man of the fleshly body and mind. A person that minds the things of this world that satisfy the needs of the flesh instead of the Spirit. He is not a Spiritual man or one of Spiritual understanding. He does not look after the needs of the Spiritual body. Paul's job was to take the carnally minded people, raise them to understand God (Spirit), and then turn them over to Peter. Peter was over the Jews, the ones with Spiritual knowledge about God and Spiritual things.

Galatians 2:8

8 For he that wrought effectually in Peter to the apostleship of the circumcision, the same was mighty in me toward the Gentiles.

Peter was over the circumcised, which was the Jews at the time. They had some understanding of the Spirit but may have yet to see how to put Spirit into action in the flesh, even if they did not understand the Spirit 100%. And that was Peter's job to know that they did.

So, that is going to take us to the book of Romans. I will be going over the whole book. By Chapter and verse with what I see as the spiritual explanations to follow. But we will cover the old man of the flesh and the new man of Spirit. To me, the book of Romans is one of the most important books of the bible. When Satan's minions worked at the conclave, they should have left the book of Romans out of the bible. This book shows how to fulfill the commandments of God. And the blueprint on how to become who we are; Spirit.

Now I warn you; I am reviewing the entire book of Romans. It may be slow from time to time in the intro and ending of the book of Romans. And Paul has a way of repeating himself sometimes, as I do. But I am sure it will also be a ride you may always remember. In any case, you will never look at the bible the same way again.

Come with me as we explore the mysteries of the book of Romans. And see how we can put off that old man of sin. And put on the new man of Spirit, and become the temple of the living God.

1 Corinthians 3:16-18

16 Know ye not that ye are the temple of God, and that the Spirit of God dwelleth in you?

17 If any man defile the temple of God, him shall God destroy; for the temple of God is holy, which temple ye are.

18 Let no man deceive himself. If any man among you seemeth to be wise in this world, let him become a fool, that he may be wise.

ROMANS 1

1 Paul, a servant of Jesus Christ, called to be an apostle, separated unto the gospel of God.

2 Which he had promised afore by his prophets in the holy scriptures.

3 Concerning his Son Jesus Christ our Lord, which was made of the seed of David according to the flesh.

Notice here where Paul explains that Jesus was made of the seed of David according to the fleshly man. Christ is the true Son of God. The flesh is not the Son of God, nor can it be. God is a Spiritual being, and so are you. And we saw earlier that the flesh cannot please God in its lower vibration of matter.

Romans 1:4

4 And declared to be the Son of God with power, according to the Spirit of holiness, by the resurrection from the dead.

Christ is the Son of God according to Spirit and power. Jesus is the Son of Mary according to the flesh.

Romans 1:5-6

5 By whom we have received grace and apostleship, for obedience to the faith among all nations, for his name.

6 Among whom are ye also called of Jesus Christ.

Satan has been alive and well, ruling this earth with his demons since the beginning of existence. There has been much monkey business with the Bible, especially during Constantine and the conclave with the Roman Catholic Church. King James did not help the matter with Sir Francis Bacon either. God is the Creator of all life; the creation (the flesh) should never be worshiped and put above the "Father" (Spirit). When you put Jesus in front of Christ you are making the creation more important than the Creator of all things. Sometimes the Bible uses the name of Jesus first to explain it is the fleshly man doing the work with the inner man. For a better explanation, we can look to Romans 1:25 below.

Romans 1:25

25 Who changed the truth of God into a lie and worshipped and served the creature more than the Creator, who is blessed forever. Amen.

The flesh is the coat of skin created for the Spirit man to dwell in and express himself. The body is more like a cocoon or a shell of a seed that contains the soul. The soul is looking for God to resurrect it within the flesh, and the flesh is not an object to be worshiped by man. It would be like making the shell of a nut more critical than the seed that held the DNA of life in it. The outside (body) does not give life. It is God that gives life to the source (soul). The shell (body) returns to the earth from which it came when the soul has experienced all that life has had to offer. In rare cases as with Jesus and Elijah. They were able to transform the lower vibration of fleshly matter into beings of light. We will talk about this more later in the book.

Romans 1:7-8

7 To all that be in Rome, beloved of God, called to be saints: Grace to you and peace from God our Father and the Lord Jesus Christ.

8 First, I thank my God through Jesus Christ for you all, that your faith is spoken of throughout the whole world.

Here again, is the mighty work of Constantine and the conclave. To have all people worship the fleshly man Jesus and not the beloved “Father" of Spirit.

Matthew 4:10

10 Then saith Jesus unto him, get thee hence, Satan: for it is written, thou shalt worship the Lord thy God, and him only shalt thou serve.

Even the fleshly man Jesus knew that only the "Father" was to be worshiped. The fleshly man Jesus and the Spiritual man Christ never wanted to be worshiped. Christ was trying to raise people into Spiritual understanding that they may be the same as he was, alive in the flesh.

Matthew 12:50

50 For whosoever shall do the will of my "Father" which is in heaven, the same is my brother, and sister, and Mother.

Whoever was to do the will of God. Whether you were a man or woman, you are not a servant to worship Jesus or Christ. But as Christ said, we are brothers, sisters, and mothers. Would you ever ask your brother, sister, or Mother to worship you? The only way to this understanding is through God's words (The Word). Not by saying the name of Jesus in prayer. As Paul says in Romans 2:13, "It is not the hearers of the law that are just before God, but the doers of the law shall be justified." We do not make it to heaven by saying we believe in Jesus. We make it to heaven by manifesting Christ (the Word) within us. By the Words that he spoke that give us those instructions to live.

Romans 1:9

9 For God is my witness, whom I serve with my Spirit in the gospel of his Son, that without ceasing, I make mention of you always in my prayers.

Paul is serving as a Spirit, not the man of the flesh. Paul says here that he serves in the Gospel of Christ. Meaning he is living in Christ (The Word of God).

Romans 1:10-11

10 Making request, if by any means now at length, I might have a prosperous journey by the will of God to come unto you.

11 For I long to see you, that I may impart unto you some spiritual gift, to the end ye may be established.

Paul is looking to impart some gifts of the Spirit to illuminate others souls in the lower vibration. Not to benefit the flesh, which cannot please God. He wanted them established in Spirit, the body of God—the one body with many members.

Romans 1:12

12 That is, that I may be comforted together with you by the mutual faith both of you and me.

Faith is the first foundation of the Word we must manifest within ourselves.

Romans 1:13-14

13 Now I would not have you ignorant, brethren, that often times I purposed to come unto you, (but was let hitherto,) that I might have some fruit among you also, even as among the Gentiles.

14 I am debtor both to the Greeks and to the Barbarians; both to the wise and to the unwise.

Notice Paul is saying that the Greeks, Barbarians, and all others were people as pertaining to the flesh. living after the man of sin or being dead in sin. That state of being not yet alive or quickened in Spirit. Paul was looking to have fruit or awaken some in the Spirit.

Romans 1:15-16

15 So, as much as in me is, I am ready to preach the gospel to you that are at Rome also.

16 For I am not ashamed of the gospel of Christ: for it is the power of God unto salvation to everyone that believeth; to the Jew first, and also to the Greek.

Christ, the Word of God, is the only way to salvation. To everyone that believes the gospel and the gospel was God's Word (Christ) speaking to the people. But who has considered his words? Look what Christ said in Matthew.

Matthew 5:48

48 Be ye therefore perfect, even as your Father which is in heaven is

perfect.

He has also said, "sin not". People have been repeatedly told in churches that no one can be perfect and that everyone sins, which is how it is today. So, who do we believe in, the churches or Christ? Either Christ got it wrong, or the churches. And if it was Christ that got it wrong. Then he was not perfect, and all religion is in vain. As Paul would say, I speak as a man. I know Christ was right, and all the world and churches got it wrong. John was bold in 1 John.

1 John 3:8

8 He that committeth sin is of the Devil; for the Devil sinneth from the beginning. For this purpose, the Son of God was manifested that he might destroy the works of the Devil.

The works of the Devil are sin. And if you are a sinner, you are not of God, but the Devil, according to this verse. Christ came here to destroy sin in the souls of men. Also, the Jews of today are not the Jews that call themselves Jews. Jews are Spiritual, inward people, not of the flesh. Anyone can be a Jew or gentile. It depends on where you are in your Spiritual unfoldment. A gentile is a man of the world outwardly. A Jew is a Spiritual man, one that is inward. That is why the Son of God or the Word was manifested in the flesh to destroy sin.

Revelation 3:9

9 Behold, I will make them of the synagogue of Satan, which say they are Jews, and are not, but do lie; behold, I will make them to come and worship before thy feet, and to know that I have loved thee.

Romans 2:29

But he is a Jew, which is one inwardly; and circumcision is that of the heart, in the Spirit, and not in the letter; whose praise is not of men, but of God.

These are the Jewish person(s) that Paul is talking about in this verse. Those that are to the letter of the law are Gentiles. Those that worship God in Spirit are Jews. The Jews of today are circumcised in their hearts, not by the circumcision of the flesh as they do today. It means to put off the heart of the fleshly man and the things he speaks and does. And put on the heart of the Spirit, and do the works of God.

Romans 1:17

17 For therein is the righteousness of God revealed from faith to faith: as it is written, the just shall live by faith.

There is nothing more important than faith. It is the cornerstone of the New Jerusalem. It is the first foundation we must build on. See my book: ***"Atom and Eve's walk in the garden",*** for more information on the foundations.

Romans 1:18

18 For the wrath of God is revealed from heaven against all ungodliness and unrighteousness of men, who hold the truth in unrighteousness.

Churches today teach that you cannot be perfect or be without sin. They teach the truth in unrighteousness when God's Word tells you to do righteousness. And still, others are telling you not to try, and there is nothing you can do. What do you think God thinks about those who teach sin as ok? They preach from up on high that it is ok for you to sin day after day and receive repentance on Sundays. Then head to Monday through Saturday and rinse, repeat, and do the same sins over again. All you need to do is read the words. The wrath of God is on "all ungodliness and unrighteousness of men". There are no exceptions that I have read here. These are the ones that hold the truth in unrighteousness.

Matthew 23:9

9 And call no man your father upon the earth: for one is your "Father," which is in heaven.

How often are men on earth called fathers? We teach our children to call us fathers. In the churches, men of sin are called fathers. Are the words written in this book in vain? Is Satan alive and at work in the world? Has he been at work while we were unaware? Are you starting to see him yet? You will need to answer these questions for yourself. As for me, I know the depths of Satan. God has shown me the dark corners that Satan dwells within.

Romans 1:19-20

19 Because that which may be known of God is manifest in them; for God hath shewed it unto them.

20 For the invisible things of him from the creation of the world are clearly seen, being understood by the things that are made, even his eternal power and Godhead; so that they are without excuse.

Notice where it says, "for the invisible things being understood by the things made". We, as souls living in the flesh, can understand the Godhead. There is no more excuse for anyone. I cannot say well; this is what the preacher told me. You must have your relationship with God. No one else can stand for you in your place.

Romans 1:21-23

21 Because that, when they knew God, they glorified him not as God, neither were thankful; but became vain in their imaginations, and their foolish heart was darkened.

22 Professing themselves to be wise, they became fools.

23 And changed the glory of the uncorruptible God into an image made like to corruptible man, and to birds, and four-footed beasts, and creeping things.

God, the All in All, must be the only one we ever worship. Not even the beloved Christ wanted to be worshiped as men do today. Notice verse 23, "changing the Glory of God into the image of a corruptible man". Jesus was a man of the flesh. Christ was a man of Spirit—a member of the All in All's body. But even today, God the All in All, his glory has been changed into the image of a man of flesh, Jesus. Even Jesus said the same in Luke.

Luke 4:8

8 And Jesus answered and said unto him, get thee behind me, Satan: for it is written, thou shalt worship the Lord thy God, and him only shalt thou serve.

Notice the words chosen in Luke: 8:39

Luke 8:39

39 Return to thine own house and shew how great things God hath done unto thee. And he went his way and published throughout the whole city how great things Jesus had done unto him.

Man has always had the most challenging time seeing Spirit. Notice Christ is telling the man to tell the people what great things God had done for him. But that man was even like the men are today. They want to worship what they can see, touch, smell, or taste. The man went out and said Jesus had healed him. Jesus did not tell this man anything of the sort. Just like today, Christ is saying to worship God. And people still worship the man of flesh, Jesus. In Jesus's name, we pray, they say. Or, in the name of Jesus Christ, people pray. They put the creation in front of the Creator, not knowing that Satan has turned them into anti-Christ. While they believe they serve God.

1 John 2:18

18 Little children, it is the last time: and as ye have heard that antichrist shall come, even now are there many antichrists; whereby we know that it is the last time.

I pray that All will wake up from this deception. And know that there is only one God, one Spirit, and one body even though there be many gods that make up the members that make up that one God and one Spirit. All can see that the All is All and the All is in All. As the ***Kybalion*** states

"While All is in THE ALL, it is equally true that THE ALL is in ALL. To him, that truly understands this truth hath come great knowledge".

Romans 1:24-25

24 Wherefore God also gave them up to uncleanness through the lusts of their own hearts, to dishonour their own bodies between themselves:

25 Who changed the truth of God into a lie and worshipped and served the creature more than the Creator, who is blessed forever. Amen.

The law is perfect, and the first Commandment is perfect. And Christ himself gave it to us. Love God with all your hearts, minds, and soul. All means 100%, not 10%, for God and 90% for Jesus. Not even 90% for God and 10% for Jesus. This first Commandment is one of the many truths about God that has been turned into a lie and upside down. The creature is being worshiped instead of the Creator. The All in All the I Am That I Am. That every knee will bow to before it is over, Amen.

Romans 1:26

26 For this cause God gave them up unto vile affections: for even their women did change the natural use into that which is against nature.

Look at the state the nation is in today, with all the gender equality. And how many of the Synagogue of Satan go along with the agenda? There is no lukewarm with God. You are either in the body of God (Spirit). Or you are in the body of the ruler of this world.

Revelation 3:16

16 So then because thou art lukewarm, and neither cold nor hot, I will spue thee out of my mouth.

There is no middle ground. You are either in the Spirit or the flesh.

Matthew 6:24

24 No man can serve two masters: for either he will hate the one and

love the other, or else he will hold to the one and despise the other. Ye cannot serve God and mammon.

You cannot serve both Spirit and flesh. It is like trying to mix oil and water, they do not mix.

Romans 1:27

27 And likewise also the men, leaving the natural use of the woman, burned in their lust one toward another; men with men working that which is unseemly, and receiving in themselves that recompense of their error which was meet.

The seed from man's productive organ feeds the brain through the spinal track. This fluid is the spinal fluid that covers the brain. That is what the man gives up to other men. It is what enables God to open the pineal gland. This fluid allows us to enter into Spiritual states of consciousness and become one with the "Father". As men and women are one flesh in the lower realm. Each helping the other to overcome this world. All men and women can be one with the Spirit ("Father") in all things.

Romans 1:28

28 And even as they did not like to retain God in their knowledge, God gave them over to a reprobate mind to do those things which are not convenient.

The reprobate mind is where most of humanity is today. The mind looks after the fleshly world or anything other than God as long as the brain is running on empty (Dry) and not having the proper fluid around the brain that provides the ability to fire on all cylinders. You cannot enter into a Spiritual state of mind. I should not say you cannot because all things are possible with God. But it is like running a car with no oil; it will run for a while, then seize up and no longer work. Plenty of fluid around the brain could do better if you understand how to handle the pressure when the fluid builds up within your body. We must use the liquid on the brain for Spiritual thoughts and purposes to release the tension correctly. It comes with much stress that must be dealt with and used in love and mercy. The power is not to be used on a physical kind of love but a

Spiritual love that we express to others. It does no good having a 1000-horsepower motor. If it blows up every time you turn it on. In rage in the form of mental masturbation as a friend of mine once said. Mental pressure must be dealt with in love.

Romans 1:29-30

29 Being filled with all unrighteousness, fornication, wickedness, covetousness, maliciousness; full of envy, murder, debate, deceit, malignity; whisperers.

30 Backbiters, haters of God, despiteful, proud boasters, inventors of evil things, disobedient to parents.

Is this different from where we are in society today? We are here today because of humankind's love of the fruit from the Tree of Good and Evil. Humanity justifies the evil that they do. Saying that their wrong is better than what others do or have done. That is not how it works. Wrong is wrong no matter what degree of wickedness it is in your actions or mind. Your consciousness knows all and judges all things within you. You can lie to the world and not get caught. But you cannot escape the conscience and the perfect law.

Romans 1:31

31 Without understanding, covenant-breakers, without natural affection, implacable, unmerciful.

This about sums up our world today. Does this sound different from our government and schools today as well? Where is the mercy for the people? Implacable according to **Oxford Languages** Implacable definition is.

"**Implacable**" *definition:*

relentless; unstoppable.

Yes, this sums up what we have going on today.

Romans 1:32

32 Who knowing the judgement of God that they which commit such things are worthy of death, not only do the same but have pleasure in them that do them.

How many houses of worship allow filth to be tolerated in the churches today? As if God has changed his laws somehow over the years. Maybe God did not know what he was doing at the beginning of creation. Perhaps he got it wrong and changed his mind. God forbid, God has not changed, rather the people's tolerance for sin has changed.

Matthew 15:3

3 But he answered and said unto them, why do ye also transgress the commandment of God by your tradition?

How many religions today have their traditions based on paganism, and they don't even know it? Preachers learn a curriculum to preach, which other men wrote. Please stay in the box and don't deviate from it. Let us look at Easter and the pagan bunny. You might say, "come on, it is not that big of a deal". How about the pagan god Eostre or Freya, the god of fertility? Where religion acquires the art of dying of the Easter eggs. They used to sacrifice children, then cut them open. Then they would dip eggs in the blood of the children. To offer to the god Freya. Or how about good old lovable Santa Claus with his Viking beginnings with the pagan god Odin? All you have to do is rearrange the word Santa and get Satan. They did not even try that hard to hide what they truly worship. Let's not even talk about Halloween and its origin. Who has questioned their religious origins? Most will tell you this was my mom's or dad's religion. Most traditions in religion come from the Roman Catholic Church and the Conclave. Where Constantine felt it necessary to mix Pagan beliefs with Christian beliefs. To get all the Pagan Romans on board with the new religion. As a Christian, you went along with it, or the Romans killed you. Those were the only two choices you had at that time. That's when many of these traditions became accepted by almost all religions. Most religions have been structured on the Roman Catholic beliefs and Bible, and the Romans put them together at the conclave. Along with all Roman beliefs, traditions, and lies about their pagan gods. The pagans loved worshipping men of the flesh as gods.

Matthew 15:4

4 For God commanded, saying, Honour thy father and mother: and, he that curseth father or mother, let him die the death.

Remember, Christ, said to call no man your father because God is our "Father". The "Father" we were to honor was God. The Mother is those who care for the Church or body of God.

Matthew 23:9

9 And call no man your father upon the earth: for one is your Father, which is in heaven.

The bible is for Spirit and Spiritual enlightenment. It is not to illuminate the flesh and the fleshly man.

Matthew 15:5-6

5 But ye say, whosoever shall say to his father or his mother, it is a gift, by whatsoever thou mightiest be profited by me.

6 And honour, not his father or his mother, he shall be free. Thus, have ye made the commandment of God of none effect by your tradition

But if you sin against God the "Father" and give a gift to the Church and repent, then all your sins are forgiven with that donation; thereby the Church can profit from your sin and make a mockery of God and his laws. Why do so many not believe in God today? Could it be that the Churches and all their preachers tell people to be good, while they get caught up in some of the biggest scandals? Thereby making a mockery of God's name.

Matthew 15:7-9

7 Ye hypocrites, well did Esaias prophesy of you, saying,

8 This people draweth nigh unto me with their mouth and honoureth me with their lips, but their heart is far from me.

9 But in vain they do worship me, teaching for doctrines the commandments of men.

God is in their mouths, and their words sound so good to the ears of the masses. As they stand and say, glory be to the fleshly man Jesus. As the Father and Christ of Spirit are far from their hearts. And how many souls are in the pit of their trap? It will do no good to say to God, “I was only preaching what I was taught to teach by other men”. All must have their own relationship with God. He is a "Father" to all of us.

1 John 2:27

27 But the anointing which ye have received of him abideth in you, and ye need not that any man teach you: but as the same anointing teacheth you of all things, and is truth, and is no lie, and even as it hath taught you, ye shall abide in him.

God is in you; God abides in you. God is not far away but closer than you think. And you alone and no one else can have a relationship with him.

Acts 17:27-28

27 That they should seek the Lord, if haply they might feel after him, and find him, though he be not far from every one of us.

28 For in him we live, and move, and have our being; as certain also of your own poets have said, for we are also his offspring.

For in God, we live in one body. We have our movement in God. And God is where we have our being. There is only one body, one Spirit with many members. God is that space between every particle. God is that space outside every atom. And God is that space between you and me. And in that space, we have our movement. We have an Energy, frequency, vibration, and rhythm all our own in God the "Father." In the "Father", we are one. All is in All, and All is All.

ROMANS 2

1 Therefore thou art inexcusable, O man, whosoever thou art that judgest: for wherein thou judgest another, thou condemnest thyself; for thou that judgest doest the same things.

No one in this life needs to judge anyone at any time. When you come to understand the perfect law of God. The perfect Law of Cause and Effect runs on autopilot without anyone intervening. It works for righteous people as well as unrighteous people. What you plant, you shall reap.

Romans 2:2

2 But we are sure that the judgement of God is according to truth against them which commit such things.

Paul knows the perfect law is always in action. Paul knows it runs on autopilot without any help needed. Paul knows that with what measure you dish it out; that dish will return to you just as full as you sent it out. You cannot leave the dinner table until you have eaten the last drop of your harvest/karma. That is why Satan works in deceptions and not outright lies. He uses the law while breaking the law because lesser causes form lesser effects. After all, it is not his fault if you read something into what he is saying. Let us take a look at what Paul's has to say for a minute in Galatians.

Galatians 6:7

6 Be not deceived; God is not mocked: for whatsoever a man soweth, that shall he also reap.

We should always be careful when we throw out rash words or emotions to someone. Whatever one person does to another person, that person is also doing to themself. If the world is running in chaos, it is because chaos has been pumped into the world by the people. By loving one another, we can do away with some of the confusion in the world.

Romans 2:3

3 And thinkest thou this, O man, that judgest them which do such things, and doest the same, that thou shalt escape the judgement of God?

It is just like it states at the: Glenn research center

Newton's Third Law: Action & Reaction

"... for every action (force) in nature, there is an equal and opposite reaction. If object A exerts a force on object B, object B also exerts an equal and opposite force on object A".

In other words, forces result from interactions. Or, as I like to call it, the perfect Law of Cause and Effect.

Romans 2:4-5

4 Or despises thou the riches of his goodness and forbearance and longsuffering; not knowing that the goodness of God leadeth thee to repentance?

5 But after thy hardness and impenitent heart treasurest up unto thyself wrath against the day of wrath and revelation of the righteous judgement of God.

Paul is not holding anything back, is he? Let's just come to an understanding of it. It is better to love and receive love. Then it is to hate and receive hate.

Romans 2:6

6 Who will render to every man according to his deeds.

Deeds, that is what it is all about for us while we are on earth. We must ask ourselves the question; which fruit are we eating? From what tree is our fruit (deeds) coming? The Tree of Good and Evil or The Tree of Life. You can find more information in my book about the two Trees; **"Atom and Eve's walk in the garden".** It is helpful to understand the two trees and the deeds of both trees.

Romans 2:7

7 To them who by patient continuance in well doing seek for glory and honour and immortality, eternal life.

Here we go, beloved Paul mixing a little salt with the pepper. Here we start to make a turning point from death to life.

Romans 2:8

8 But unto them that are contentious, and do not obey the truth, but obey unrighteousness, indignation, and wrath.

Here you can find the penalty for not living in the perfect law of God. The hell that the people of this earth live in today. By living in the understanding of the fleshly carnal man instead of the understanding of the Spirit man.

Romans 2:9

9 Tribulation and anguish, upon every soul of man that doeth evil, of the Jew first, and also of the Gentile.

First, notice upon every soul and not flesh. Why does it come to the Jew first? Because the Jew is a Spiritual person with an understanding of the law. That person knows better than to do what they had done. The Gentiles are lost in this world and do not know who they are. Therefore, they need to understand what they have done.

Romans 2:10

10 But glory, honor, and peace to every man that worketh good, to the Jew first, and to the Gentile.

Those who do God's will, receive God's reward, before the unlearned or wicked person because they follow the perfect law of God. God is just in all things. The Jews working on a Spiritual level for example. Feeding the soul with food. The Gentiles working on the fleshly or lower vibration for example. Taking care of the needs of the flesh by feeding people with food for the flesh.

Romans 2:11

11 For there is no respect of persons with God.

Whether it be Jesus, Buda, Muhammad, or you and me. We are all that we do in the soul and not as much as what we do in the flesh.

Romans 2:12

12 For as many as have sinned without law shall also perish without law: and as many as have sinned in the law shall be judged by the law.

The world is without the spiritual law of God. It is a world of chaos and wickedness. People die every day at random. Because they allow themselves to be governed by the lower laws of cause and effect. Instead of moving into the upper realm of holiness. Whereby they become one with the law. For most of mankind the Almighty God is not their God. That might be a hard pill to swallow, but it is true.

Mark 12:27

27 He is not the God of the dead, but the God of the living: ye, therefore, do greatly err.

If you are in the Spirit, God is your God and "Father". If you live by the world and its laws. You are dead by sin, as well as being dead in sin. In any case, you are dead because of sin, and God is not the God of the dead but living. No matter how much someone might think that he is their God they are mistaken. God can know of you. But if you are not worshiping God in Spirit. Satan is the god of those that live in the flesh and are dead in sin. And just as people do not know, they have a God that is their "Father". They do not know that Satan is their father and god here and now. Welcome to the world of deception by Satan. He is good at what he does, isn't he?

Luke 9:60

60 Jesus said unto him, Let the dead bury the dead: but go thou and

preach the kingdom of God.

Jesus was talking about those dead in sin having an unawaken soul burying those who died in the flesh. Christ was saying follow me; I have the Words of life.

Matthew 22:32

32 I am the God of Abraham, and the God of Isaac, and the God of Jacob. God is not the God of the dead but of the living.

The only way to be alive is to be resurrected or reborn as a Spiritual being in the flesh. And that is what we are talking about now, how we can be reborn or resurrected as a Spirit in the flesh. Abraham, Isaac, and Jacob had all overcome the flesh.

Romans 2:13

13 For not the hearers of the law are just before God, but the doers of the law shall be justified.

The world is full of hearers of the law. I can show you a million every Sunday morning. But the law's doers are fewer in-between in today's world. The sad part is a lot of people think they are doers. And it is easy to believe that when you judge what you do by the world's standards.

Romans 2:14-15

14 For when the Gentiles, which have not the law, do by nature the things contained in the law, these, having not the law, are a law unto themselves.

15 Which shew the work of the law written in their hearts, their conscience also bearing witness, and their thoughts the mean while accusing or else excusing one another.

Some people of the flesh who do not understand God's law have good hearts. They try hard to please God in the things they do. God is merciful and judges them by their hearts. Because they have yet to learn the law, they could sin and not know that they had sinned. God would never see it because he would not look at the sin. God is judging you by looking at your heart and consciousness. And your heart and conscience are right with God, even if your flesh is not. You do not understand that you were sinning. But God will find a way to bring it to your mind to show you so that you can have God make a change in your habit. That is the Spirit of truth that dwells within you. That little voice that says you shouldn't do that.

For instance, when Paul consented to the death of the disciples. Paul believed in his heart he was doing the right thing. But when Christ (The Word) came to Paul within him. He showed Paul what he was doing was wrong, then Paul made the change. If Paul had not changed when learning the truth. It would have been another story altogether.

Romans 2:16

16 In the day when God shall judge the secrets of men by Jesus Christ according to my gospel.

That day is now. The Word of Christ, the Spirit of truth, and the comforter live inside you. And it knows all your dirty little secrets if you have any. And we are judged according to the gospel or Word of God. We all undergo an internal judgment and rebirth from the old fleshly carnal man to a quickened Spiritual man.

Romans 2:17-20

17 Behold, thou art called a Jew, and restest in the law, and makest thy boast of God.

18 And knowest his will, and approves the things that are more excellent, being instructed out of the law.

19 And art confident that thou thyself art a guide of the blind, a light of them which are in darkness.

20 An instructor of the foolish, a teacher of babes, which hast the form of knowledge and of the truth in the law.

These verses have put the fear of God in me for years. They have kept me from expressing the truth about God, fearing I might lead someone astray and down the wrong path. I have been shown much mercy from God and Christ over the years. After all these years, I only feel comfortable and confident in my writing. And that is the God I know and Love. More importantly, the God that knows and loves me. But here, Paul is talking about today's religious instructors, telling people on Sunday not to sin. When preachers themselves do the same sins that all others do, these kinds of religions are built upon faulty foundations that say you cannot be perfect—all the while judging you for the sin you do. It is an oxymoron if you think about it.

Romans 2:21

21 Thou therefore which teachest another, teachest thou, not thyself? Thou that preaches a man should not steal, dost thou steal?

All people should wait on teaching until they obtain Spiritual enlightenment from God, and have established a relationship with him. Then and only then does he tell you what he has in mind. Sometimes the Word speaks in you and is a part of you. And it is fantastic when this happens. When this happens, you learn as the other person learns as you talk with them. While you listen to the Word spoken through you. It is hard to explain, but it is beautiful to experience. How can a person help someone if they need help overcoming a thing?

Romans 2:22

22 Thou that sayest a man should not commit adultery, dost thou commit adultery? Thou that abhorrest idols, dost thou, commit sacrilege?

I can't tell you the times some preacher on TV or some bishop has been caught with their pants down around their ankles, making a mockery of God. Christ is our bridegroom in the body of the Spirit. We are spiritual beings and must present ourselves to Christ as pure souls entering the one body of Spirit. So, if we are married to this world and the things of the flesh. We are committing adultery. Our soul cannot join to who it is supposed to be with, Christ (the Word). You are committing blasphemy by turning the Temple of God, which you are, into a vessel of sin by living in the fleshly man and his desires for this world.

2 Corinthians 11:2

2 For I am jealous over you with godly jealousy: for I have espoused you to one husband, that I may present you as a chaste virgin to Christ.

Suppose you are breaking one facet of the law. How can you teach something that has not been overcome within you yet? Can you teach someone how to rebuild a motor if you have never opened a car's hood to see an engine?

Romans 2:23-24

23 Thou that makest thy boast of the law, through breaking the law dishonourest thou, God?

24 For the name of God is blasphemed among the Gentiles through you, as it is written.

How many people have bad taste in their mouths and hearts, when you bring up God in a conversation? How many eyes roll back up in the head when you bring up God? How many people say they believe in God but refuse to have anything to do with a church because of the actions of the preachers or members? Is the church of today about God or money? How many so-called preachers of today have made a mockery of God? And these same preachers turn out to be disciples of Satan. Standing on a pulpit preaching what they believed to be the word of God. Then they become caught up in the scandal of the day. These same preachers then say the same thing, "I am sorry; I am only a man after the flesh and a sinner". They say, "I am only human, after all". Well, they are right about one thing; they are human. They are of the flesh. And if you are not in the Spirit, you should not preach the Word of God. I do not get out of balance too often nowadays. But making a mockery of God's name has made me take a deep breath on more than one occasion. I try to understand that some are lost souls in the deception of it all.

Romans 2:25

25 For circumcision verily profiteth, if thou keep the law: but if thou be a breaker of the law, thy circumcision is made uncircumcision.

Suppose you have a good heart and keep the laws of God. It will be a profit unto your soul if you have a good heart and keep the commandments of God. Having only a good heart will not get you into the kingdom of heaven. There are a lot of people that are kind to other people. And are still sinful and do so regularly.

Romans 2:26

26 Therefore, if the uncircumcision keeps the righteousness of the law, shall not his uncircumcision be counted for circumcision?

Suppose you have a heart that is not loving in nature towards others. But you are righteous in all your doings with others. Shall not your uncircumcised heart be counted as the circumcised heart?

Romans 2:27-28

27 And shall not uncircumcision which is by nature, if it fulfils the law, judge thee, who by the letter and circumcision dost transgress the law?

28 For he is not a Jew, which is one outwardly; neither is that circumcision, which is outward in the flesh.

Back in the old days, the church people lived by their families' traditions, much like today's people. Paul plainly says what he is trying to say in verse 28. The only way to be called a Jew is to be Spiritual or be an inward person. You can be white, black, red, brown, Irish, Greek, Indian, or an alien from space. It does not matter if you have cut off the tip of your penis. If you are Spiritual, you are a Jew. If you are Gentile, you are of the flesh or carnal man.

Romans 2:29-30

29 But he is a Jew, which is one inwardly; and circumcision is that of

the heart, in the Spirit, and

30 not in the letter: whose praise is not of men, but of God.

The only reason they started doing circumcision of the flesh. Was because the people in that time period of history learned by doing, not hearing. I am the same way in life. You can talk and explain something to me a hundred times. I will not get it; ask my wife. But let me do it one time, and I will understand it. God had Moses and Abraham show circumcision of the body. To try and have the people understand circumcision of the heart—something they would need to do in lifetimes to come.

Hebrews 3:8

8 Harden, not your hearts, as in the provocation, in the day of temptation in the wilderness.

Now is the time for us to cut off the foreskin of our hearts. How many times have I seen people harden their hearts? When I talk about God in any other way than people have been taught, as I have done myself in the past. Again, you could ask my wife about that as well. But she will also tell you no matter how I feel about something that I have heard. That night I will take it straight to the altar of God. To get the low down on whatever the subject was. God has the final say in what will become a part of me. And she will tell you when I am wrong on a matter, I will lay that false belief down and not pick it up again. Even though it can be tough at times to lay a thing down. I dislike pride, it is hard telling my wife she has been right on multiple occasions. Sometimes I think God has put us together so she can teach me humility. And only she can tell you if that is working. Again, God has a beautiful sense of humor. And I thank him for his humor and my wife.

Hebrews 3:9-10

9 When your fathers tempted me, proved me and saw my works forty years.

10 Wherefore I was grieved with that generation, and said, they do always err in their heart, and they have not known my ways.

Notice the grieving was in the heart. In the heart lies all the feelings of the soul. It is the love we feel. It is the hurt we feel when a loved one is not well. The heart is the brain to the soul, and the mind is the brain to the body.

Hebrews 3:11

11 So I swore in my wrath, they shall not enter into my rest.

You cannot enter God's Day of rest until your heart is circumcised. And the outer man of the fleshly nature is done away with. Until then, you are still working in the six days of creation in your heart (6) days, mind (6) days, and soul (6) days. The six days of the creation of yourself. When you enter the 7th day, you no longer are working in the world. But God is working in you. You have rested from you trying to be the one to do it all and started letting God do it in you. Or, let go and let God. You have faith God will do it all in you, and you become pure faith. And you now have the perfect works, which is walking in that new direction, having faith that God will do the works in you. Let us look at what Paul was referring to in the book of James.

James 2: 26

26 For as the body without the Spirit is dead, so faith without works is dead also.

A soul is to a spirit, what a child is to an adult, what a seed is to a tree, what an atom is to the universe, and what an Adam is to God. A soul is a seed of a god on its way to becoming one with God.

ROMANS 3

1 What advantage then hath the Jew? Or what profit is there of circumcision?

2 Much every way: chiefly, because that unto them were committed the oracles of God.

There are seven seals in the little black book called the Bible, talked about in Revelations. Those seals have been done away with in Spiritual understanding. There are seven levels in which to read the Bible. Most people read the Bible on one level: by the fleshly man. Humanity has been taught to read the Bible on one level by mainstream religion. That level is of the fleshly man, which cannot please God in the first place. When people try to interpret the Bible through the fleshly man. That becomes the only seal they can see in the book. Everything is interpreted and seen through a fleshly man's perspective. The Bible was for awakening the soul and is of a spiritual interpretation.

2 Peter 1:20

20 Knowing this first that no prophecy of the scripture is of any private interpretation.

Here we read that it is not by any one person's understanding that we understand the Bible. But it comes of the divine inspiration of the Spirit. Knowledge comes from seeking and asking God for the understanding and wisdom.

2 Peter 1:21

21 For the prophecy came not in old time by the will of man: but by holy men of God spake as they were moved by the Holy Ghost.

Here we see that we do not understand the Bible by flesh or the will of man. We can appreciate all levels of the Bible when moved by the Holy Ghost, only when moved by God's Spirit. There are seven locks that we must take a look at to understand the Bible in total. They would be 1 the past, 2 the present, 3 the future, 4 the inner man, 5 the outer man, 6 heavens, 7 and earth as a whole people. The Bible needs to be understood by society in a fuller Spiritual sense. Unfortunately, this has yet to happen so far in our lifetime. It is like reading the phone book when you need information that is only obtained in an encyclopedia. But for some unknown reason, you still believe you can receive the information you need from the phone book.

This verse talks about a Spiritual person with their heart circumcised within them. This person has become right with God in their heart, mind, and soul. As seen in verse 2 a Jew is one inwardly, not outwardly. Those are the kind of people that are the oracles of God. Yes, there can be certain souls doing specific jobs that God created. Remember, many members, one body. 1 Corinthians 12:12, which says, ***"For as the body is one, and has many members".*** According to Oxford Languages, an oracle is;

Oxford Languages

"Oracles"

"A priest or priestess acting as a medium through whom advice or prophecy was sought from the gods in classical antiquity".

Galatians 3:28

28 There is neither Jew nor Greek, there is neither bond nor free, there is neither male nor female: for ye are all one in Christ Jesus.

Paul is also saying when you enter the Spirit. That you are a spiritual light being. You are an Adam in the Body of God. You are neither male nor female but something resembling both. You become a being with masculine and feminine traits, like androgynes being, if not one. You are a creator with all the attributes of creating.

Romans 3:3-5

3 For what if some did not believe? Shall their unbelief make the faith of God without effect?

4 God forbid: yea, let God be true, but every man a liar; as it is written, that thou mightiest be justified in thy sayings, and mightiest overcome

when thou art judged.

5 But if our unrighteousness commends the righteousness of God, what shall we say? Is God unrighteous who taketh vengeance? (I speak as a man)

Notice where Paul says I speak as a man. Paul was the man of the flesh or lower realm, as Christ was the Spirit that dwelt in Jesus. There was a Spiritual being which Paul was living in Paul, the fleshly man. Paul decided to go down in the (lower vibration) into a fleshly man's state of conscious to make that comment. We can ascend as well as descend in Spirit. See **Romans 10:6-9** for fuller detail. It is essential to know you will become that new Spirit being. By undergoing a metamorphosis of sorts.

Romans 3:6-10

6 God forbid: for then how shall God judge the world?

7 For if the truth of God hath more abounded through my lie unto his glory; why yet am I also judged as a sinner?

8 And not rather, (as we be slanderously reported, and as some affirm that we say), Let us do evil, that good may come? Whose damnation is just.

9 What, then? Are we better than they? No, in no wise: for we have before proved both Jews and Gentiles that they are all under sin.

10 As it is written, there is none righteous, no, not one.

All have sinned and fallen short of the Glory of God. Whether you are a Jew or Gentile. All have died the death of sin and become dead in sin. Here is where religion has left off, and goes no further. But we must put off this old way of thinking. We must move forward and put off sin and become alive in Christ (The Word).

Romans 3:11

11 There is none that understandeth, there is none that seeketh after God.

What does it mean to seek after God? Well, it means to seek after him with 100% of your heart, 100% of your mind, and 100% of your soul. That would total up to 100% of all of you. Except for flesh because it cannot please God in its lower vibration.

Romans 3:12

12 They are all gone out of the way; they are together become unprofitable; there is none that doeth good, no, not one.

Who truly loves God with All their heart, mind, and soul today? Who truly loves their neighbor as themselves? Who truly loves themselves in today's World? And if you are not fulling the commandments, then you have become unprofitable.

Romans 3:13

13 Their throat is an open sepulchre; with their tongues, they have used deceit; the poison of asps is under their lips.

I don't know if there is anyone that cannot relate to this verse. Can you think of anyone at work that would talk about another co-worker behind their back? Have you seen this happen at church? No one would try to make someone look bad, would they? They might get that promotion instead of you, not in today's World. You get the point I am trying to make. We are living in a world that cares about me and mine. We are not living in a world of you and yours and us.

Romans 3:14

14 Whose mouth is full of cursing and bitterness.

Because of this very thing, my wife and I cancelled all social media platforms. It would amaze me that someone would say something so disturbing online. But in person, I don't think that same person would ever tell you the same thing to your face.

Romans 3:15

15 Their feet are swift to shed blood.

Can you think of any protest groups that might fit this bill?

Romans 3:16

16 Destruction and misery are in their ways.

Do you think everyone is happy in today's World? People have become so mad, and I mean all the time. People had to come up with names to describe the rage. Do the words “Karen”, “road rage”, “libtard’s”, or “right winger” ring a bell? You could come up with plenty yourself.

Romans 3:17

17 And the way of peace have they not known.

There is no compromise today from anyone. All people and sides have to be right all the time. People's own opinion is the only thing that matters. Satan has the World divided up against itself. And that is just how he likes it. The more division he can create, the less unity he has to deal with.

Romans 3:18

18 There is no fear of God before their eyes.

Fear it seems is a tool used to get people to seek God. I have found that it is Love of God, and a love for God that keeps you close to God.

Romans 3:19

19 Now we know that what things soever the law saith, it saith to them who are under the law: that every mouth may be stopped, and all the World may become guilty before God.

The letter of the law lets you know that you are dead in sin. Being dead in sin lets you know you are guilty of living selfishly in the flesh. But if you live under the law of Moses and not the law of faith, then you are subject to all the laws and shall be judged by the laws in the Bible. That is impossible to do while in the flesh. It is much easier to live under the law of faith. Faith in God that he can and will do all things. This includes perfection while living in the flesh. Trust in God that he has all things handled at all times. But if you have all the faith in the World yet do not have a relationship with the "Father", where are you? How do you know you are heading in the right direction in life? You are still lost if God gives you instructions and you cannot understand his language. I know from personal experience. But I also know, by the grace of God, go I.

Romans 3:20

20 Therefore by the deeds of the law there shall no flesh be justified in his sight: for by the law is the knowledge of sin.

Preach it, Paul; No flesh shall be justified before God by the letter of the law. So, if people are trying to do good in the flesh to please God, it did not happen yesterday, today, or tomorrow, and it will never work. They that are in the lower vibrations of the flesh cannot please God. You must be in Spirit. To be in Spirit, your soul has gone through a rebirth and quickened into Spirit. By the law's letter, we understand what sin is. So that we can see sin within ourselves; it's hard to comprehend sin if you do not know what sin is. Paul addresses this later down in another chapter.

John 4:24

24 God is a Spirit: and they that worship him must worship him in Spirit and in truth.

Spirit is the only way forward for any that want to overcome the flesh. And that is only done one way, in the Word of Christ. And that is only accomplished one way; through the "Father" sending you the Word of Christ. Then the Word or Christ will bring you to the understanding and oneness with the "Father". In the "Father" and the Word of God is the only place you can find true truth.

Romans 3:21

21 But now the righteousness of God without the law is manifested, being witnessed by the law and the prophets.

It is the righteousness of God that saves us. Not you doing the letter of the law on your own. What, then, should you continue in sin? God forbid. We will be going over this a little later in the book. All things are possible with God, but we must rest in God and allow him to do the work in us.

Romans 3:22

22 Even the righteousness of God which is by faith of Jesus Christ unto all and upon all them that believe: for there is no difference.

Notice the words ***"faith of Jesus Christ".*** And not the words ***"faith in Jesus Christ".*** Sometimes it is the smallest of words that lead to the most significant understanding. We must have faith (Peter), Christ's foundation in the kingdom of God. We understand that the World will be made right by the "Father" and through the Word of God. And that Word of God lives in you. And God sets before the Altar, waiting on your free will offering of love. The key to opening the door is your faith in God that God will open the door.

John 14:16

16 And I will pray the Father, and he shall give you another Comforter, that he may abide with you forever.

That comforter lives within you. It is that little soft voice that always leads you to the truth.

John 14:17

17 Even the Spirit of truth; whom the World cannot receive, because it seeth him not, neither knoweth him: but ye know him; for he dwelleth with you, and shall be in you.

The World does not see or listen to the Spirit of truth. Most do not even believe in the Spirit of truth. But again, Christ says it dwells in you and lives in you. So,

Christ's words are either valid, or Christ misspoke; then he was imperfect. And again, I say God forbid. Let the Word be true and every man a liar. There is a world within you, just waiting to be discovered by the true believers of God. And that world is a world of Spirit.

John 14:18

18 I will not leave you comfortless: I will come to you.

I will not leave you comfortless, means you have not been left comfortless. Who is it that is going to come to you? How can he come if you are not looking for him? And it is only possible if you have faith. Faith that it is going to happen and is happening right now.

John 14:19

19 Yet a little while, and the World seeth me no more, but ye see me: because I live, ye shall live also.

If Christ said you should live. It means Christ is saying you are dead. And this is a true statement because all are dead in sin. And Christ said you shall see him. And you can if you look inside yourself. You will find the Word of God that will lead you into all truth, and then you shall live.

John 14:20

20 At that day ye shall know that I am in my "Father", and ye in me, and I in you.

When you wake up in Spirit, you will find. God lives in the Spirit; Christ lives in the Spirit, and you live in the Spirit. You will find that there is only one Spirit, that there is only one body, and that there are many members to that body. I talk to God, and God speaks with me. You can talk to God, and God will talk to you. I can talk to Christ, and Christ talks with me. You can talk to Christ, and Christ will speak with you. But it would help if you stopped looking outside and started looking inside yourself, if God is not speaking with you now.

John 15:14

14 Ye are my friends, if ye do whatsoever, I command you.

But first, to be Christ's friend, you must do the commandments. Love God with all your heart, mind, and soul. And love your neighbor as yourself. There are no shortcuts to the one Spirit. Many thieves today are trying to work and break their way into heaven. But there is only one proper way to enter the kingdom of the "Father". Any person preaching or teaching anything other than doing the commandments of God can be a false prophet. God does all the work; we need to rest. If someone is teaching you how to open the pineal gland without the purification set up by God, they are a thief trying to work their way into heaven. Where is the faith? There is only work of the flesh being done by the people. God can overcome all shortcomings and vitamin deficiencies. If God wants you in, who can keep you out? If God wants you out of Spirit, who can give you entrance to heaven? Be not deceived; faith and love for the "Father" is the only way.

Romans 3:23

23 For all have sinned and come short of the glory of God.

I believe this verse to be religion's favorite verse in the Bible. It is one of Satan's favorite tools as well. Although it is true, it is taken out of context by many. Yes, all have sinned, but where does the Bible say you must stay in sin? Where does it say in the Bible to continue in sin? It does say, "you must be reborn". It does say, "you must put off the old man". It does say; "Be perfect as your "Father" in heaven is perfect." And it does say, "you must be reborn and resurrected, and that the mortal must put on immortality". It also says, "we must reach forth our hands and partake of the Tree of Life." The deception of Satan and the third of heaven, his demons have never disappeared. And that deception runs very deep in today's World.

Romans 3:24

24 Being justified freely by his grace through the redemption that is in Christ Jesus.

Our redemption is in Christ (The WORD of God)—Christ's words. But yet, people let others of sin interpret those words for them instead of having a relationship with the Word of God and the Creator. When they allow themselves to listen to other men of sin who understand nothing of God, they become blinded when listening to them and fall into the same illusions which that person themself fell.

2 Thessalonians 2:11-12

11 And for this cause God shall send them strong delusion, that they should believe a lie.

12 That they all might be damned who believed not the truth but had pleasure in unrighteousness.

Unrighteousness has nothing to do with God. If a man tells you that it is impossible to be perfect. You should question everything that man has ever told you. If someone says to you, putting off the old man of the flesh is impossible. It would be best to question anything that person has ever told you. The Bible says no such thing at all.

Romans 3:25

25 Whom God hath set forth to be a propitiation through faith in his blood, to declare his righteousness for the remission of sins that are past, through the forbearance of God.

Faith is the only way to take advantage of the blood of Christ. It is through faith (Peter) that we accept the blood of Christ (the Word). Through the Word, we welcome the words written. And put on the new man of Spirit by our "Father". By doing so, we are putting on Christ (the Word) and receiving remission for our sins. According to Bing on word search, remission means.

"Remission"

"The cancellation of a debt, charge, or penalty"

There is no more debt, so we need to quit working!

John 1:1-2

1 In the beginning was the Word, and the Word was with God, and the Word was God.

2 The same was in the beginning with God.

How can the Word both be with God and be God? Have you ever read this and asked yourself that question? Because the truth is there is only one Spirit and one body, with many members to that body. One Adam dwells next to another Adam in the body of God (Space). That space between you and me is the body of God. All is Spirit, and All is God. Everything in life seen and not seen is Spirit. It has its Energy which is in God. It vibrates at its Frequency within God. It dances to the Rhythm that God gave it. We all live in the mind of God at his pleasure.

Romans 3:26

26 To declare, I say, at this time his righteousness: that he might be just, and the justifier of him which believeth in Jesus.

God the "Father" justifies us through the Word of God (Christ). It is through the Word we make our changes. All else is an illusion from the Romans of old.

Romans 3:27

27 Where is boasting, then? It is excluded. By what law? Of works? Nay: but by the law of faith.

God's first commandment is to love God with all your heart, mind, and soul. Doing so allows us to do away with the ego of man. When we love God with all our hearts, minds, and souls, we see that God does all the work according to our faith. We put our sin on the altar and start walking in the direction away from that sin. Walking away from that sin is the works. We are walking in a new direction in our life. It is our faith in God that he will burn it out of us. That makes that sin disappear in us and is no more. God takes the desire from us when he burns it on the altar as a free will offering. It is God that must clean you of all sin. It was God's gift to the World, as long as you are trying to cleanse yourself of sin. God will stand by and allow you to try and do so because you are not surrendering yourself to him. You are continuing to work in the six days of creation. It is up to you to want to rest from these works of the flesh. You must put forth your hands and partake of the Tree of Life, a gift from God, the Almighty Creator of all things seen and unseen.

Romans 3:28

28 Therefore, we conclude that a man is justified by faith without the deeds of the law.

Peter (rock/faith) is the only way to start this incredible journey with God. Your faith is the key that will open or close all doors. Faith is the cornerstone and first foundation of the new spiritual city of New Jerusalem. If you lack a relationship with Peter (faith). Ask God the "Father" to have a better relationship with Christ (the Word) for one. And the Spirit of Truth will explain how to go about it. It is not by your works of the flesh that you overcome this World. It is through faith in God. That God will overcome the World in you. Notice it is without the deeds of the law.

Matthew 16:19

19 And I will give unto thee the keys of the kingdom of heaven: and whatsoever thou shalt bind on earth shall be bound in heaven: and whatsoever thou shalt loose on earth shall be loosed in heaven.

Peter (Faith) is that key in which nothing or everything happens. All power comes from above. All power comes from within you. All power comes from a higher vibration. Vibrate at a higher vibration and become one with the "Father". Where you can say I and the "Father" are one. So, through your faith, you can have all things or nothing. It is up to you and how much faith you have in God. I will tell you though, putting your trust in yourself, or the flesh, will get you nowhere. Well, it will get you where you are today in a world of chaos.

John 10:30

30 I and my "Father" are one.

We cannot separate ourselves from God except in our minds. We are all gods living in the body of God. And for as long as people want to believe they are some mere mortals, they will be mere mortals. Because of their lack of faith in the "Father" and The Word of God. In Christ's words, which were the "Fathers."

John 10:34

34 Jesus answered them, is it not written in your law? I said, Ye, are gods?

Nobody can make you believe the Words spoken by Christ. But it would be best to question where your information has come from throughout your life. Does that information line up with the words in the Bible? Only God, you and Christ can answer that question. Not another man, for what if he is wrong? God is within you, and God is omnipresent. But God must be sought out as fine Gold has been sought for through-out history.

Romans 3:29

29 Is he the God of the Jews only? Is he not also of the Gentiles? Yes, of the Gentiles also.

God is not exclusive to any race, creed, or people of one land or another. God is the God of all because God is All, and All is the All. There is no respect for persons with God. There are only those in Spirit and those in the flesh—or those of lower vibrations (Gentiles) and those of higher vibrations (Jews).

Romans 3:30

30 Seeing it is one God, which shall justify the circumcision by faith, and uncircumcision through faith.

The Spiritual beings (Jews, awakened ones) in the flesh. Are justified by the faith in which they exercise. The uncircumcised ones (the Gentiles, waking up ones) are the ones that live after the flesh. The Gentiles become justified by God through the works of their faith in God—the walking in that direction away from sin.

Romans 3:31

31 Do we then make void the law through faith? God forbid: yea, we establish the law.

We establish our works (deeds) through our faith in God. We put our trust in God to wake us up. We demonstrate the law by manifesting the law within us. Then what is that law we must manifest within us?

Matthew 22:37-40

37 Jesus said unto him, thou shalt love the Lord thy God with all thy heart, and with all thy soul, and with all thy mind.

38 This is the first and great commandment.

39 And the second is like unto it; thou shalt love thy neighbor as thyself.

40 On these two commandments hang all the law and the prophets.

Christ never came to do away with the old commandments but to fulfill them. And then to give us new commandments.

Matthew 5:17-19

17 Think not that I am come to destroy the law or the prophets: I am not come to destroy, but to fulfill.

18 For verily I say unto you, till heaven and earth pass, one jot or one tittle shall no wise pass from the law, till all be fulfilled.

19 Whosoever, therefore, shall break one of these least commandments, and shall teach men so, he shall be called the least in the kingdom of heaven: but whosoever shall do and teach them, the same shall be called great in the kingdom of heaven.

Those that teach us that it is impossible to do the law. That is what this verse is explaining. Those that teach you that it is impossible to do something Christ told you to do. Now either they are wrong, or Christ was wrong when he told us to be perfect. As for me, I am taking the side of the Son of God on this one.

Matthew 5:20

20 For I say unto you, that except your righteousness shall exceed the righteousness of the scribes and Pharisees, ye shall in no case enter into the kingdom of heaven.

So, who are the scribes and Pharisees? They were the ones that learned the Bible and every word it says. But the Pharisees never understood what the Bible was saying because their hearts were in doing the traditions of their fathers of old. And not in learning the truth about who and what they were. They became the blind, leading the blind. They are still with us today, as they were back then. They still stand in their synagogues and preach from the highest pulpits. When Christ came last time, none believed in his word, except a few that learned to believe him. It is the same today; there is nothing new under the sun.

Isaiah 53

53 Who hath believed our report? And to whom is the arm of the Lord revealed?

Christ (the Word of God) is that report. But who has believed that report today? Who believes it is possible to be a perfected spirit in the flesh? I have met one other person who believes it is possible. What I preach, if I preach to anyone, is this. Love God with all your heart, mind, and soul. Love your neighbor as yourself. And if I have missed anything at all. I will say love the one body (Spirit); we are all members of.

ROMANS 4

1 What shall we say then that Abraham our father, as pertaining to the flesh, hath found?

2 For if Abraham were justified by works, he hath whereof to glory; but not before God.

Here we see the differences between the actions of work and the action of faith in God. God did not justify Abraham for the works that he did but for the faith that he had. God told Abraham he would have a child in old age. In Abraham's heart, God was not questioned but believed. He did not set out to make anything happen. Like Abraham, we must believe God's Word and enter into the Spirit through faith in God, not through the works of the flesh. How can anyone become perfect when they do not see or believe God can make them perfect? How can you become a god if you do not see you are a god? You have lost the race before getting out of the gate. All have stumbled at a stumbling block of Satan.

Romans 4:3

3 For what saith the scripture? Abraham believed God, and it was counted unto him for righteousness.

What applied in Abraham's time also applies to us today. Abraham believed in God by having faith (Peter) in God. That faith is what was seen as righteousness by God. Abraham had faith that God would do what he promised. So, it is not by works in the flesh that we please God. It is in faith in things unseen, the "Father" which dwells within us, which is Spirit.

Hebrews 11:1

1 Now faith is the substance of thing hoped for, the evidence of things not seen.

We trust something we do not see to fix our problems. We put our faith in things unseen to purify us now. How can you have faith in something when you are dead? If you return to Spirit, you see as Spirit. Where is your hope for the calling when things are made clear to us? When I write this book even now. The task feels daunting; many are asleep and dead in sin. But my faith is in the "Father" that he will call all, that he will justify all, and that he will glorify all. I think back to the time when Christ lived in Jesus. I realize that Christ started with nothing. God called twelve Disciples, leading to a movement that exists today. Even though Satan has sidetracked that movement for a while. I know in my heart; it will not be forever. I know everything has happened and is happening as God intends.

We must look to the promises made by God and believe. Just look at John 14:12 below.

John 14:12

12 Verily, verily, I say unto you, He that believeth on me, the works that I do shall he also do; and greater works than these shall he do; because I go unto my "Father."

The problem is today finding authentic faith in God. If people did, they would fulfill the first two commandments. And not treat them like they were the first two suggestions. The first commandment is to Love God with All (100%) of your heart, mind, and soul. The second is to love your neighbor as ourselves. Learning to love yourself is a challenging task. And I am not talking about the love of the ego. Plenty of people have that kind of love. I am talking about the type of love where you lay down your carnal man and all the desires for this world. To give yourself freely as a will offering to God. Now, I am not talking about killing oneself physically. I am talking about giving up the deeds that you do—and becoming a new kind of being living in the flesh. A being resurrected into a living quickened Spirit living in a flesh body.

Romans 4:4

4 Now to him that worketh is the reward not reckoned of grace, but of debt.

Read this verse over and over and over again. You must understand it to its entire meaning. You cannot work your way into heaven in the flesh. God does not owe us anything at all, rest is a gift from the "Father" to us all. Every time you think in your head. I should do this, or I should have done that; you are working. You should have let go and let God. You go to the "Father" with everything. You become one with the "Father" in thought, Word, and Spirit. I know this is a hard thing to understand. Just look at your own human body for just a minute. Try to see all the pieces of your body as separate independent parts living in one body. Do you tell your feet where to walk every minute? Do you ask them to step left and then right? Do you tell your hands what to grab? Or ask your eyes what direction to look? All these members work separately in the body. But all these members work as one body. Your body has one consciousness, one voice from which all words proceed forth that all hear. Seven octillion Atoms, all independent, working as one. If you can start seeing your body and the true wonder it is. Then you can begin to be like a flea on an elephant's back trying to understand the elephant. But at least you would be on the back of the elephant trying to understand it.

Romans 4:5

5 But to him that worketh not, but believeth on him that justifieth the ungodly, his faith is counted for righteousness.

Faith is the only way to the "Father" within heaven, which is in you. Seek the Word from the "Father." And the Word shall lead you to the "Father". God justifies the ungodly through faith in him to do it.

Romans 4:6

6 Even as David also describeth the blessedness of the man, unto whom God imputeth righteousness without works.

I know this can be confusing to some that understand the Bible. Because the Bible also says faith without works is dead in the book of James. You cannot buy your way into heaven by works. But you must still do the actual works of God. The course is going before the mercy seat of God. You must go to the altar of God in the Temple of God, and you are that, Temple. I will show you below how it works.

1 Corinthians 3:16

16 Know ye not that ye are the Temple of God, and that the Spirit of God dwelleth in you?

First off, you are the Temple of God. In every Temple, there is an Altar. You are no different, and you have an Altar within you. It has a veil between the inner (Spirit) and outer (flesh) court.

Revelation 11:2

2 But the court which is without the Temple leave out, and measure it not; for it is given unto Gentiles: and the holy city shall they tread under foot forty and two months.

We know that the Gentiles are the ones that have not overcome the flesh yet. The inner court is reserved for those that overcome the sinful man of the flesh by God's grace. It is the mortal putting on immortality. Until now the Gentiles are still treading the Holy City under foot.

Ezekiel 8:16

16 And he brought me into the inner court of the Lord's house, and behold at the door of the Temple of the Lord, between the porch and the altar, were about five and twenty men, with their backs toward the Temple of the Lord, and their faces towards the East, and they worshipped the sun towards the East.

The inner court or the other side of the veil within you is where the "Father" dwells. That is where you and I want to make our dwelling. So, how do we do it? Well, we don't. God does, and here is how this all happens.

1. You go inside yourself into the quiet of your mind. There you pray to the "Father," who sees in secret and rewards you openly.

Matthew 6:4-5

4 That thine alms may be in secret: and thy "Father" which seeth in secret himself shall reward thee openly.

5 And when thou prayest, thou shalt not be as the hypocrites are: for they love to pray standing in the synagogues and in the corners of the streets, that they may be seen of men. Verily I say unto you; they have their reward.

A relationship with your "Father" is personal. It is between you and him; your journey is not the journey you can take with someone else.

Matthew 6:6

6 But thou, when thou prayest, enter into thy closet, and when thou hast shut thy door, pray to thy "Father" which is in secret; and thy "Father" which seeth in secret shall reward thee openly.

Treat it with the respect the "Father" deserves. You should know that we all stand there by the grace of God, and there is nothing anyone has done to deserve being there.

2. You tell the "Father" you want to offer up yourself as a freewill offering on the Altar. You ask God to burn out of you (the Temple) all the dross (impurities) of sin that exist in you. Put everything on the Altar and ask God to burn all dross (rubbish) out of your being, your mind, heart, and soul. Remember to cleanse first the inside of the mind (cup). You have faith in the (Father) that he will do all the work, not that you will be doing the work.

Matthew 23:25-26

25 Woe unto you, scribes and pharisees, hypocrites! For ye make clean the outside of the cup and of the platter, but within they are full of extortion and excess.

26 Thou blind Pharisee, cleanse first that which is within the cup and platter, that the outside of them may also be clean also.

3. Then you walk in that new direction (this is the work). You must have faith in the "Father" as well. You have faith that God will do everything and change you into a new creation by burning the desires out of you.

And knowing God will perfect you by burning out the dross. Ok, so let's look at the whole thing as God talked about it back then.

Ezekiel 22:18

18 Son of man, the house of Israel is to me become dross: all that are brass, and tin, and iron, and lead, in the midst of the furnace; they are even the dross of silver.

God is saying all have become impure and have sinned.

Ezekiel 22:19-20

19 Therefore thus saith the Lord God; because ye are all become dross, behold; therefore, I will gather you into the midst of Jerusalem.

20 As they gather silver, and brass, and iron, and lead, and tin, into the midst of the furnace, to blow the fire upon it, to melt it; so, will I gather you in mine anger and in my fury, and I will leave you there, and melt you.

Welcome to hell; this is where we are today. We are still gathered and burned in a carnal state of mind as mortals. And you could see this better if you could picture yourself being stuck here on earth and being a god. Thinking you were a mere mortal, full of sin.

Ezekiel 22:21-22

21 Yea, I will gather you and blow upon you in the fire of my wrath, and ye shall be melted in the midst thereof.

22 As silver is melted in the midst of the furnace, so shall ye be melted in the midst thereof; and ye shall know that I, the Lord, have poured out my fury upon you.

We must understand who the "Father" is and that this is not the life he wants for us. But it is a life that humanity has chosen for itself. No matter how hard God has tried to show us a new way. Refining Gold or Silver in a furnace does no harm to the metal. It just cleans out the impurities (sin) from the metal (you).

Ezekiel 24:11

11 Then set it empty upon the coals thereof, that the brass of it may be hot, and may burn, and that the filthiness of it may be molten in it, that the scum of it may be consumed.

Here God foretells how he will do the firing, not us. We have tried, but humankind needed help to get the job done. God was going to melt the scum or sin from within us. That is where we are at in the unfoldment today. Everyone on earth is still trying to do the job themselves by pleasing God in the flesh. It is not going to happen, ever. Just as long as people try to please God, they continue to work in the six days of creation.

Ezekiel 24:16

16 Son of man, behold, I take away from thee the desire of thine eyes with a stroke: yet neither shalt thou mourn nor weep, neither shall thy tears run down.

God is doing the purification, not you and I. At its completion when the desire for sin and the things of this world are taken away from us by God. They will not be by the works of the fleshly man. All glory goes to God, not 20% for ourselves and 80% to Jesus. It is 100% for the "Father".

4. When you walk in this new direction of life, you will be tried by fire; (again, this is the works) all things are tested by fire. But remember, God, tempts no man. They tempt themselves with their thoughts dwelling on the issue. And when a man dwells on sin, he will enter into evil. If not for the grace of God.

James 1:13-15

13 Let no man say when he is tempted, I am tempted of God: for God cannot be tempted with evil, neither tempteth he any man:

14 But every man is tempted when he is drawn away of his own lust

and enticed.

15 Then when lust hath conceived, it bringeth forth sin: and sin, when it is finished, bringeth forth death.

Desire (Eve) starts in the eyes and leads into the lust of the heart and soul, finally corrupting your mind (Adam). Adam and Eve must work together as one in the body.

5. We can look to Matthew to see what happens when you are faithful until the end of the trial by fire through and by faith in God.

Matthew 24:13

13 But he that shall endure unto the end, the same shall be saved.

The reward goes to them that endure all things.

Matthew 24:14-15

14 And this gospel of the kingdom shall be preached in all the world for a witness unto all nations; and then shall the end come.

15 When ye, therefore, shall see the abomination of Desolation, spoken of by Daniel the prophet, stand in the holy place, whoso readeth, let him understand.

According to *Oxford Languages on Google search*. The definition of

"Abomination"

"A thing that causes disgust or hatred."

"Concrete abominations masquerading as hotels"

Similar: atrocity disgrace horror obscenity outrage curse torment evil crime monstrosity violation bugbear anathema bane a feeling of hatred.

"Their abomination of indulgence"

Also, the definition of Desolation from the same source is.

"**Desolation**"

a state of complete emptiness or destruction.

"The stony desolation of the desert"

anguished misery or loneliness.

So, do you understand yet, and do you see it? You are the Holy place where God dwells. You are the Temple of the living God. The soul lives in your fleshly man, the mortal man people see in the mirror and think they are.

6. When the "Father accepts the offering". Then God will burn whatever the sin is out of the Temple (your soul). You will no longer have the desire to do whatever it is. It is truly on another level when this happens. You must remember all these things did not take place in a day. You have acquired and learned them throughout your life. It takes distance for the purification to happen. But there are no limitations put on you. Let it be so according to your faith.

1 Peter 1:7

7 The trial of your faith, being much more precious than of gold that perisheth, though it is tried with fire, might be found unto praise and honour and glory at the appearing of Jesus Christ.

James 2:14

14 What does it profit, my brethren, if someone says he has faith but does not have works? Can faith save him?

You must have the works to go along with your faith.

James 2:15-16

15 If a brother or sister is naked and destitute of daily food.

16 And one of you says to them, "Depart in peace, be warmed and filled", but you do not give them the things which are needed for the body, what does it profit?

What people need is knowledge, wisdom, and understanding. To clothe them because of the nakedness of their sin. The words I am speaking now are that food that feeds the soul. If you take them to heart, these words will become new raiment.

James 2:17

17 Thus also faith by itself, if it does not have works, is dead.

It is essential to understand you must have faith in God alone. You must walk in that direction (works), believing and knowing in your heart, mind, and soul that God is working in you. You must see yourself as becoming even as Christ was and is.

John 5:30

30 I can of mine own self do nothing: as I hear, I judge: and my judgement is just; because I seek not mine own will, but the will of the Father which hath sent me.

Christ was and is one with the "Father", look at his words. "I can of mine own self do nothing" Christ is the Word, God is the thought behind the Word Christ, and they are one. The "AS I HEAR I, JUDGE". We must manifest the "Father's" will and not our own. We must hear the "Father" within his Temple, which we are that, Temple.

James 2:18-20

18 But someone will say, "You have faith, and I have works." Show me your faith without your works, and I will show you my faith by my works.

19 You believe that there is one God. You do well. Even the demons believe-and tremble!

20 But do you want to know, O foolish man, that faith without works is dead?

Faith is not a word; it is an action.

7. <u>Once purified by fire, be sure not to reenter back into that sin again that God has cleansed and freed you from that desire from which you had.</u>

Hebrews 10:26

26 For if we sin willfully after that we have received the knowledge of the truth, there remaineth no more sacrifice for sins.

The second kind of work is doing it yourself. Like when you do your new year's resolutions and the like. You say I am going to quit something. These resolutions only sometimes work for long periods. But this would be like telling God; I can do it alone. Now, God, I owe you nothing for doing the work of quitting whatever it was. If God did owe you, then it would not be a gift from God. It would become a payment God owed you for work done. Then you are saying you can do it yourself and that Christ's death meant nothing. God would never find this acceptable. These are called works of the flesh. In the one you have faith in, God to do the works. And in the other one, you have faith in yourself. Thank Satan for another grand deception.

Romans 4:7-8

7 Saying, Blessed are they whose iniquities are forgiven, and whose sins are covered.

8 Blessed is the man to whom the Lord will not impute sin.

After all the purification, your sins become covered with new clothing, clothing of light, Spirit, and you become forgiven by the "Father." You have become blessed by the "Father' of all. According to

<u>Oxford Languages on Google</u>

"<u>Impute</u>"

"Represent (something, especially something undesirable) as being done, caused, or possessed by someone; attribute".

We will no longer have undesirable sins within us. It becomes altogether burnt out of who we were.

Romans 4:9-12

9 Cometh this blessedness then upon the circumcision only, or upon the uncircumcision also? For we say that faith was reckoned to Abraham for righteousness.

10 How was it then reckoned? When he was in circumcision or in uncircumcision? Not in circumcision but in uncircumcision.

11 And he received the sign of circumcision, a seal of the righteousness of the faith which he had yet being uncircumcised: that he might be the father of all them that believe, though they be not circumcised; that righteousness might be imputed unto them also.

12 And the father of circumcision to them who are not of the circumcision only, but who also walk in the steps of that faith of our father Abraham, which he had being yet uncircumcised.

We must walk in the same steps that Abraham walked. We must manifest Peter (faith) in God, who dwells within us. All have had uncircumcised hearts. And all hearts need to be circumcised by God.

Romans 4:13

13 For the promise, that he should be the heir of the world, was not to Abraham, or to his seed, through the law, but through the righteousness of faith.

It does not matter if you have received circumcision in the flesh. What matters is if you have become circumcised in your heart. Your righteousness is manifested through your faith (Peter) in God as in the old time and even today. God uses the matter things in this world to explain spiritual things.

Romans 4:14-15

14 For if they which are of the law be heirs, faith is made void, and the promise made of none effect:

15 Because the law worketh wrath: for where no law is, there is no transgression.

Suppose there was no law telling us what sin is. There would be no sin because no one would know about sin. But we can tell the difference between right and wrong because we have a law.

Romans 4:16

16 Therefore it is of faith, that it might be by grace; to the end, the promise might be sure to all the seed; not to that only which is of the law, but to that also which is of the faith of Abraham; who is the father of us all.

The more we have faith in God, that God is doing all the works and making all of the changes within us. The more we are brought into the promise of God's grace. Just as long as we make the changes ourselves, we will fail. The gift of the remission of sins was free from God. The problem is people go about trying to justify themselves before God. God does the work in you through the Word that no flesh may glorify themselves before God.

1 Corinthians 1:29-30

29 That no flesh should glory in his presence.

30 But of him are ye in Christ Jesus, who of God is made unto us wisdom, and righteousness, and sanctification, and redemption.

Just as long as people do the work of justifying themselves. People are still working in the six days of creation. The seventh day of rest is to "Let go, Let God". God gives you knowledge, wisdom, and understanding. You also receive sanctification and redemption from the workings of the deeds of the fleshly man. And your soul has been resurrected from death of the body. You will have become reborn in Spirit from the man of the flesh.

Romans 4:17

17 As it is written, "I have made thee a father of many nations",

before him whom he believed, even God, who quikeneth the dead, and calleth those things which be not as though they were.

Again, the dead are those dead in sin. When God quickens you, he is stirring your soul and waking it up. Then the soul is reborn and grows into a living spirit within the flesh. Raising the flesh to a higher vibration of light being. It is no longer flesh but light. He calls those things that are flesh or carnal into things that are (spirit). But in truth matter is also spirit, just at a low vibration to be seen in this realm. All things are spirit because God is all things, and God is the one Spirit, though there be many spirits. Everything is energy, vibration, frequencies and rhythm. Everything is Spirit and Spirit is everything. God is All in All and God is All. It can be no other way.

Romans 4:18

18 Who against hope believed in hope that he might become the father of many nations, according to that which was spoken, so shall thy seed be.

That seed that shall be is the seed of faith in God. To do what he promised he would do. We need to quit trying to do it ourselves. We should never judge or justify the sin within us. Just see it for what it is, and put it on the Altar within us. It is not who we are; we are not sin. We have chosen to dwell in sin. We choose to work when we can enter into rest. We choose to believe we are mortals when we are gods. We choose to see ourselves as imperfect beings. When we have been created in the image of our loving "Father". And all your choices have made you who you are today. And your causes now will make you who you are tomorrow; choose wisely.

Matthew 7:1-2

1 Judge not, that ye be not judged.

2 For with what judgement ye judge, ye shall be judged: and with what measure ye mete, it shall be measured to you again.

People make the mistake of playing around with sin. What I mean is they fight with themselves over sin in their heads. Sin is sin is sin is sin. See it for what it is, then turn it over to God to burn on the Altar. It does not say, do not judge except for yourself; it says, "Judge not".

And here is another trap of Satan's. To get you to judge yourself forever. For something that happened in the past. I have news for you, friend. You can never change what happened, ever! It was a learning experience; that is all it ever was or will be. Lay it down on the Altar, and live in the now. God will burn it out of you and be reborn in the Spirit. Let God resurrect you from death in the body of sin. Be free in the Spirit, the body of God.

Romans 4:19

19 And being not weak in faith, he considered not his own body now dead, when he was about a hundred years old, neither yet the deadness of Sarah's womb.

Abraham did not see the limitations of the flesh. Abraham put his trust in Spirit; he put his belief in the "Father". He did not believe in another man to fix his problems but God alone.

Romans 4:20

20 He staggered not at the promise of God through unbelief; but was strong in faith, giving glory to God.

Peter (faith) can be your best friend in the Spirit as an Apostle. Or your worst nightmare in the flesh as a disciple. You must have Christ (the Word) train him through the "Father".

Romans 4:21-22

21 And being fully persuaded that, what he had promised, he was able also to perform.

22 And therefore it was imputed to him for righteousness.

Through faith is where righteousness is obtained. My friend Bobby used to say that righteousness meant "<u>right</u> <u>use</u> <u>ness</u> of the law". We should all look for the right use of the law. And ask God to manifest that right use into our being. And realize that we are all prodigal Sons lost in the world of flesh.

Luke 15:18-19

18 I will arise and go to my father and will say unto him, "Father," I have sinned against heaven, and before thee.

19 And am no more worthy to be called thy son: make me as one of thy hired servants.

To think that we are mere mortals is the trap of all traps. To believe that we are sinners and there is nothing we can do about it is a trap of traps. God is waking us from this deep sleep that Satan has had upon our souls. It is time to return home, and there is nothing for us here. Satan is the god of this world, and we have our world, the body of God, the "Father", the All. That body has no limitations because all things are possible. When you become one with the "Father". Maybe you grab an empty, unused portion of space in the "Father." And create another universe with him, as Christ did in this one. Raising more souls to do the same as Christ has. Are not all things possible with the "Father"?

Luke 15:20

20 And he arose, and came to his father. But when he was yet a great way off, his father saw him, and had compassion, and ran, and fell on his neck, and kissed him.

God has never stopped loving you. He is waiting for you to return home. We are where we are in this life because we have put ourselves where we are right now. Through the causes and effects, we have chosen. When you are tired of working in the six days of flesh and this world, you can lay it down anytime and return home. It is all up to you what you want to do. You have the choice to take the blue pill or the red pill.

Morpheus from the movie **The Matrix by: Larry and Andrew Wachowski**

"This is your last chance. After this, there is no turning back. You take the blue pill, the story ends. You wake up in your bed and believe whatever you want to.

You take the red pill, you stay in Wonderland, and I show you how deep the rabbit hole goes. Remember, all I'm offering is the truth. Nothing more".

James 4:8

8 Draw nigh to God, and he will draw nigh to you. Cleanse your hands, ye sinners, and purify your hearts, ye double-minded.

Be of one mind, the mind of Spirit. Circumcise your heart, and have faith in God. That God will cleanse you with the Water (Word-Christ). Do not continue in sin, but overcome evil with the "Father".

Luke 15:21

21 And the son said unto him, Father, I have sinned against heaven, and in thy sight, and am no more worthy to be called thy son.

Confess your shortcomings, and ask for strength. Fill the Altar with many will offerings, blessings, and prayers (incense). Ask to be led into the light and life.

Luke 15:22

22 But the father said to his servants, bring forth the best robe, and put it on him; and put a ring on his hand, and shoes on his feet.

Shoes on your feet represent you walking in a new direction. You are no longer naked in sin but are clothed by God with light.

Revelation 3:5

5 He that overcometh, the same shall be clothed in white raiment, and I will not blot out his name out of the book of life, but I will confess his name before my "Father," and before his angels.

This world must be overcome now. The resurrection is now, not after you die in the flesh.

Romans 4:23-24

23 Now it was not written for his sake alone, that it was imputed to him.

24 But for us also, to whom it shall be imputed if we believe on him that raised up Jesus our Lord from the dead.

All that read the Word and come to God the "Father". God is waiting on you to quit working in this world. He is waiting for you to understand you can't do it yourself. It is a gift from God to all that receive it. We must believe in God and his Word (Christ) that he sent us. You must see the possibility of perfection before you can obtain it. If you can't see that, all is lost before you have begun.

Some need to realize what happened when the crucifixion took place. The Almighty God of the All in All. God gave his Son the (bright shining one) as an offering for all souls. Jesus was not the son of God; he was the son of Mary. Christ (The Word) was the son of God. And Christ was given for an offering that day, along with Jesus. Christ is over all of God's works. Christ sits on the right hand of God. But Jesus was made a little lower than the angels for the suffering of death. The flesh cannot please God; only Spirit can. When my flesh does not exist any longer, I will go on. We already know the flesh cannot please God from Romans 8:8 But I believe the flesh can be redeemed and transformed into a being of light. Entering heaven as Jesus did. Remember flesh and blood cannot inherit the Kingdom of God. But Jesus and Elijah did enter heaven.

Hebrews 2:9

9 But we see Jesus, who was made a little lower than the angels for the suffering of death, crowned with glory and honour; that he by the grace of God should taste death for every man.

Romans 4:25

25 Who was delivered for our offences and was raised again for our justification.

It is essential that when we are speaking the Word (Christ). We know Jesus was a man of the earth, the son of Mary and Joseph. When you say Christ Jesus, you recognize the Son of God that dwelt in Jesus on earth. You should never put the creation before the creator. It sets up a false idol in the Temple (your soul and mind) before God.

Matthew 1:16

And Jacob begat Joseph, the husband of Mary, of whom was born Jesus, who is called Christ.

It can be challenging to understand Christ. Even his disciples did not know who Christ was. They were still trying to figure it out while training to be Apostles.

Matthew 16:13

13 When Jesus came into the coasts of Caesarea Philippi, he asked his disciples, saying whom do men say that I, the son of man, am?

Let's look at a couple of things carefully.

1. The first thing is that a disciple is in learning, not yet a master.
2. Second, I the son of man, not the son of God.
3. Third, Jesus said, "I the son of man", son of man is the son of the flesh.

Matthew 16:14

14 And they said some say that thou art John the Baptist: some, Elias; and others, Jeremias, or one of the prophets.

The disciples here are saying we don't know either. They would have said he was the Christ in man if they did. Christ was trying to see which disciples were waking up to the truth in Spirit.

Matthew 16:15

15 He saith unto them, but whom say ye that I am?

Christ comes straight out with the question. That he genuinely wanted to be answered all along. He wanted to see who could see the Spirit awakened in man.

Matthew 16:16

16 And Simon Peter answered and said, Thou art the Christ, the Son of the living God.

It was Peter (faith) that was waking up in the Spirit. Notice Peter did not say thou are Jesus, son of God. Peter could see the spirit man (Christ) living in the fleshly man (Jesus). He saw the Son of God Christ residing in the son of man, Jesus.

Matthew 16:17

17 And Jesus answered and said unto him, Blessed art thou, Simon Barjona: for flesh and blood hath not revealed it unto thee, but my "Father" which is in heaven.

The flesh is not able to reveal this to you. The "Father" is the only one that can reveal these truths to you. The true Word (Christ) dwells in the body of God the All and in us all, just as the "Father" does.

Matthew 16:18

18 And I say also unto thee, that thou art Peter, and upon this rock, I will build my church; and the gates of hell shall not prevail against it.

Peter's name means rock and faith. We, as souls, are members of the Spirit that make up the church of God. And that spiritual building must be built on faith. Hell, a (carnal mind), cannot prevail against faith in the "Father".

Matthew 16:19

19 And I will give unto thee the keys of the kingdom of heaven: and whatsoever thou shalt bind on earth shall be bound in heaven: and whatsoever thou shalt loose on earth shall be loosed in heaven.

And here is the big secret of faith and what it can and cannot do. God does all things for us that we ask of him. It takes distance to travel between cause and effect. Faith is the foundation between cause and effect. Whatever you bind (doubt) in your faith in your mind. You have tied God's hands; you might say you will not receive anything through your unbelief or lack of faith in God. Whatever you loosen or have faith in God in your mind. You will receive whatever you ask for in the Word. There are no limitations as long as you work in the law and live within the Word and fulfill God's commandments. Those commandments are to love God and one another.

John 15:12

12 This is my commandment, that ye love one another, as I have loved you.

This verse does not say to love only members of the church you go to or of people of your beliefs. It does not say to love only people of your Nation. It does not say people of your skin color, women, men, or your status. It means to love all people. Knowing this that all are lost, and God can save to the utmost. Some are more lost than others. That only means they have higher to climb out of the traps they have put themselves in. Knowing that we have all been in a low spot once or twice in our own lives.

ROMANS 5

1 Therefore being justified by faith, we have peace with God through our Lord Jesus Christ.

God the "Father" justifies in faith through the Word of God (Christ).

Romans 5:2

2 By whom also we have access by faith into his Grace wherein we stand and rejoice in hope of the glory of God.

When you leave a free will offering on the Altar within yourself, you receive Grace from the "Father" for the offering. You can rejoice to know that the "Father" will accept the offering and burn your sins on the Altar. Or knowing he will purge you from your sins of the fleshly man. Or the dross that dwells within the gold.

Romans 5:3

3 And not only so, but we glory in tribulations also: knowing that tribulation worketh patience.

When you put your gift on the Altar before God, you must do the work of walking away from those sins. Knowing there will be a period of trials and tribulations. Be patient, and keep walking in that direction away from that sin. Say to your faith; do you love God more than this? It will be soon that you will no longer have the desire to do whatever it was that you were doing. It will be like you had never had the will or desire to do whatever it was. Remember earlier in Ezekiel 24:16 when God said, ***"Son of man, behold, I take away from thee the desire of thine eyes with a stroke".*** Notice he also said Son of man. So, he is burning the desire out of the flesh. Lust and desire come from the eyes of the fleshly man.

For example, A company I used to work for sent some of our employees out of town to work on a building in California. I had a friend at work to whom I explained the trials and tribulations. He decided he wanted to try and stop smoking. He said he could not think of anything more challenging. He had tried many times and could not quit the habit. That night he went to the altar and placed his offering upon it. He asked God to burn it out of himself so that he may no longer have the desire within himself to smoke cigarettes. The next couple of days were very tempting for my friend. Satan does not like to see people leaving gifts at the altar. Satan walks up and down in the earth. Or Satan walks up in down in the garden within you. And he will do all he can to tempt you to fail. Even Jesus went through the same trials.

Matthew 4:1

1 Then was Jesus led up of the Spirit into the wilderness to be tempted of the devil.

Notice how Jesus was led and taken up by the Spirit into the wilderness. The Spirit and wilderness are within you; all things are within you, every sane and wild thought you have. We become tempted by Satan (random thoughts) when we allow ourselves to dwell on a random thought. We must watch over our garden constantly for weeds that start to grow (random thoughts). For example, if you were to say, I would love God even if I lost my house and were living in the streets. By dwelling on these thoughts, you are a creator who can bring them into existence. That is why Christ said you should not tempt God in vain. If you go back and read the story of Job, it can be read in a brand-new light now.

Matthew 4:2

2 And when he had fasted forty days and forty nights, he was afterward an hungred.

The act of fasting weakens the flesh, allowing the Spirit to become stronger. We can see Christ talking about this in Matthew.

Matthew 26:41

41 Watch and pray that ye enter not into temptation: the Spirit indeed is willing, but the flesh is weak.

The Spirit of the "Father must overcome the flesh". But at the same time, the flesh is weak in most. Just look at the health problems today, the obesity levels in humanity. We could all solve these problems with proper diet and exercise. But then why do we have the problem in our society in the first place? Because of improper desire within ourselves. Humanity sees a donut and wants a donut. Humanity sees some kale, and they do not desire the kale. Fleshly, man wants the self-gratification of the sweet desire. Satan knows that as well. Do you think he and his have not used this to keep you down in Spirit? But as long as you keep trying not to eat the donut. You will be eating that donut. If you turn it over on the Altar, you will never have the desire to eat one again. Also, God will show you everything they are trying to do to you by having you eat that donut. It is more than your desire for the right things that you lose. But the knowledge, wisdom, and understanding that come with it.

Matthew 4:3

3 And when the tempter came to him, he said, if thou be the Son of God, command that these stones be made bread.

Every thought you have ever had about doing something ungodly is the evil that dwells within you. Suppose you listen to this voice and do what it tempts you. Then you became that evil that you do. Or, you became one with that evil. Again, you became one with your father, the devil.

Let's get back to the conversation about my friend. Over the next couple of days, he went through some trying times, overcoming cigarettes in faith. We worked construction, and in the morning. My friend went to get on a lift to work and do some painting on the exterior of a building. And found a cigarette on the control panel of the boom lift he was using that day. He told me later it was just sitting there as though someone left it for him. I told him someone did put it there for him. Satan works in the minds of many people. Some do not even realize it to be true.

Walking back to our hotel room, he told me how hard it was to tear up that cigarette. But he did and prayed for strength. I told my friend that Satan does not give up without a fight. He told me God had shown him the war, and now he could fight when we returned to the hotel room. We both had seen a brand-new pack of cigarettes on the stairs while walking to our rooms. We looked at each other and laughed out loud. I told my friend that Satan had left a gift for him; it appeared so apparent some other forces were working in our world. My friend tossed those cigarettes in the garbage.

In the morning, my friend informed me about the war he had within himself that night. Digging them out of the trash and having one of those cigarettes was tempting. He told me how often he would pray to the "Father" for strength that night. He told me he finally fell asleep. The following morning God had taken my friend's desire to smoke from him. It was like he had never smoked, he said. That is how it all works with God. We must be strong and have faith until the end. We know that it is God that overcomes all things, not ourselves. And it is done through faith in God alone and none other. We get that faith through the Word of God. Which is one with the "Father".

John 21:15

15 So when they had dined, Jesus saith to Simon Peter, Simon, Son of Jonas, lovest thou me more than these? He saith unto him, Yea, Lord; thou knowest that I love thee. He saith unto him, Feed my lambs.

All our faith must be in God. Faith must feed all our other eleven foundations. And the only way to do that is through the "Father". The twelve foundations are talked about in greater depth in my book **"Atom and Eves walk in the garden"**. This topic takes another book to explain. While it is important to understand, just remember God does the work.

John 21:16

16 He saith to him again the second time, Simon, Son of Jonas, lovest thou me? He saith unto him, Yea, Lord; thou knowest that I love thee. He saith unto him, Feed my sheep.

It is Peter (faith) that feeds all other disciples that dwell within us. Without Peter (faith), you cannot lay the first foundation of your temple which is faith. Know you not that you are the temple of the living God that must be built?

John 21:17

17 He saith unto him the third time, Simon, Son of Jonas, lovest thou

me? Peter was grieved because he said unto him the third time, lovest thou me? And he said unto him, Lord, thou knowest all things; thou knowest that I love thee. Jesus saith unto him, Feed my sheep.

Christ asked Peter three times if Peter loved him. Christ was confirming Peter's faith in his heart, mind, and soul. Faith wavers in and out of love for God and the things of this world. Faith has to be rooted in strength and love. We must always ask ourselves whether we love God more than this or that. Peter was grieved that Christ asked him three times if he loved Christ. We must love the Word of God with all our hearts, mind, and soul. We do that by loving the "Father" with all our hearts, mind, and soul. Because the "Father" (thought) and Son (Word) is one. Your thoughts and words are one, only the earthly mind and thoughts are in chaos.

Matthew 7:24

24 Therefore whosoever heareth these sayings of mine, and doeth them, I will liken him unto a wise man, which built his house upon a rock.

That rock is Peter; that rock is faith, which holds the keys to the kingdom of heaven.

Matthew 7:25

25 And the rain descended, and the floods came, and the winds blew, and beat upon that house, and it fell not: for it was founded upon a rock.

What can come against you when you have built your foundation upon a perfected faith?

Matthew 7:26

26 And everyone that heareth these sayings of mine, and doeth them not, shall be likened unto a foolish man, which has built his house upon the sand.

That sand is a quicksand that will pull you under. It is a lack of faith in God. And more confidence in yourself.

Matthew 7:27

27 And the rain descended, and the floods came, and the winds blew, and beat upon that house; and it fell: and great was the fall of it.

Significant was the fall of this world. That fall is where we all are right now. Who has the faith to move a mountain? No one can answer this question but you alone. We must find out all we can about Peter. Peter denied Christ three times in the past. Continuously tested are our two thoughts within desire. Within our ideas of the mind is where the firing process happens. Faith is unstoppable when faith is rooted in the "Father" through the Word of God. Your thoughts move between heaven and hell or proper reasoning and improper reasoning.

Hebrews 11:1

1 Faith is the substance of things hoped for, the evidence of things not seen.

We should not have faith in something we can see. But the Spirit within us and the unseen world around us. The "Father" is all things unseen.

Hebrews 11:2-3

2 For by it, the elders obtained a good report.

3 Through faith, we understand that the worlds were framed by the Word of God so that things which are seen were not made of things which do appear.

It is faith that gives us discernment. When you exhibit faith, God sends you the Word (Christ). What is unseen in the Spirit realm makes all we see in the matter world.

Hebrews 11:4-6

4 By faith Abel offered unto God a more excellent sacrifice than Cain, by which he obtained witness that he was righteous, God testifying of his gifts: and by it, he being dead yet speaketh.

5 By faith Enoch was translated that he should not see death; and was not found, because God had translated him: for before his translation he had this testimony, that he pleased God.

6 But without faith, it is impossible to please him: for he that cometh to God much believe that he is and that he is a rewarder of them that diligently seek him.

Not having faith is like trying to please God in the flesh. It is never going to happen. God is Spirit, and we must worship God in Spirit, seek God in Spirit. The land of Spirit dwells within you. It is more beautiful than any fairy tale movie you have ever watched.

Romans 5:4

4 And patience, experience; and experience, hope.

The more you try your faith in the fire, the more progress you will see and the more patient you will become. From experience, you obtain from the Altar and faith. Your faith and hope in God will grow as you see the changes within you.

Romans 5:5

5 And hope maketh not ashamed; because the love of God is shed abroad in our hearts by the Holy Ghost given unto us.

Your heart will become lighter and happier. The things of this world will not matter as much to you as your soul awakens and begins moving within your body. It is like what a woman feels when a baby moves within them; you feel it in your whole being. Sometimes the energy is so overwhelming you feel like you will break out of your skin.

Romans 5:6-8

6 For when we were yet without strength, in due time, Christ died for the ungodly.

7 For scarcely for a righteous man will one die: yet peradventure for a good man some would even dare to die.

8 But God commendeth his love toward us, in that, while we were yet sinners, Christ died for us.

And there it is, the mercy of it all. Christ (the Word-the Son of God) died for us. Yes, a fleshly man died that day as well. But God's Son, who was and is Spirit, was crucified that day. He entered into hell to free those there as well. You and I are in that hell now. To be in a carnal state of mind is hell. And to be unable to see your way out of that state of mind is hell. Hell is being a god made in the likeness and image of your "Father". Then being deceived into thinking you are nothing more than a mere mortal. Then living that lie repeatedly—lifetime after lifetime after lifetime. Let's look at Acts for a moment. To see what hints, we can gather.

Acts 2:31

31 He seeing this before spake of the resurrection of Christ, that his soul was not left in hell, neither his flesh did see corruption.

We can see the soul, a seed that is the Spirit man of Christ, has been resurrected from the dead. It also shows the fleshly man. The man born of Mary did not see corruption. His flesh was raised to a higher vibration into a being of light, before ascending. Notice where it says his flesh—showing that the man called Jesus was the dwelling place of a spirit called Christ. It is making a clear distinction between the soul and the flesh.

Christ was a living Spirit living in the body of Jesus. A Soul is a seed, and it is a seed that can grow into a living, quickening Spirit.

Romans 5:9-10

9 Much more then, being now justified by his blood, we shall be saved from wrath through him.

10 For if, when we were enemies, we were reconciled to God by the death of his Son, much more, being reconciled, we shall be saved by his life.

Christ was the Son, a son of Spirit. We all have the same capability as Christ. For we are also Spirit in the image of our "Father". The beloved Christ is also in the image of the "Father".

John 1:1

1 In the beginning was the Word, and Word was with God, and the Word was God.

"The Word was with God, and the Word was God" ...sounds like a contradiction. When you try to understand this from the mind of a fleshly man, it is impossible to understand. But if you can see it from the Spirit, it makes perfect sense. As a fleshly being, you have a voice that comes out of your body. The question becomes; is your voice separate from you and your body? Are you that voice that comes out of your body and nothing else? Is that voice no longer a part of you when it leaves your body? When your voice leaves your body, it goes into the ether and creates an effect for the cause of those thoughts and words spoken. Remember, there is only one body but many members to that body of Spirit. So as God is perfect knowledge, wisdom, and understanding at conception. Christ (The Word of God) is perfect knowledge, wisdom, and understanding at expression. Christ is God's voice in the body of God. Just as your voice is one with your body. And when Christ goes forth, he fulfills the thought of God. Science will one day have to recognize that this explains the big bang theory. Christ spoke God's will and thought into existence in one mighty expression of the Word of God. Sending out vibrations into the body of God.

Isaiah 55:11

11 So shall my word be that goeth forth out of my mouth: it shall not return unto me void, but it shall accomplish that which I please, and it shall prosper in the thing whereto I sent it.

What do you think God is talking about here? So shall my beloved Christ, the Word of God, go forth out of my mouth, and Christ shall not return empty. Christ will accomplish that which I please. The Word (Christ) shall prosper where I send him, the Word.

John 1:2

2 The same was in the beginning with God.

Christ was in the beginning with God. Christ was and is the big bang that science is trying to understand. Creation is God's thought, Christ spoke creation into existence, and they are one.

John 1:3

3 All things were made by him, and without him was not anything made that was made.

Nothing has ever been created and come into existence without the Word of God's thought. It is like me talking to you in person. The voice that came out of me that you heard. It would be a part of me, even though it left me when I spoke it. It would be the same as if you were talking to God. And heard the voice coming out of him, this is the Word of God. That is the best way possible I can explain it. I hope it helps you with your understanding.

John 1:4

4 In him was life, and the life was the light of men.

Christ is Spirit, and Spirit is life. Spirit is the light of men. The Word brings light to the soul and shines in the darkness (flesh). Unfortunately, sometimes the darkness comprehends it not.

John 1:5

5 And the light shineth in darkness; the darkness comprehended it not.

And the Spirit shined in the soul, and the flesh could not comprehend it. Because all the flesh could see was flesh. They could not understand anything they could not see, touch, smell, or taste.

Genesis 1:1-3

1 In the beginning God created the heaven and the earth.

2 And the earth was without form and void, and darkness was upon the face of the deep. And the Spirit of God moved upon the face of the waters.

3 And God said, let there be light: and there was light.

And God said it with the Word of God (Christ), and they are one.

Romans 5:11

11 And not only so, but we also joy in God through our Lord Jesus Christ, by whom we have now received the atonement.

We receive the atonement through the Word, which is one with God. And all glory goes to the "Father". All must understand that there is but one body with many members. We cannot worship any member of the body. But only the whole body, which is the "Father". The totality of the body, the All in All, and the All is All.

Romans 5:12

12 Wherefore, as by one man sin entered the world, and death by sin; and so, death passed upon all men, for that all have sinned.

The death that passed upon all men was spiritual. Sin is the reason for all death; you cannot sin and remain in the Spirit.

Romans 5:13

13 For until the law sin was in the world: but sin is not imputed when there is no law.

How can you know anything about sin? If you have nothing telling you what sin is and that sin is wrong. If we have no law, then there is no sin. But we do have a law now that tells us what sin is. Since the law, all have died and are dead in their sins.

Romans 5:14

14 Nevertheless death reigned from Adam to Moses, even over them that had not sinned after the similitude of Adam's transgression, who is the figure of him that was to come.

Adam was the figure of him that was to come—through Adam, sin entered into the world. Through Adam, God will take sin out of the world. Adam is the same soul as Christ. Christ has come back many times, leading people back to redemption. He has been in many different human fleshly bodies. God and Christ have never had any limitations on them except for the ones men have put on them in their minds. In other words, the flesh cannot comprehend the things of the Spirit. The flesh desperately wants to take God and put God (Spirit) into a box. The problem is All that you see and can't see is God. So, God cannot be placed in a box because God would be the box as well. God is All things. Christ was also David in the fleshly man. We can reach this conclusion in John.

John 10:34

34 Jesus answered them, "Is it not written in your law, I said, Ye are gods"?

Christ said very plainly, "in your law". It shows that he spoke those words himself in history. The problem becomes the flesh can't believe all things are possible for God. The reason is that the fleshly mind cannot comprehend things beyond the box of limited reality. Take note that Christ said: "I said".

Psalm 82:6

6 I have said, Ye are gods, and all of you are children of the Most High.

Here you can find David talking about the souls dwelling in fleshly men being gods in Psalms. Again, David is saying "I have said". Showing that Christ was the same soul in David as that of the one in Jesus. Just like John the Baptist was Elijah. The Bible talks about regeneration, and religion again gets it wrong.

Matthew 19:28

28 And Jesus said unto them, Verily I say unto you, that ye which have followed me, in the regeneration when the Son of man shall sit in the throne of his glory, ye also shall sit upon twelve thrones, judging the twelve tribes of Israel.

Man must stop with this notion that God is sitting on some throne in heaven, looking down on you as just a judge. God is All things, and God is Spirit. And Spirit is All that there is to life. The ones sitting on the twelve thrones judging the twelve tribes are the twelve Apostles. The twelve tribes are the souls that dwell in the flesh of men and women. The Kingdom of God is within you, along with Christ, the Apostles, and the "Father".

Luke 17:20

20 And when he was demanded of the Pharisees when the kingdom of God should come, he answered them and said, The kingdom of God cometh not with observation.

People of flesh and religion always look for a sign in this world. They are expecting Christ to come down from the clouds and save them. It is not going to happen that way. I know it will be hard for people to accept, even after reading this. You will not see the Kingdom of God coming on the outside. But you will see changes coming to the outside world.

Luke 17:21

21 Neither shall they say, Lo here! Or, lo there! For, behold, the

kingdom of God is within you.

Everything you need and are looking for is within you. Satan took over religion a long time ago. He has some people so convinced of his lies. Even after reading the truth for themselves. Thanks to the Romans, people will still believe the lie that he set up in their minds long ago. God has an experience in all things at the same time. God truly is Omnipresent. But so are Christ and the twelve Apostles. Spirit has no limitations except for your lack of faith in God.

Romans 5:15

15 But not at the offence, so also is the free gift. For if through the offence of one many be dead, much more the Grace of God, and the gift by Grace, which is by one man, Jesus Christ, hath abounded unto many.

Awaking from the fleshly man is a gift from the All of All things, the "Father". And that is done by manifesting the Word of God in our members. The Word cannot be obtained by working for it. Repenting and saying to yourself you have to do better the next time is working for the gift of God. You must enter into rest from your works in your heart, mind, and soul. Surrender and turn your soul over to God. God calls, justifies, glorifies, and to God goes all glory. When you work, you are glorying in yourself and not God. The only work we do is at the Altar within us. Even that is not work when you do it with free will and a loving heart. We must remember Romans 6:1-4 as well. This does not give us the illusion that we are able to continue in sin either. Thinking that we are mere sinners and there is nothing we can do. As taught by mainstream religion today.

Romans 5:16

16 And not as it was by one that sinned, so is the gift: for the judgement was by one to condemnation, but the free gift is of many offences unto justification.

Again, it is a free gift from God. The blood of Christ has already paid for it. The justification comes from God alone.

Romans 8:33

33 Who shall lay anything to the charge of God's elect? It is God that justifieth.

God alone justifies us and no other. And the "Father" does this through the Word of God.

Romans 5:17

17 For if by one man's offence, death reigned by one; much more they which receive abundance of Grace and of the gift of righteousness shall reign in life by one, Jesus Christ.

Souls are dead in sin within the body of flesh. Through righteousness, they shall be made alive by and through the Word of God. Again, this is a gift from God. God has blessed us, and nothing is expected in return except surrender from work. All we must do is enter God's rest and quit working for it.

Romans 5:18

18 Therefore as by the offence of one judgement came upon all men to condemnation; even so by the righteousness of one the free gift came upon all men unto justification of life.

The justification of life comes by way of the Altar within you. Notice where it says it is a free gift. It is not something you can work for.

Romans 5:19-21

19 For as by one man's disobedience many were made sinners, so by the obedience of one shall many be made righteous.

20 Moreover, the law entered that the offence might abound. But where sin abounded, Grace did much more abound.

21 That as sin hath reigned unto death, even so, might grace reign through righteousness unto eternal life by Jesus Christ our Lord.

Death of the living soul came by way of sin. God made Adam a living soul, not a living flesh, when God breathed the breath of life into him. Now (right-use-ness) must be used to obtain eternal life.

Genesis 2:7

7 And the Lord God formed man of the dust of the ground and breathed into his nostrils the breath of life, and man became a living soul.

The sin of people causes the death of the soul. It is through the righteousness that we obtain eternal life. Or, as my friend Bobby used to say, "Right use ness of the law", Adam and Eve started as living souls, which are Spirit. After sin, they were given a coat of skin (flesh).

ROMANS 6

1 What shall we say then? Shall we continue in sin, that Grace may abound?

2 God forbid. How shall we, that are dead to sin, live any longer therein?

Which religion today tells you to be free from sin? Which religion today tells you it is possible to be perfect? I know of none, and I have looked for years. The message that religion spreads today contradicts everything the Bible says about sin. Even Paul tells us that we should not continue in sin any longer. Paul goes as far as saying, "God forbid". Paul tells us that we are all dead to sin. Our souls are just dead seeds. Our souls are waiting to be planted in truth and watered by the living water of the Word of God. Water that bubbles up within you. Grown, glorified, and justified by the Grace of God.

John 4:10

10 Jesus answered and said unto her if thou knewest the gift of God, and who it is that saith to thee, give me to drink; thou wouldest have asked of him, and he would have given thee living water.

So, let's look at this verse closely. Jesus says, "If thou knewest the gift of God, and who it is that saith to thee, give me to drink; thou wouldest have asked of <u>him</u>, and <u>he</u> would have given thee living water". So, who are the "him" and "he" that Jesus refers to here? Should the words not have been "me" and "I"? Was it not Jesus the lady was talking with? Who is "him"? Was she supposed to ask? Who else was there to have given her the living water? Jesus is speaking in the flesh about Christ and the "Father" that lived within him. He was saying if you knew it was the Christ that lived within me that you were talking with, he would give you the living water (the Word of God). There is so much in that little verse to see.

John 4:11

11 The woman saith unto him, Sir thou hast nothing to draw with, and

the well is deep: from whence then hast thou that living water?

As then, as today, people only see flesh and the fleshly world around them.

John 4:12-13

12 Art thou greater than our father, Jacob, which gave us the well, and drank thereof himself, and his children, and his cattle?

13 Jesus answered and said unto her, whosoever drinketh of this water shall thirst again.

People that live in the flesh and by the fleshly man live to the needs of this world.

John 4:14

14 But whosoever drinketh of the water that I shall give him shall never thirst; but the water that I shall give him shall be in him a well of water springing up into everlasting life.

Now Christ is talking here, telling the women that the Word of God is life. That Christ will bubble up from within you as Spirit. As well as these Words will give you everlasting life; Spirit is life.

Romans 6:3

3 Know ye not that so many of us were baptized into Jesus Christ were baptized into his death?

We are baptized into Christ's death, not life. We souls, beings of Spirit, are buried deep within our coat of skin made for us by God. Just like Adam and Eve's coats of skin were made for them so long ago. When Adam and Eve sinned, God mixed the serpent's seed (soul) with Eve's seed (soul). Our souls became created from the same spiritual DNA of both Eves and Satan. Some might find that hard to believe, but nonetheless, it is true. Let's look at Genesis for a second.

Genesis 3:15

15 And I will put enmity between thee and the woman, and between thy seed and her seed; it shall bruise thy head, and thou shalt bruise his heel.

Data from **Oxford Languages**

"Enmity"

"The state or feeling of being actively opposed or hostile to someone or something."

"Decades of enmity between the two countries" "family feuds and enmities"

"SIMILAR: hostility, animosity, antagonism, friction, antipathy, animus, opposition, dissension, rivalry, feud, conflict, discord, contention, acrimony, bitterness, rancor, resentment, aversion, dislike, ill feeling, bad feeling, ill will, bad blood, hatred, hate, loathing, detestation, abhorrence, odium, malice, spite".

How many of us can do all of these things? Yes, we all have both good and evil within us. We have both Eve and the serpent seed mixed within us. But it is not a seed of flesh, but a seed of the soul. You have the free will to believe whatever you want and do whatever you want to do. And just as Eve was deceived back so long ago by Satan; we find ourselves being deceived by him today. If you look closely, you can see the war that goes on within you as well as without. It is a war within the mind of all of us. When we say to ourselves to do this, or not to do that, or speak to ourselves, why did I do that? When you knew it was wrong to do in the first place. Then moments after, you did what you knew to be incorrect. You started feeling bad about yourself and what you did. Welcome to the war of Good and Evil. It is a very wrong mindset to live in, but millions of people do it every day. Just take a look at our society—race wars, Gender wars, etc., etc. You know the drill; no one has to tell you. It is an endless world of conflict. But not you, because you are above all this, right? Well, maybe in the flesh, but are you in the soul? Do you war in your mind with yourself, as stated above? If so, then whose voice are you listening to? Which one of those voices are you? Think about it for a moment if you say to yourself do something. Then say to yourself you should not do it at the same time, then who are you? Sometimes people even try to convince themselves it is ok to do something, even when they know it is wrong. Are you all of these voices in your head? How come you have more than one opinion? It is quite a pickle if you stop to think about it. Who are you in the midst of all the chaos and those voices? And who the heck is everybody else if they are not you? Come on; they all have to be you because they sound alike. If Satan were trying to deceive you, he would not use your voice to do it, would he? When Paul started looking this deeply at everything. I am sure this is the point where they thought Paul was going mad. These are hard questions to ask yourself, but they must be asked. And if God and Christ also talk to you from within, you should know who they are, right? Are you adhering to God's Word and eating from any Tree of life in the Garden of Eden? Or, are you deceived by Satan and eating of the Tree of Good and Evil? If Satan deceives you, your soul is dead because of sin. If you are dead in sin, then you must be resurrected from the death you are living. This is what Paul is talking about, the death of being dead in sin. Again, remember Christ's words; "let the dead bury the dead".

Romans 6:4

4 Therefore, we are buried with him by baptism into death: that like as Christ was raised up from the dead by the glory of the Father, even so, we also should walk in newness of life.

Again, our souls are buried in the flesh, awaiting resurrection into our Spirit being. Paul is telling us if we understand what is going on. Then we would walk in a new direction with our lives. A new life where we move in a direction away from sin, understanding that it is possible to manifest perfection.

Romans 6:5

5 For if we have been planted together in the likeness of his death, we shall be also in the likeness of his resurrection.

The changes we will be going through are a <u>likeness</u> of what Christ had gone through, not the same thing. When God resurrected Christ, he was able to take different bodies. Not just the body of Jesus that he used. Let me pose a question to you. Why did the disciples not recognize and know it was Jesus in

John 21:12? They knew that it was the Lord. But there was something different about him. Notice that they are still being called disciples and not Apostles here. Also, we need to keep in mind nothing is impossible for Spirit.

John 21:12

12 Jesus saith unto them, Come and dine. And none of the disciples durst ask him, who art thou? Knowing that it was the Lord

Why would they have to ask him if he was Christ? Was he in the body of Jesus? If so, why did they not recognize Jesus? They knew it was the Lord, but they could not tell by looking at him for some reason. The Bible tells us a lot of information if we seek it. And stop asking other people what it says. You must have your relationship with God. He will if you ask God to take the veils from the eyes and wax from the ears.

Romans 6:6

6 Knowing this, that our old man is crucified with him, that the body of sin might be destroyed, that henceforth we should not serve sin.

As the young kids of today would say, Paul, is spinning some truth here. Our old man living after the flesh, dwelling in sin, is put to death. Thereby the deeds of the fleshly body of sin are destroyed. We are no longer to live in sin, but we become free from our graves, dirt, or dust from the ground, that thing called flesh or coat of skin.

Romans 6:7

7 For he that is dead is freed from sin.

We are all dead in sin. In this, all religions would agree. But what we need to understand is. We have become free from our sins. They no longer have dominion over us. But it is by you and Peter (your faith) in the "Father".

Romans 6:8

8 Now, if we be dead with Christ, we believe that we shall also live with him.

We must see now; we can put off sin and live with Christ as our true spiritual selves living in fleshly bodies. We are dead souls (seeds) looking for salvation from the death of sin by the breath of life and becoming a quickened Spirit. Just look around you. Does nature not teach us that most things have a seed in them? Look at the seeds of plants; seeds die (dry out) before you bury them in the ground. Then they come alive and grow into a plant. We do not plant seeds when they are green. But we wait until they dry out and die. Then plant the seeds the following season. Now that the seed (soul) has died, you also must be given water (The Word of Christ) to grow. The flesh is soil, the soul is the seed, the Spirit is the Tree, and our deeds are the fruits. Go to any church or religion and ask them to explain the flesh, soul, and Spirit to you. Then ask God what the truth is.

Romans 6:9

9 Knowing that Christ being raised from the dead dieth no more; death hath no more dominion over him.

Death has no more dominion over Christ. But it has no more dominion over you. If you believe, you are only a fleshly mortal person. Then that is the reality you have created for yourself. Because of your faith in that deception, it becomes your reality. You have the keys to heaven and earth. What you decide to do with them is up to you. No one can force you into eternal life. We must all reach out our hands and partake of the Tree of Life.

Romans 6:10

10 For in that he died, he died unto sin once: but in that he liveth, he liveth unto God.

We have to live unto God; to live unto God is life. To be in sin is death. And you will do it over and over and over again until you live and quit dying.

Romans 6:11

11 Likewise reckon ye also yourselves to be dead indeed unto sin, but alive unto God through Jesus Christ our Lord.

We reckon ourselves to be dead in sin (fleshly man). But alive in Spirit by Christ (The Word of God). So, we are resurrected in the Word (Christ) of the living God.

Romans 6:12

12 Let not sin therefore reign in your mortal body, that ye should obey it in the lusts thereof.

Again, it is said not to sin. Or let it not be a part of you. If sin is not a part of you, then you are perfect in God's eyes. You become forgiven of your sins. Where do the words "let not", turn into, 'it is ok because you are only human'? God will understand if you sin because you are only human. God forbid we are not human, even if we live as humans. We are Spirit in the image of our "Father", which is Spirit.

Hebrews 8:12

12 For I will be merciful to their unrighteousness, and their sins and their iniquities will I remember no more.

Once all is overcome, God no longer reflects on your sins. But how can he forget your sins if you never stop doing them? They are always before him as a reminder.

Romans 6:13

13 Neither yield ye your members as instruments of unrighteousness unto sin: but yield yourselves unto God, as those that are alive from the dead, and your members as instruments of righteousness unto God.

You must be able to see the resurrection as if it has already happened within yourself. You must see it to become it. True faith knows God is of his Word, and His Word is true. You must see yourself as living to become alive. You must understand that you are Spirit to become Spirit. God is Spirit, and you were created in his image and likeness. You are Spirit; how could you be anything other than Spirit? But for now, most are dead seeds (souls) waiting to be reborn in the flesh. People are looking and working for a resurrection after they die. People only see what they see in the mirror—undergoing the programming that has taken place. How many songs has Satan given you to sing? With verses telling you that you are only human. If you keep singing them, what are you creating with your voice but an illusion. The deception runs deep, very, very deep.

Ecclesiastes 5:3

3 For a dream cometh through the multitude of business; and a fool's voice is known by multitude of words.

There is nothing new under the Sun.

Romans 6:14

14 For sin shall not have dominion over you: for ye are not under the law but under Grace.

Paul was a master with words. You do not need to live in sin any longer. You can put off sin in Christ (The <u>Word</u> of God). Sin does not have power over you. You become under a new law of Grace. The Law of Cause and Effect still applies. But the swing of the pendulum is milder than it was. You are now being reborn, learning all over. You become as a disciple in learning. Because you find out that everything you have been taught has been a lie. And as a child, you must learn all over again, and you will make mistakes because you do not honestly know right and wrong. God understands that and gives you his Grace while you are under discipleship. You are learning to be an Apostle. You are in the process of being reborn.

John 3:3

3 Jesus answered and said unto him, Verily, verily I say unto thee, except a man be born again, he cannot see the kingdom of God.

Being born again does not mean joining a religion and calling yourself a born-again Christian. As a soul being, it means you wake up within the flesh and grow into a quickening spirit. You become like Christ in Jesus. And that is the woke we all want to be. Not what they call woke in today's world. A faithful born-again Christian cannot sin because God has purified them from within.

John 3:4-5

4 Nicodemus saith unto him, how can a man be born when he is old? Can he enter the second time into his mother's womb and be born?

5 Jesus answered, Verily, verily, I say unto thee, except a man be born of water and of the Spirit, he cannot enter into the kingdom of God.

The water is the Word of God. The truth that you receive from the Word leads you into enteral life. The soul is born by the Water and Spirit of God. Then the soul becomes a quickened spirit.

1 Corinthians 15:45

45 And so it is written, the first man Adam was made a living soul; the last Adam was made a quickening spirit.

First comes the dead soul, after that the living soul, then the quickened Spirit. Adam was not flesh but the living soul of a man.

1 Corinthians 15:46

46 Howbeit that was not first which is spiritual, but that which is natural; and afterward that which is spiritual.

The natural is the body and soul in man. That lives in the fleshly world. From the natural living soul comes the spiritual man.

1 Corinthians 15:47

47 The first man is of the earth, earthy; the second man is the Lord from heaven.

The first man is from your mother and dad, a fleshly man in which you live. The second man is Spirit and is from your "Father".

John 3:6

6 That which is born of the flesh is flesh, and that which is born of the Spirit is Spirit.

People need to wrap their heads around this. Jesus was born to Mary and is of flesh. Christ is of Spirit and is Spirit. The Romans set Jesus up as a god of the flesh for all to worship. They knew if they could get people to worship the flesh, they would always be able to enslave them. Also, the Roman pagan gods were men of flesh.

That which you see in the mirror every morning is not you. That is the coat of skin that houses the soul within man. The flesh belongs to this world, from your fleshly man, mom, and dad. You have a "Father" of Spirit, and you are Spirit. You remain dead in sin unless you do wake the soul. Living after the fleshly man is the flesh your seed (soul) will die in, just as a seed you saved for planting in your garden the following year. Then you wound up never planting a garden. Then those seeds never wound up having a purpose. It is like a merry-go-round; it goes on around and around. There is only one way to free yourself from the grave. That is to be resurrected and be reborn again in Spirit. That is the only way for your soul (seed) to have a purpose.

John 3:7-8

7 Marvel not that I said unto thee, Ye must be born again.

8 The wind bloweth where it listeth, and thou hearest the sound thereof, but canst not tell whence it cometh, and whither it goeth: so is every one that is born of the Spirit.

You could be talking to someone in the Spirit and never know it. I know that to be true because they never saw Christ back then, or even today. All that people see is Jesus. They put the creation before the Creator back then as well as today. It is like putting the ground ahead of the fruit from the Tree. Both are needed, but it is the fruit that gives life. How else do I know this to be true?

Hebrews 13:2

2 Be not forgetful to entertain strangers: for thereby some have entertained angels unawares.

If we are the Sons and Daughters of God, then what are we? But gods and angels ourselves. And some have entertained angels and not known about it. Because you can't look through the ground to see the roots of the trees. You can't look through the flesh to see the Spirit. Looking at the trees (persons) and fruit (deeds) would be best.

Revelation 22:13

13 I am Alpha and Omega, the beginning and the end, the first and the last.

Christ was the first, everything in the middle, and Christ will be the last manifestation of the Word. He was Adam, David, Jesus, and many others.

John 10:16

16 And other sheep I have, which are not of this fold: them also I must bring, and they shall hear my voice, and there shall be one-fold, and one shepherd.

Christ went to many others, in many lands, in many different bodies of flesh. But always the same Christ in those bodies.

John 3:9

9 Nicodemus answered and said unto him, how can these things be?

They did not understand what Christ was saying then or now. Man looks at the Bible with a fleshly man's mind and heart. The Spirit of the "Father can only understand it".

Romans 6:15

15 What, then? Shall we sin because we are not under the law but

under Grace? God forbid.

Again, Paul is telling people not to sin. It is unacceptable to sin six days a week and repent on Sunday. It is like spitting on God's sacrifice and altar six days a week and then getting a rag out on Sunday to clean it off.

Romans 6:16

16 Know ye not, that to whom ye yield yourselves servants to obey, his servants ye are to whom ye obey; whether of sin unto death or of obedience unto righteousness?

Satan is the god of sin and this earth. If anyone lives in sin, that person belongs to the god of this earth. They would have made him their master. You cannot serve the God of righteousness and Satan, the god of sin at the same time.

1 John 3:8

8 He that committeth sin is of the devil; for the devil sinneth from the beginning. For this purpose, the Son of God was manifested, that he might destroy the works of the devil.

If you sin, you are dead in sin; Satan is your god. Now, I know that is a difficult pill to swallow. I had to eat it myself. But if you take a lot of water (the Word Christ) with that pill, it will go down much more effortlessly. God is the God of the living, not the dead.

Mark 12:27

27 He is not the God of the dead, but the God of the living: ye, therefore, do greatly err.

If you are dead in sin, God is not your "Father". You can be under the law of Grace if you are moving into Spirit. But if you do not see perfection and live in sin. Then you may like it less. Because you are of the flock of Satan's fold. But there is still time to switch teams, and we always need some good players.

2 Corinthians 4:4

4 In whom the god of this world hath blinded the minds of them which believe not, lest the light of the glorious gospel of Christ, who is the image of the God, should shine unto them.

Satan, the god of this earth, has blinded the people.

Matthew 6:24

24 No man can serve two masters: for either he will hate the one and love the other, or else he will hold to the one and despise the other. Ye cannot serve God and mammon.

God is Spirit and must be worshipped in the Spirit. You cannot serve flesh and Spirit at the same time. You cannot sin six days a week and ask for forgiveness from the "Father". Then expect to receive forgiveness.

Romans 6:17

17 But God be thanked, that ye were the servants of sin, but ye have obeyed from the heart that form of doctrine which was delivered you.

Suppose you can see the deception in this life. Then this doctrine is for you. The "father" will bring you out of sin and allow you to grow in the words of truth. Because God knows it is in your heart to do so.

Romans 6:18

18 Being then made free from sin, ye become the servants of righteousness.

The story begins here with the transformation from death to life. We are being made free from that sin that held us in the prison of our minds—allowing us to move into a more righteous (right-use) body.

You will be made free from sin. You will become children of the living God. You will be a member of the one actual body of Spirit, not of the god of the dead, and being dead in sin. You are <u>made</u> free from sin by God. By your faith and works in God.

Romans 6:19

19 I speak after the manner of men because of the infirmity of your flesh: for as ye have yielded your member's servants to uncleanness and iniquity unto iniquity; even so now yield your member's servants to righteousness unto holiness.

Notice Paul was saying I speak after the manner of a man, and Paul does this more than once. It would help if you took note of it. Paul is showing you a clear separation between the fleshly lower man of this earth. And the higher Spiritual man of heaven. Paul is not saying you leave this world to serve God. But we must change and worship God now. We move from iniquity and move into holiness. When you are holy before God, you are perfect in his eyes.

Romans 6:20-21

20 For when ye were the servants of sin, ye were free from righteousness.

21 What fruits had ye then in those things whereof ye are now ashamed? For the end of those things is death.

As in the Garden of Eden, the Fruit that Adam and Eve partook of was never a natural fruit of this world. They did the deeds that day when they partook of the forbidden knowledge. There was no profit in the deeds that they partook in that day. Just as today, there is no profit in sin for the Spirit. The statement when Paul says, "***for the end of those things is death***", some can find it confusing in the meaning. Paul is not only talking about spiritual death. But a physical death of the body.

Romans 6:22

22 But now being made free from sin, and become servants to God, ye have your fruit unto holiness, and the end everlasting life.

Again, you have your fruit (deeds) in holiness. The end of that is awakening in the Spirit to everlasting life.

Romans 6:23

23 For the wages of sin is death, but the gift of God is eternal life through Jesus Christ our Lord.

If you live in sin, it leads to death in the soul as well as the flesh. Perfection leads to eternal life through Christ. Christ is the (Word) of God. His words give you as a soul being life. The Spirit of truth leads you into life eternal.

ROMANS 7

1 Know ye not, brethren, for I speak to them that know the law how that the law hath dominion over a man as long as he liveth?

We were all governed by the old law of Moses, to do the law in the Old Testament. But we are no longer governed by that law because we have died and are dead in sin. The flesh has never, and can never, please God. This law goes hand in hand with the perfect Law of Cause and Effect. If you have a glass bottle into which you put your change. And you put $58 worth of change into that jar. You could only take out $58 and nothing more. That is the perfect Law of Cause and Effect in a nutshell. Whatever you put into life, you will get back out of life and not a penny, more or less. But the change does not come out of the jar the same way it went into the jar. Our effects can also come in a different order than the causes that we put out. The only way the law can change is by the law of grace. That is when you are moving from death to life. You are still receiving the effect, but you are receiving instructions on why you are accepting the effect. In other words, you are learning to be an Apostle. Thereby learning from God to make better causes in your life.

Romans 7:2

2 For the woman which hath an husband is bound by the law to her husband so long as he liveth; but if the husband be dead, she is loosed from the law of her husband.

When you are dead in sin and living in the world. You are married not only to this world but to the god of this world.

Romans 7:3

3 So then if, while her husband liveth, she be married to another man, she shall be called an adulteress: but if her husband be dead, she is free from that law; so that she is no adulteress, though she be married to another man.

You cannot be married to the body of God at the same time as being married to the world. You would be entering into adultery, which is what Paul is communicating to the people. But now that you have understood that you are dead in sin. You no longer have to be married to this world. You can now be married into the body of Christ. You would no longer be an adulteress. Seeing now, you are only living in Spirit. And you have crucified the flesh.

Romans 7:4

4 Wherefore, my brethren, ye also are become dead to the law by the body of Christ; that ye should be married to another, even to him who is raised from the dead, that we should bring forth fruit unto God.

We have lived in sin for so long. And have been married to this old-world way of thinking. Until Christ came back, we were under this old law of sacrifices of animals and rituals, which God has never taken pleasure in. Moses started all this to explain the Spirit by using things of the matter world or the world of visual reality. To illustrate what was coming and needed to be done in the Spirit. All of this speaks to the free will offerings I talked about earlier. We are free of all the old traditions when Christ died on the cross. On the outside of the flesh, the killing of goats and cows and the like.

God does not want those kinds of sacrifices. God wants us to use our free will offering from our heart—the willfully giving up of the old man of sin and death of the flesh. Giving up the wrong we do in this world. Now that Christ died for us, we are free from the marriage of Satan (sin). And we can marry a new one into the body of Spirit. We are no longer bound to our old lives. We are free to marry Christ at the wedding feast. That does not mean that we are not bound to the new laws. A commandment from God is a commandment, and to fulfill the new commandment. Remember what Christ was saying. If you even think about sleeping with your neighbor's wife, you have already done it. You have already done the deed in your mind. And have yet to clean the inside of the cup (the mind).

Matthew 22:12

12 And he saith unto him, Friend, how camest thou in hither not having a wedding garment? And he was speechless.

How can you be married to the body of the Spirit if you are naked in sin? If you are naked in sin, you are still married to another (Satan). If you are still married, you cannot marry another.

Matthew 22:13

13 Then said the king to the servants, bind him hand and foot, and take him away, and cast him into outer darkness, there shall be weeping and gnashing of teeth.

Outer darkness is where everyone is now. We see the weeping and gnashing of teeth. All you have to do is open your eyes to this world.

Matthew 22:14

14 For many are called, but few are chosen.

All that are God's chosen ones must put on God's armor and wedding apparel. Or face being cast into outer darkness. Exactly where we find humankind is today, with the weeping and gnashing of our teeth in the land of chaos. We see Satan ruling with a firm grip and a steel rod.

Hebrews 10:6

6 In burnt offerings and sacrifices for sin, thou hast had no pleasure.

God only cares for the sacrifice deeds of the soul in man, made of a willing heart. You are putting your soul on the altar of God to be cleansed of all sins—by living the new commandments.

Romans 7:5

5 For when we were in the flesh, the motions of sins, which were by the law, did work in our members to bring forth fruit unto death.

While we souls live in the flesh, we live under the laws of the fleshly man. We are under the direction of the sins of this world. Our fruits (deeds) lead to our spiritual death, then to the body's grave, and the soul moves on.

Romans 7:6

6 But now we are delivered from the law, that being dead wherein we were held; that we should serve in newness of Spirit, and not in the oldness of the letter.

I laugh because Paul can say things the same way, a million different times, and still say the same thing. My wife says I do the same thing. Our souls are in a dormant state for a period. Like seeds, you keep them on a shelf at your house until the season is right to plant them. But once we learn the truth about God and his Word (Christ). We have God, awaken our souls into spiritual beings, and serve God without sin. In a newness of life in the Spirit. And not the old man of the flesh. Or the old letter of the law, but by the new commandments. Love, love, and a little more love. And if I have forgotten anything else, remember more love. True love has no judgment or self-motive. They could not keep the old ten commandments because they were trying to do it by the flesh. But inside, they were still doing the sins in their minds. That is why the commandment of love came into play. Because when you truly love someone. You could do them no injustice. So, we have moved from trying to do the law in the flesh to overcome it in the Spirit.

Romans 7:7

7 What shall we say then? Is the law sin? God forbid. Nay, I had not known sin, but by the law: for I had not known lust, except the law had said, thou shalt not covet.

So why are we here today? Earth is a training ground for the gods. We are here to learn about the Tree of Good and Evil and understand what the Tree of Life is all about. We are here to understand what hate is, as well as love. The "Father" has held nothing back from us. God could have left us as perfect beings, as in the beginning. But then we would not be as our "Father" knowing all things. God wanted us in his image and likeness because of his love for us. And this was the only way to make all this happen. God made it an adventure for every one of us. And since there is no such thing as time in Spirit. You have had a short journey in what you believe to be a long time to get it done, many lifetimes. You are only limited to the mind of the carnal person you see in the mirror.

Romans 7:8

8 But sin, taking occasion by the commandment, wrought in me all manner of concupiscence. For without the law, sin was dead.

The word ***concupiscence***, according to **Oxford Languages on Google**, means:

"Concupiscence"

"Strong sexual desire; lust".

Paul was a sinner like any other man until the Lord called on him. Paul was consenting to the torturing and killing of the Apostles of Christ. Paul thought he was doing the right thing, when he was not. Just as the Spirit of God was lifted within Paul in that period, today, the Word (Christ) will also arise within us.

Acts 9:4

4 And he fell to the earth and heard a voice saying unto him, Saul, Saul, why persecutest thou me?

We will all understand that we are living in sin and are dead in sin. And if we are not reborn a new, and if we do not resurrect our souls through the "Father". Then all souls that are not reborn or resurrected will be parted from their bodies when they die. The flesh will be put in the ground of this earth. We will have missed our opportunity for the resurrection this go around. And Satan, the god of this world, would have had his way with us again.

Romans 7:9

9 For I was alive without the law once: but when the commandment came, sin revived, and I died.

All have sinned and do so daily. Some, not even knowing that they have sinned against others and themselves at times, and this has led us all to spiritual death. When we start to wake up and see we are more than flesh. We find we have been living a lie and outside of the commandments. We know that we are dead in sin, and becoming aware we need to be reborn and resurrected.

Romans 7:10

10 And the commandment, which was ordained to life, I found to be unto death.

When you seek eternal life, you must first die in the old man of the flesh. To be able to receive everlasting life in the Spirit. That does not mean you kill yourself literally in the flesh. It says you must put off the old deeds of the sins of the body of flesh. Or, as Paul calls it, the deeds of the carnal man. So, if we all want to live in God, we must die in the acts of the flesh.

Romans 7:11

11 For sin, taking occasion by the commandment, deceived me, and by it slew me.

We are all part of God's perfect creation when born in the flesh. But when we grow older and enter into sin, we are slew, as Paul puts it, and we all die in sin, as Adam and Eve did so long ago. What started me on this vast journey for knowledge in the first place was I remember the day I died in Spirit. It has always stuck with me in one form or another. It has always troubled me. I always thought that I was somebody else other than myself. But the truth is we are all somebody. And we are all somebody other than ourselves. We are Spirit, and we are gods. We are children of the highest "Father". The All in All and the All is All—part of that one body and one Spirit with many members. We float within God, as do snowflakes in a snow globe.

Romans 7:12

12 Wherefore the law is holy, and the commandment holy, and just, and good.

The commandments are Holy and must be kept by all. God did not give them to us as suggestions. They were for us to learn to be more like our "Father".

Romans 7:13

13 Was then that which is good made death unto me? God forbid. But sin, that is might appear sin, working death in me by that which is good; that sin by the commandment might become exceedingly sinful.

It's all sin within us that must die. We must put on the new person of perfection through the "Father". "And be perfect as our "Father" in heaven is perfect". as it says in Matthew 5:48.

Romans 7:14

14 For we know that the law is spiritual: but I am carnal, sold under sin.

God did not make the law death to the fleshly man. But to the old man of the flesh (sinful man). Here Paul is telling you that you do not have to die in the flesh to live. But that you must stop your old deeds. The law has always been for the spirit man, not the carnal man. The problem is the carnal man tries to interpret the Bible. The Bible must be interpreted by and through the Spirit.

Romans 7:15

15 For that which I do I allow not: for what I would, that do I not; but what I hate, that do I.

What Paul is talking about here can be found in Galatians.

Galatians 5:17

17 For the flesh lusteth against the Spirit, and the Spirit against the flesh; and these are contrary the one to the other: so that ye cannot do the things that ye would.

Paul is talking about a war that goes on within himself and the one you have within you when you begin the awakening process. It can be overwhelming. Hopefully, you do not make the mistake I have made over the years. The biggest one is, trying to change myself. It is an exercise in futility. God must be the one that does the work within you. You must see the sin for what it is, nothing more than sin, a bad experience you have had or are having. Then put it on the Altar and let God go to work. Cleaning out the Temple, which you are. Once the Temple, the dwelling place of God, is cleaned or purified, God has a place to dwell within you. Do not judge sin or yourself. Christ said, "do not judge". That includes yourself.

Jude 1:9

9 Yet Michael the archangel, when contending with the Devil he disputed about the body of Moses, durst not bring against him a railing accusation, but said, The Lord rebuke thee.

Michael could not bring himself to judge the Devil. Then who are we to judge God's creation, which we are?

Romans 7:16

16 If then I do that which I would not, I consent unto the law that it is good.

I cannot tell you how much sleep I have lost over this verse. It took years of praying to God to understand this verse. God gave me the answer in his mercy, so I will now share with you what Paul said when he was doing wrong, it was good. More than once, I told myself. What the hell is Paul saying? When is it ever good to do evil? Then after years of seeking the answer, God told me Paul was changing from fleshly to spiritual. Paul was waking up and could now see the war within himself. The differences between the two, the flesh (the old man) and Spirit (the new man). He started seeing both sides of the Tree of Good and Evil in him. Plus, he could see the Tree of Life in himself as well. That's why it was good because up until that point. Paul did not know the war that was going on within himself. Now that he saw the fight, he could war against it. So, now Paul saw the evil within himself and could battle it by putting it on the Altar. You cannot fight a war if you cannot see a war is going on.

Romans 7:17

17 Now then it is no more I that do it, but sin that dwelleth in me.

Sin is still a part of us, but we see it as old programming running in our minds. It is like elevator music running in the background. Sometimes you dislike listening to that particular kind of music. But you find yourself trapped in this elevator and can do nothing about it. It's from all the years of the lies we have been taught and have come to believe. We cannot put off all that old programming in a day. We have to learn all over; we must become as a child and start all over again. We must reprogram the mind as we do computers. We must kill the old man of ego through the Altar. We must be crucified in like manner that Christ was. All of our sins must be nailed to the cross or laid upon the altar of God in the Temple. And you are that, Temple; the altar is within you if we are the Temple of the living God. Ask yourself the question, what is a Temple, and what is in a Temple? Then you can come up with the answers of who and what you are. And what actions are needed in a Temple?

1 Corinthians 6:19

19 What? Know ye not that your body is the Temple of the Holy Ghost which is in you, which ye have of God, and ye are not your own?

The Temple is a place of worship. It has an Altar, candlesticks, and stained glass, representing the veils over your eyes.

1 Corinthians 13:12

12 For now, we see through a glass, darkly; but then face to face: now I know in part; but then shall I know even as also I am known.

That is what is being talked about here in 1 Corinthians 6:19.

Romans 7:18

18 For I know that in me (that is, in my flesh) dwelleth no good thing: for to will is present with me, but how to perform that which is good I find not.

We are souls that dwell in the body. In the flesh dwells sin, which is why Paul says in the flesh dwells no good thing. But in the soul dwells God the "Father" which body we are, for we are not flesh but souls capable of becoming quickened spirits.

Paul is also explaining the war within himself. The old programming collides with the new learning. He saw that there was nothing that he had ever learned in his life. That could help him enter eternal life; it had all been a lie. He saw part of the new law but could not manifest it within himself. That's because God does the work. You do the sacrificing on the altar. Then walk in that direction in faith. That is the actual works and faith together. If you do the work, it is a debt owed to you and not a gift of God. Now, Paul could see the differences in the different kinds of labor between the Spirit and flesh.

Romans 4:4

4 Now to him that worketh is the reward not reckoned of grace, but of debt.

God loved us enough to give us this gift. All we have to do is accept it from him.

Romans 7:19

19 For the good that I would I do not: but the evil which I would not, that I do.

Paul was trying to change into Spirit. But he was getting trapped in his old habits. He was finding it hard to turn over a new leaf. We can all relate to Paul on this one. But he shows you that he was making the change. Not only that, but he did the change through the Word of the "Father". Because we know Paul overcame and became filled with the Holy Ghost.

Acts 19:6

6 And when Paul had laid his hands upon them, the Holy Ghost came on them; and they spake with tongues, and prophesied.

We know Paul overcame the world because of the deeds and works of the "Father" he did. Remember, you shall know a tree by its fruit. These were the fruits or deeds of Paul.

Romans 7:20

20 Now if I do that I would not, it is no more I that do it, but sin that dwelleth in me.

Paul saw he was becoming a new creation. But as yet, he still had old programming within him. Paul also noticed that it was not who he was anymore. This old programming took time to come about. It would take time for that old program to be replaced by proper programming in his mind. But it was not going to stop him from moving forward. Paul saw that he was the Spirit and not the old man he once was. It was just an old program running on autopilot. And like all programs they must run their course. Paul was becoming as a child again. He was becoming reborn in Spirit and putting off the old man of sin.

1 Corinthians 13:11

11 When I was a child, I spake as a child, I understood as a child, I thought as a child: but when I became a man, I put away childish things.

Suppose you stay caught up living in the past. You can never change the past. And after all, memories are only memories, and you are not memories. You are a conscious being, and you are Spirit. We are all gods on this significant training ground that we call earth. Learning what it is to become loving and caring gods. Living in our most remarkable example, our "Father".

Romans 7:21

21 I find then a law that, when I would do good, evil is present with me.

Paul saw that he was a spirit. But the old man of the ego was still inside him. He finally saw the war between that seed of Eve and the seed of the serpent. The two seeds were both a part of him. As it said in

Genesis 3:15

15 And I will put enmity between thee and the woman, and between thy seed and her seed; it shall bruise thy head, and thou shalt bruise his heel.

We must all come to see this war; we must all fight. There is no getting away from it. This war is won by the "Father" through his Word.

Romans 7:22

22 For I delight in the law of God after the inward man.

Paul, with his soul, loved the law of God. He was moving in the right direction. But it takes work; the old man will not give up without a fight.

Romans 7:23

23 But I see another law in my members, warring against the law of my mind, and bringing me into captivity to the law of sin which is in my members.

Please make no mistake about it, you are in a war. Most of the civilization is losing this war. They are on the canvas, and the ten count has begun. But there is hope when we reach for the Word instead of the towel. I will tell you the quickest and easiest way to see the war Paul is talking about here. We should all have power over ourselves, but some give it away to others, that being said. I should add some disclaimer to appease the world of flesh here. Consult a doctor before trying this. You will need to fast for one or two days without food or water.

Pray for strength from God the "Father". After a few hours, you will hear a voice telling you to eat or drink something. Tell it 'No', then continue. That voice will start speaking to you about nonsense by the end of one day, let alone two. I say this because that voice is not you. It is the voice of fear, and there is no fear in God. God created you in his image; there is no fear in the true you. That person of fear is the person you are trying to put off by reprogramming it. You are the weaker one, praying to God and looking to God for help. You will find out how genuine the war is. You are the voice that says I will do this through God, my "Father"; he is my strength. Anything other than that is the old man of the flesh. If you do this fast, you will see the war. That voice of the lower vibration will lie to you over and over. It will tell you that this is all B.S. it will tell you, 'You are crazy'. It will say 'I am getting sick', or 'you will die if you don't drink water or eat food'. But in any case, this is the war Paul was discussing. Fasting is the fastest way to weaken the flesh and allow the soul to grow. Just remember to do all things in moderation. In time the flesh gets weaker and weaker, and the soul gets stronger and stronger. You will reach the point where you no longer hear the voice of the flesh. But it all starts with God and the Altar within you. Again, consult a doctor or health expert before fasting.

Romans 7:24

24 O wrethched man that I am! Who shall deliver me from the body of his death?

You will need to find strength when you see this war within you because you will see that it is impossible for you to overcome your old self and this world. You cannot raise your soul from the grave. I tried doing it for years before learning it was a gift from God. I had to get out of the way and allow God to do the work through the Word (Christ).

Romans 7:25

25 I thank God through Jesus Christ our Lord. So then with the mind I myself serve the law of God; but with the flesh the law of sin.

Paul says that he cannot make the change himself. He needs to be delivered from the body of death (flesh). Paul is showing that he is dead and needs resurrecting. Then he thanks Christ (The Word of God). The Word (Christ) of truth is the only way to be saved from the body of flesh in this life. The "Father" remember sends you that Word (Christ). So, now he is cleaning his thoughts, which will change the body of the fleshly man. But Paul also shows a clear separation between the two beings he is at the time. The mind is the source of conception and creation in thought, a conscious mind. Our words are that place of expression of that thought. See what Christ is saying in Matthew.

Matthew 23:25-26

25 Woe unto you, scribes and Pharisees, hypocrites! For ye make clean the outside of the cup and of the platter, but within they are full of extortion and excess

26 Thou blind Pharisee, cleanse first that which is within the cup and platter, that the outside of them may be clean also.

Christ did not care for cups or platters. It is the mind Christ was referring to in this verse. Suppose you renew the mind by becoming like children again. You are learning all over from the Spirit (Word) of God. Then your outer man of the flesh will fall in line and make the changes. Christ could say it no more plainly than in Matthew.

Matthew 5:27-28

27 Ye have heard that it was said by them of old time, thou shalt not commit adultery:

28 But I say unto you, that whosoever looketh on a woman to lust after her hath committed adultery with her already in his heart.

Christ has doubled down on the old law. Christ did not do away with that law. Christ now says righteousness or unrighteousness starts in mind as a seed. And those seeds (causes) will grow into effects. If you have thoughts about doing any sin, you have already done the sin or unrighteousness. Just as if you had done the act in and through your body. Because you already played it out in the Temple of God, which you are. You have come to defile the Temple. The mind must undergo a new reprogramming, moving into holy thoughts. Through good ideas, you will receive proper realizations from those thoughts.

"The mind is a beautiful garden, a paradise from God. Plant seeds that grow well in the soil of the ether. But watch for seeds of chaos that grow and are scattered to the winds. They grow the weeds of destruction to your soul". "Ray Roberts"

ROMANS 8

1 There is therefore now no condemnation to them which are in Christ Jesus, who walk not after the flesh, but after the Spirit.

According to ***Oxford Languages***, the meaning of the word condemnation is.

"**Condemnation**"

"The action of condemning someone to a punishment; sentencing."

We can now walk in the Spirit or the Word of God and not as a man after the flesh. There is no more sentencing or imprisonment of the Soul into the lower vibration of the flesh. You become free of the lower realm, and your Soul can grow into a quickened spirit. You are moving from mortal to immortal, which is talked about in two places in 1 Corinthians 15:45 and Romans 8:11.

1 Corinthians 15:45

45 And so it is written, the first man Adam was made a living soul; the last Adam was made a quickening spirit.

When my wife reviews my books, she leaves little side notes for me. When something does not make sense. Or she is looking for more information on the topic. Here Mary left me a little sidenote. It reads, "Why not address why the bible tells us there were multiple versions of Adam"? Well, that is a very good question, and harder to explain. If, you cannot buy into the regeneration, what some call reincarnation. Well, I do not know if I buy into reincarnation myself. But I do believe in regeneration. Reincarnation where you come back as a fish or rabbit or something else. Regeneration is where you come back as a soul in the flesh over and over.

I am not asking anyone to buy into my beliefs or any new religion. This is how I see it from all my years of seeking and praying to God, for his understanding. I think it is important for every person to seek for themselves and go to the "Father" for all understanding. What I see happened was in the beginning was Christ the Word of God. This Christ was Adam. The first Adam was made a living soul. Where does the Bible talk about Adam being made into living flesh? A living soul was one that was made in perfection. Not knowing good or bad right or wrong. It was perfect in its creation. Christ has lived many lives on earth, as well as we all have. Even in this book I talk about how Christ said through Jesus. "Is it not written in your law, I said, Ye are gods'?

John 10:34

34 Jesus answered them, "is it not written in your law, I said, Ye are gods"?

How could Christ be the one that said it, when David was the one that spoke those words in.

Psalms 82:6

6 I have said, Ye are Gods; and all of you are children of the Most High.

Now I know I have covered this in the book. But it is important to understand. That the Romans have changed a lot in this book. But that the mysteries were hid for Gods children to see. If only they would use their hearts more instead of their minds or reason. More than once the bible talks about the hidden mystery. Meaning the knowledge and wisdom of God is hidden from us. We must be seekers and seek it out as if it were fine gold.

Ephesians 6:19

19 "And for me, that utterance may be given unto me, that I may open my mouth boldly, to make known the mystery of the gospel.

Colossians 1:26

26 "Even the mystery which hath been hid from ages and from generations, but now is made manifest to his saints".

The mystery back then was manifested to the saints, not the world. Adam was Christ, it was important for him to fall from perfection to show the way back to all souls. Those souls were created by God in the beginning from himself. Christ lived in David and Christ lived in Jesus. The Word has always come back to the people in times of need to show them the next progression in soul unfoldment.

Christ partook of the Tree of life, becoming the tree of life. Christ has been trying to show us how to partake of the Tree of Life for ourselves. This is the knowledge that has been hidden in the Vatican in Rome for so long. Once people understand that they can raise their vibration and redeem the man of flesh. by raising him or her to a higher vibration becoming like Christ. Then this thing we call death ceases to exist. The human is changed from low level of vibration into a being of light. People are no longer a slave to this world. But souls become one with God in all things.

Genesis 3:22

22 And the Lord God said, Behold, the man is become as one of us, to know good and evil: and now, lest he put forth his hand, and take also of the tree of life and eat, and live forever.

Once you partake of the tree of life, (Christ, the Word of God) you become a quickened spirit. The last Adam (Christ) was made a quickened spirit. This is the act of the Soul undergoing a metamorphosis. It is the act of the Soul becoming a new creation. While you are still living in the flesh, not after you die. After you die, it is too late to inherit the prize. You must raise the vibration of the soul which raises the vibration of the lower man. Whereby he may now enter into the heaven, as Christ did with Jesus. That is why Jesus was made a little lower than the Angels and Christ went on to sit at the right hand of God. The fleshly (lower vibration of spirit) person was redeemed into a higher vibration of spirit. This is the rapture that everyone talks about, but has gone without understanding.

Philippians 3:13-14

13 Brethren, I count not myself to have apprehended: but this one thing I do, forgetting those things which are behind, and reaching forth unto those things which are before.

14 I press toward the mark for the prize of the high calling of God in Christ Jesus.

This prize can only be obtained in the "Father" when he sends you the Word (Christ).

1 Corinthians 15:53

53 For this corruptible must put on incorruption, and this mortal must put on immortality.

For this sinful, fleshly, minded man of this world. Must put on the perfection of Holiness. This Soul being dead in the flesh, must put on the true Spirit that he is and become immortal. According to **Bing word search** immortal and immortality means:

"Immortal"

"Living forever; never dying or decaying."

"Immortality"

"The ability to live forever; eternal life".

Immortality must be acquired and put on by us while living. It is not a place to go to after we die. And for those that believe that Satan has done an excellent job at deceiving them. But if he could deceive Adam and Eve, two perfect beings. How hard would it be for him to deceive imperfect beings?

1 Corinthians 15:54

54 So when this corruptible shall have put on incorruption, and this mortal shall have put on immortality, then shall be brought to pass the saying that is written, Death is swallowed up in victory.

So, when this sinful man of the flesh. Shall have put on the Holy Spirit and becomes a quickened spirit. There is no more death in the flesh for the Soul to go through over and over again. Death is swallowed up and is no more. You have obtained victory over Death.

1 Corinthians 15:55

55 O death, where is thy sting? O grave, where is thy victory?

The grave no longer has any power over you. Because the Spirit has been lifted in the flesh by the "Father". That is what happened when the Apostles were all filled with the Holy Ghost at the Pentecost.

I have always asked myself, "If the Apostles were full of the Holy Ghost, how could they be killed"? God told me, "They were not able to be killed". Then he showed me this verse.

Mark 15:37

37 And Jesus cried with a loud voice and gave up the Ghost.

None of the Apostles or Christ could be killed. But it was not time yet, for all things of God to be fulfilled. So, they gave up the Ghost; no one ever took it from them. Or, in Stephens's case, he just fell asleep.

Romans 8:2

2 For the law of the Spirit of life in Christ Jesus hath made me free from the law of sin and Death.

The Spirit is life, and it is acquired in Christ (The Word of God). Where there is no sin, there is no death. Spirit has its law, and it is not of this world. Death happens because of sin, and the Spirit of God does not overcome the fleshly man. Because of your lack of faith in God to do all things he said he would.

Romans 8:3

3 For what the law could not do, in that it was weak through the flesh, God sending his own Son in the likeness of sinful flesh, and for sin, condemned sin in the flesh.

Since Adam and Eve fell into sin, humanity has been trapped in sin. Society has always had the most challenging time. They do not even try to look past the person they see in the mirror. Man says he believes in the Spirit of God. But they do not understand what the Spirit of God is. Even today, if Christ were here walking around and working miracles. There would be a lot of people calling him a son of Satan. People have a hard time genuinely being able to discern between good deeds and evil deeds—things they cannot see, touch, smell, or taste. You cannot use any of these senses to see Spirit. You must use your heart to see and feel the Spirit of God. Over the years, I have told many people that it is possible to become perfect. I have never heard the words show me how. Or how do you believe that is possible?

I have been told nine times out of ten times, "well, you are not perfect". But that is where humankind is at in its unfoldment process. That is where humanity has always been, lost in the fleshly mind of humanity's world of judgment. We are in a world where people eat the Tree of Good and Evil daily. What people do not understand is God looks at the heart, mind, and Soul of a person. He does not look at the flesh of men. God looks at the Soul because the flesh is unable to please God. Christ came in the likeness of sinful flesh, in a man named Jesus. To show humanity how putting off the fleshly man is possible.

Romans 8:8

8 So then they that are in the flesh cannot please God.

The flesh does not please God at any time and never will. But that is where humanity does all its judgment. They think in the flesh, and they judge by the flesh itself. We need to understand the mercy of the Spirit and judgment of the Spirit. I tell you now, "It is all another trap of Satan and his demons of this world".

1 Corinthians 15:50

50 Now this I say, brethren, that flesh and blood cannot inherit the Kingdom of God; neither doth corruption inherit incorruption.

So, tell me did Jesus in the lower vibration of flesh inherit the Kingdom of God? If so, God is a respecter of people. If that is true, eat, drink, and be merry, for all is a lie. I speak in the flesh, knowing in the Spirit all is true. Jesus was transformed by Christ Spirit into a being of light through the "Father". He was no longer flesh but a being of a higher vibration. To live, you must challenge your old beliefs about God. Flesh, sinners, or ones of corruption will never enter the Kingdom of God. The Kingdom of God is reserved for those that overcome the flesh or lower vibration, through and in the "Father". You cannot be one of corruption (sinner) and inherit (enter) incorruption (the Kingdom of God). And if it is true that flesh cannot inherit the Kingdom of God. And God has no respect for persons, which I believe is true. Then Jesus as a lower vibration could have never entered into the Kingdom of God. Only the Son of God Christ (Spirit) could have entered the Kingdom. Unless Christ had raised the vibration of Jesus. Whereby this mortal (lower vibration) has put on immortality (Higher vibration of Spirit).

John 7:24

24 Judge not according to the appearance but judge righteous judgement.

If you look closely in John. It is telling you not to judge in the flesh or that which you can see. God's righteousness can only be found in Spirit; we must be in Spirit to execute that proper judgment. As well as the deeds of the Spirit done with the "Father" through men that dwell on this earth.

Romans 8:4

4 That the righteousness of the law might be fulfilled in us, who walk not after the flesh, but after the Spirit.

John led us very nicely into this next verse. God's righteousness is fulfilled in all by awakening the Soul from the grave of the flesh. Thereby we are putting on the whole armor of God. The Bible is not about suggestions; it is about commandments. As of the days of old, just as today. God is still saying to the masses, as he always has been doing from the beginning of time.

Isaiah 9:17

17 Therefore the Lord shall have no joy in their young men, neither shall have mercy on their fatherless and widows: for everyone is an hypocrite and an evildoer, and every mouth speaketh folly. For all this, his anger is not turned away, but his hand is stretched out still.

God's hand is still stretched out, waiting for someone to take hold of it. But most try to justify their salvation or earn their way into heaven on their own merits.

Ephesians 6:11

11 Put on the whole armour of God that ye may be able to stand against the wiles of the devil.

To withstand the devil, you must put on the whole armor of God. There is no other way to fight the deceptions and distractions of Satan.

Ephesians 6:12

12 For we wrestle not against flesh and blood, but against principalities, against powers, against the rulers of the darkness of this world, against spiritual wickedness in high places.

Not many in the world see this war that the world is in now. You will never see a red-horned guy with a pitchfork running around. It is not a war of flesh and blood. But spirits living in men and women of this world. And if you do not believe this has and is happening. Then they have done their job very well indeed.

Ephesians 6:13

13 Wherefore take unto you the whole armour of God, that ye may be able to withstand in the evil day, and having done all, to stand.

Again, this is not a suggestion by Paul. Paul says, if you want to make it through this point and time of where we are in this cycle, put the armor on.

Ephesians 6:14

14 Stand, therefore, having your loins girt about with truth and having on the breastplate of righteousness.

Speak nothing but the truth and be righteous. Judge not anything of this world. Knowing that you are not of this world and have no part of it.

Ephesians 6:15

15 And your feet shod with the preparation of the gospel of peace.

Preach the first two commandments because love is the fulfillment of the law. Be peaceful with all, knowing God has all things under control. God truly is Omnipresent and Omni-powerful. If you know that to be true, we are where we are because this is where we should be. Love all, and enjoy the ride. Establish your relationship with the "Father" and the Word. Learn about your brothers, the Apostles, and your sisters in Christ.

Ephesians 6:16

16 Above all, taking the shield of faith, wherewith ye shall be able to quench all the fiery darts of the wicked.

Manifest Peter (faith) in your Soul and all your mortal members. Exercise him more than any other member. Put your trust in God and no other. Go to him for all things, no matter how small it seems. Remember, 100% nothing less than that will do.

Ephesians 6:17

17 And take the helmet of salvation, and the sword of the spirit, which is the Word of God.

Manifest Christ (the Word) within your Soul, for this, is your salvation. The Word in Spirit is the sword when spoken in truth. If the "Father" uses the rod on you, you should not use the sword on others; remember the boomerang effect of the perfect law.

Ephesians 6:18

18 Praying always with all prayer and supplication in the Spirit and watching thereunto with all perseverance and supplication for all saints.

Find yourself; you are Spirit. Go within yourself; shut the door to the outside world. That is where you will find peace in this world. That is the place you will find the "Father”. Watch for those that do the deeds of the "Father." Become one member of one body in one Spirit with them. Just know that there are many members.

Ephesians 6:19

19 And for me, that utterance may be given unto me, that I may open my mouth boldly, to make known the mystery of the gospel.

These are some of the mysteries of the gospel. That has been hidden from the beginning of time. Now is the time to awaken into God's glorious Kingdom. It is the time to find your place in the one body, the one Spirit with many members.

Romans 8:5

5 For they that are after the flesh do mind the things of the flesh; but they that are after the Spirit the things of the Spirit.

Those that mind the things of this world are of the flesh. Those that mind the things of God and his body are of the Spirit. It is up to us to manifest love in its most tangible form. It is up to us to go to God and allow him to recreate us into that perfect creation that God had designed us to be. It is up to everyone to acquire their relationship with the "Father".

Matthew 7:7

7 Ask, and it shall be given you; seek, and ye shall find; knock, and it shall be opened unto you.

Ask in faith, seek in faith, and knock in confidence. Knowing that all things are possible in and through God. With (100%) faith in your heart, mind, and Soul.

Matthew 7:8

8 For every one that asketh receiveth; and he that seeketh findeth; and to him that knocketh it shall be opened.

Everyone that asks will receive, seek God, and you will find him. The "Father" is not far away; the "Father" is within you. Waiting for you to knock on the temple door, which you are. And place a will offering on his Altar. To start the cleaning process, from all the years of neglect. It is time to open the windows and let in the light. It has been dark for way too long. It is time to clean the temple from top to bottom. It has much dust and debris from all the years of neglect.

Romans 8:6

6 For to be carnally minded is Death; but to be spiritually minded is life and peace.

To be carnally minded is to mind the things of this world and that of the worldly person. It is anything that you want more than the Spirit world. That mentality leads to the grave for your body and Soul. Spirit mind is everlasting life to all that seek its understanding.

Romans 8:7

7 Because the carnal mind is enmity against God: for it is not subject to the law of God, neither indeed can be.

According to **Oxford Languages***:* The meaning of the word

"**Enmity**"

"The state or feeling of being actively opposed or hostile to someone or something".

The fleshly mind or carnal mind is hostile to the Spirit's mind. And Paul is making it about as clear as he can here. The fleshly mind wars against the Spirit mind. Now, here is a question to ask ourselves. If we live in the flesh, how hostile are we to Spirit? Now that might seem like a stupid question at first. But have we ever put off God for this world? If we are to love God with all our heart, mind, and Soul. What percentage of all are we hitting a day? I can tell you this much I know about God. "God is merciful and patient." I know from many years of trial and errors that I have made. My goal with this book is to save you from having to travel some of that distance that I traveled. The carnal mind cannot be subject to God's laws because the carnal mind cannot comprehend the mind of God. If people try to understand God with the minds of flesh, they will fail. The fleshly mind sees in boxes. The fleshly mind sees in limitations. God is so much more than anything the fleshly mind can conceive.

1 Corinthians 2:14

14 But the natural man receiveth not the things of the Spirit of God: for they are foolishness unto him: neither can he know them, because they are spiritually discerned.

So, anyone living in the mind of the flesh cannot know the things of God. As well as not being able to interpret the Bible. The Bible is for spiritual interpretation and understanding. The only way to know God is in Spirit so that you can discern all things spiritually.

Numbers 23:19

19 God is not a man that he should lie; neither the Son of man, that he should repent: hath he said, and shall he not do it? Or hath he spoken, and shall he not make it good?

God calls, justifies, glorifies, and does everything without limitations. We have ***faith*** in God to do them. Even that we do through the measure of faith that he gives us, pray for more faith; when he gives you more, pray for more faith. Peter (faith) is the best friend you will ever have in Spirit, besides John (love). Get to know them both through the "Father". It is the "Father" that sends you the Word. It is the Word that leads you to the "Father".

John 6:37

37 All that the "Father" giveth me shall come to me; and him that cometh to me I will in no wise cast out.

All things that come to Christ, the "Father" gave him. All starts with the "Father" and end with the "Father". Because when it comes to the Word, it will not return empty.

John 6:44

44 No man can come to me, except the "Father" which hath sent me draw him: and I will raise him up at the last day.

The "Father" sends us the Word (Christ). The Word (Christ) lifts us from mortal to immortal, from flesh to Spirit.

Romans 8:8

8 So then they that are in the flesh cannot please God.

Again, the flesh cannot please God and never has and never will in its lower vibration. So, if people live in the flesh and have no idea what living in the Spirit is like. Then who is it that is pleasing God? Even if people believe they are pleasing God right now, they are not if they reside in the flesh (lower vibrations). They are the ones which Christ called the scribes and Pharisees of old.

Romans 8:9

9 But ye are not in the flesh, but in the Spirit, if so be that the Spirit of God dwell in you. Now if any man has not the Spirit of Christ, he is none of his.

Suppose a person is unaware they are a spirit living in a fleshly body. Then they are still dead in sin. Knowing you are a spirit living in the flesh is not enough. You must have God manifest himself in the temple which you are. It's like you are a caterpillar going into a cocoon. You must go into yourself, and God must change you into the new you, the new you of Spirit. Like the caterpillar becoming a butterfly, you become a new creator, a spiritual being. You undergo the same kind of metamorphosis that the caterpillar goes through. If that seems impossible, look at the caterpillar for reference. Does that not seem impossible? Look at the tadpole turning into a frog; does that not seem impossible? Did not God create both of these wonders? Look at a mother giving birth to a child. If God can do all these things in the flesh, imagine what he can do in Spirit. Free your mind from limitations, and see all things are possible. Since we were children in school, Satan has been programming our imagination to fall asleep. It is time to awaken Bartholomew (imagination) to reign within the body again.

Matthew 19:28

28 And Jesus said unto them, Verily I say unto you, that ye which have

followed me, in the regeneration when the Son of man shall sit in the throne of this glory, ye also shall sit upon twelve thrones, judging the twelve tribes of Israel

Christ was talking to the apostles sitting on the throne of his glory. The "Father" is that glory. Christ was saying they were going to be one in the body. That their job was going to be judging the twelve tribes of Israel. Look to my book **"Atom and Eve's walk in the garden"** for a full explanation of the Apostles and their meanings in the body. But the Apostles are members of the body as all are. They represent twelve fruits from the Tree of Life and foundations in the Kingdom of God. Also, refer to a book called ***"The Twelve Powers"*** for a fuller understanding of the Apostles and their functions within the body of God. ***Charles and Cora Fillmore wrote it.*** With reading this book, remember all happens within the one body of God. And as God and Christ are omnipresent, so are the Apostles; they are a part of God as well. If God is in all places, so are we because we are all a part of God in Spirit.

John 6:63

63 It is the Spirit that quickeneth; the flesh profiteth nothing: the words that I speak unto you, they are Spirit, and they are life.

Here we can see in John the quickening of the Soul that takes place by the Spirit. The flesh is a vehicle; it does not give you life. If you see yourself as the person in the mirror, what profit does that person have? For that person does not profit you at all. These words I speak to you are Spirit. They are not for the fleshly man. Are you asking yourself the question of who you are yet? It is time to wake up from this nightmare illusion of the fleshly world and leave it behind. There is nothing here for you in this world of fleshly mind but the experience of pain. There is no true happiness except in Spirit. It is time to put on the "Father", the All in All, and All is All.

Matthew 24:24

24 For there shall arise false Christs, and false prophets, and shall shew great signs and wonders; insomuch that, if it were possible, they shall deceive the very elect.

False prophets have deceived the world for years and lifetimes now. And if it were possible, to deceive the elect. What hope was there for the rest of humankind not to be deceived? Humanity had made many idols for themselves when they started worshiping the flesh instead of the Spirit. God is Spirit, and Christ is Spirit just as you are Spirit. Or a soul with the capability to manifest Spirit.

John 4:22

22 Ye worship ye know not what: we know what we worship: for salvation is of the Jews.

People who worship God as if he is like a man, sitting on some throne in the sky, will be lost for a long time, except for the mercy of the "Father". God is not a man, nor can he be compared to one. God is All there is to it All. There is only <u>one body</u> with <u>many members</u>. Also, a Jew is not a race of people of the flesh. Return to Romans 2:29. A Jew is inwardly a man of Spirit. He is also saying that people look in the mirror to see themselves. They see the fleshly person and do not know who they are or what they worship. To worship God as Spirit, you must see yourself as Spirit. And not the person you see in the mirror, the coat of skin, the reflection of your true self. It is like seeing yourself as a jacket hanging on a hook. You are no more that jacket hanging on a hook than you are the person you see looking in the mirror. The flesh is skin deep, and beauty is of the Soul.

1 Corinthians 12:12

For as the body is one, and hath many members, and all the members of that one body, being many, are one body: so also, is Christ.

I say this a lot in this book. And I do it purposefully because of how important it is to understand. There is only one Spirit, just as your body has many atoms, yet it is still one body. The spirit body has many Adam's, but yet still one body.

Revelation 2:9

9 I know thy works, and tribulation, and poverty, (but thou art rich), and I know the blasphemy of them which say they are Jews, and are

not, but are the synagogue of Satan.

When it is said, "I know thy works and tribulation, and poverty, (but thou art rich"), It means that those that seem to be poor in the flesh but have the knowledge of God are truly rich. Those that call themselves Jews and worship God in and as a fleshly man are not faithful Jews of God. Christ went so far as to call them the synagogue of Satan. I know what Christ is saying here, for indeed they are. He is talking about the heads of all the religious movements. There are decent people in all religions today. But most of the leaders of all religions are corrupted by Satan. To go into it further would take more paper than we have trees. Let's say anyone, Jew or Gentile, can awaken in Christ.

John 4:23

23 But the hour cometh, and now is, when the true worshippers shall worship the Father in Spirit and truth: for the Father seeketh such to worship him.

Christ foretells the coming of the faithful followers of God. Those that would worship God in Spirit and truth. These are those that the "Father" seek to communicate with. It is the only way to have a relationship with God. I have talked with many people from different religions about this verse. Telling them, they must worship God in Spirit. I almost always get the same response as if programmed for the answer they give. I hear, "and in truth". Never wanting to talk about the "you must be in Spirit" part. For the record, you cannot be in the Spirit unless you are in truth. So, yes, in truth would apply. But let us remember the in-spirit part. Because without that, you would never enter the Kingdom of God.

John 4:24

24 God is a Spirit: and they that worship him must worship him in Spirit and in truth.

For all the times that Christ spoke in parables. He could not have made it any plainer here than he did. God is Spirit; you are a soul that can become an awakened Spirit. There is only one Spirit and one body with many members. And whether you are in the body or out of the body, it is hard for people to tell.

Except if you have a relationship with the "Father". If you have a question and the answer comes out of the blue in your mind. Who gave you the answer to the question? Who do you thank for the reply if you do not see it as coming from the "Father"? is it all just a coincidence the answer came to you? Try to see God as a game of hide and seek. The more you seek God, the more often you will find him. How can you find him if you do not seek him? Attending church on Sunday and listening to someone else talk about a God they do not know is not seeking God. That is listening to someone who learned from another person who learned from another person. My friend that I love with brotherly love. He asks me to go to his church every once in a while.

I always laugh and say, "why, do they need someone to give a talk today"? He laughs and says no, it's the same every time. Churches do not like to get out of the box and ask questions. Religions do not like hitting any bumps in the road. Man has formed all beliefs at the end of the day. These were men of the flesh and not Spirit. You as a person whose Soul depends on it and your families' souls. All should know their religion's foundation, and a lot is riding on the answers you get.

2 Corinthians 12:2

2 I knew a man in Christ above fourteen years ago (whether in the body, I cannot tell: or whether out of the body, I cannot tell: God knoweth;) such an one caught up to the third heaven.

Even Paul had a hard time in his early years. Being able to see whether someone was in the Spirit or not. The disciples were just as confused as most today, trying to understand Spirit first. Remember, it took them a long time to see the Son of God (Christ) past the Son of man (Jesus). And yes, there are many levels of heaven and the first one starts right here within you.

Romans 8:10

10 And if Christ be in you, the body is dead because of sin; but the Spirit is life because of righteousness.

The only way to awaken the Spirit is in righteousness. Notice the Words <u>in you</u> again. Also, you are dead because of sin. Through righteousness, the resurrection takes place. The Soul is dead because of sin. But the Spirit (Word) gives life, and the Soul can grow in the "Father".

Romans 8:11

11 But if the Spirit of him that raised up Jesus from the dead dwell in you, he that raised up Christ from the dead shall also quicken your mortal bodies by his Spirit that dwelleth in you.

First and foremost, all people of religions of today; you should read this verse very carefully. Jesus, as well as the Son of God, was raised that day. Go back up to verse 10 and read. It is Christ (The Word of God) that is in us. The Word is what raised Jesus from the dead. God raised the soul man Christ from the dead, Into a quickened spirit. To quicken means to speed up. God speeds up your vibration to a higher vibration. He is turning this mortal into an immortal. Or this fleshly man's Soul into a quickened spirit. But all glory must go to the "Father".

John 2:19

19 Jesus answered and said unto them, destroy this temple, and in three days I will raise it up.

The Soul is the temple of the living God. I know it says Jesus said, but remember these verses to understand this one. It was always the "Father", Christ and Jesus speaking as one.

John 14:10

10 Believest thou not that I am in the “Father”, and the “Father” in me? The words that I speak unto you I speak not of myself: but the “Father” that dwelleth in me, he doeth the works.

John 12:49

49 For I have not spoken of myself; but the “Father” which sent me, he gave me a commandment, what I should say, and what I should speak.

John 5:30

30 I can of mine own self do nothing: as I hear, I judge: and my judgement is just; because I seek not mine own will, but the will of the "Father" which hath sent me.

Let's look at the story of Peter and Ananias for more clarity.

Acts 5:1-3

1 But a certain man named Ananias, with Sapphira, his wife, sold a possession,

2 And kept back part of the price, his wife also being privy to it, and brought a certain part, and laid it at the apostles' feet.

3 But Peter said, Ananias, why hath Satan filled thine heart, to lie to the Holy Ghost, and to keep back part of the price of the land?

Peter knew everything because he and the "Father" were one. Just as Jesus was one with Christ and Christ one with the "Father".

Acts 5:4

4 While it remained, was it not thine own? And after it was sold, was it not in thine own power? Why hast thou conceived this thing in thine heart? Thou hast not lied unto men, but unto God.

Here Peter states that he did not lie to men. But unto God. Now I am sure Ananias is saying to himself. "Who do you think you are?" or "I am talking to you, Peter, and not God". Nonetheless, that Soul (grown-Spirit) dwelt in Peter was one with the "Father". Just as Christ was one with the "Father".

Acts 5:5

5 And Ananias hearing these words, fell down, and gave up the Ghost: and great fear came on all them that heard these things.

No matter what Ananias thought, he and his wife died for lying to a god living within God. You could say a minor 'g' god who was making up a part of the body of the large 'G' God. Which is the totality of the body of the one Spirit.

Romans 8:12

12 Therefore, brethren, we are debtors, not to the flesh, to live after the flesh.

Modern-day religion teaches us that we will never be perfect. That people will always live after the flesh and sin. That is not what Paul is saying here.

Romans 8:13

13 For if ye live after the flesh, ye shall die: but if ye through the Spirit do mortify the deeds of the body, ye shall live.

According ***to*** **Oxford Languages**, we can look at the definition of the word

"***Mortify***"

"subdue" (the body or its needs and desires) by self-denial or discipline.

Showing us, we must subdue our desires (Eve) in the flesh with the Spirit. Again, Paul makes it very clear as long as you live as a mere mortal, as a fleshly man. The dirt of this earth should become your new home. But if you change your deeds and subdue your desires (Eve) for the things of this life. Suppose you would stop eating from the Tree of Good and Evil. And put forth your hands and eat from The Tree of Life. You shall be as Enoch and never see Death. Again, men and women have Adam and Eve as part of their makeup. It has nothing to do with the sexes of the fleshly person.

Genesis 3:22

22 And the Lord God said, Behold, the man is become as one of us, to know good and evil: and now, lest he put forth his hand, and also take of the tree of life, and eat, and live forever.

We must put forth our hands to change our deeds. We must willfully want to love God with all our hearts, minds, and souls. Remember, you cannot be lukewarm. Every bowl of warm soup becomes cold sooner or later.

Romans 8:14

14 For as many as are led by the Spirit of God, they are the sons of God.

Suppose God has called you from your sleep, and you are waking up to the truth about how Satan has had the world under a massive lie and a great deception all these years. You are a Son (Sun) of God, a bright, shining one. And I welcome you with open arms into the body of God. Because you, as a male or a female, are a son (sun or bright shining one) of God. You are discovering that you are more than you can ever imagine. God will lead your travels on a beautiful journey for your soul and its metamorphosis into a quickened spirit.

Romans 8:15

15 For ye have not received the Spirit of bondage again to fear; but ye have received the Spirit of adoption, whereby we cry, Abba, "Father".

When you see that there is only one body, you are a part of that body. Then you can proclaim, just as Christ did, the "Father" and I are one. You see that you and all things are one. It is hard to explain. It is peace, peace in mind, body, and Soul. The Spirit of adoption is becoming one with all things.

Romans 8:16

16 The Spirit itself beareth witness with our Spirit, that we are the children of God.

Our Soul is woken up and communicates with the Spirit of God himself. And we know that we are Spirit, and it is not of this world. This world is the playground of Satan and his demons. For us in Spirit, it is the training ground for the gods.

Romans 8:17

17 And if children, then heirs; heirs of God, and joint-heirs with Christ, if so be that we suffer with him, that we may be also glorified together.

If we become glorified, then we become heirs of God. What do the children inherit when they overcome? Revelations says we inherit all things. What are all things? Let's look at Revelations 21:7 and Philippians 2:5-6 to see what they say.

Revelation 21:7

7 He that overcometh shall inherit all things; and I will be his God, and he shall be my Son.

Philippians 2:5-6

5 Let this mind be in you, which was also in Christ Jesus.

6 Who, being in the form of God, thought it not robbery to be equal with God.

If I had said this in Christ's time, they would have picked up stones to stone me. But all things mean all things. When people grow old, they want to leave everything to their kids when they pass. We are talking about wicked people in an evil world. Now, God does not grow old or will never pass away. But does not God, love all of us and his creation, and want to do the same thing? That's why we are here, to learn how to use this power properly. To manifest perfection and overcome the world by the "Father". Becoming one with the "Father" in all things.

Matthew 7:11

If ye then, being evil, know how to give good gifts unto your children, how much more shall your "Father" which is in heaven, give good things to them that ask him?

God is Good!

Romans 8:18

18 For I reckon that the sufferings of this present time are not worthy to be compared with the glory which shall be revealed in us.

People do not know what is waiting for those that overcome.

Romans 8:19

19 For the earnest expectation of the creature waiteth for the manifestation of the sons of God.

Once you wake up to the fact that you genuinely are a Soul, capable of becoming like the Apostles, you do war with your old self through the "Father". Then when you win that war through the "Father". Even your flesh will fall in line and wait for the Soul's resurrection. The flesh will start to see its own redemption as well. As it can be raised to a higher vibration, as Christ did with Jesus and Elijah also did.

1 John 3:2

2 Beloved, now are we the sons of God, and it doth not yet appear what we shall be: but we know that, when he shall appear, we shall be like him; for we shall see him as he is.

There comes the point when you know who you are. And you go in and out of sleep, you might say. It can become confusing to some. You think you have done something wrong because you keep falling asleep again. Most likely, you have done everything correctly. But just as plants have a season of growth, so do souls. You may be waking up one day and asleep the next. It's okay; remember this verse, and you will be fine. Because one day, you will be a mighty Oak that no one can shake.

Romans 8:30

30 Moreover, whom he did predestinate, them he also called: and whom he called, them he also justified: and whom he justified, them he also glorified.

If you ask, God, he will show you what you do right and wrong. When he points out a flaw in your thinking, put it on the Altar, and walk in that new direction. Letting God justify you and then Glorifying you. It takes a short period, but God will burn it out of you. God does all the work. Our job is to walk in that new direction and have faith in him to do the rest. Remember when we first started in Romans?

Romans 1:17

17 For therein is the righteousness of God revealed from faith to faith: as it is written, the just shall live by faith.

We must live by and through faith in God to do all things. But we must believe that perfect is possible. Believe righteousness is possible, believe Holiness is possible, believe all things are possible in God and by God. God has no limitations except the ones you put on him, even then those are illusions.

Romans 8:20

20 For the creature was made subject to vanity, not willingly, but by reason of him who hath subjected the same in hope.

The lower part of man's vibration is considered the creature. According to **Merriam-webster.com,** A creature is defined as a lower animal or human.

"**Creature**"

1: something created either animate or inanimate: such as a lower animal

especially: a farm animal

b: a human being

c: a being of anomalous or uncertain aspect or nature

Romans 8:21

21 Because the creature itself also shall be delivered from the bondage of corruption into the glorious liberty of the children of God.

Here we see the creature that shall be brought from the Son of man to the Son of God into Spiritual light and life.

Remember, it said Jesus was made a little lower than the Angels for the suffering of Death. Christ was exalted above all others.

Hebrews 2:9

9 But we see Jesus, who was made a little lower than the angels for the suffering of Death, crowned with glory and honour; that he by the grace of God should taste Death for every man.

Hebrews 1:1-2

1 God, who at sundry times and in divers manners spake in time past unto the fathers by the prophets,

2 Hath in these last days spoken unto us by his Son, whom he hath appointed heir of all things, by whom also he made the worlds.

Christ made heir of all things. Christ is the Word of God that made the world and all things with the "Father".

Hebrews 1:3

3 Who being the brightness of his glory, and the express image of his person, and upholding all things by the word of his power, when he had by himself purged our sins, sat down on the right hand of the Majesty on high.

Christ sits on the right hand of God, by becoming one with God.

Hebrews 1:4

4 Being made so much better than the angels, as he hath by inheritance obtained a more excellent name than they.

God promoted Christ so much higher than the angels. He had inherited a new name; he is the Word of God. Christ, the Son of God, was not made a little lower than the angels as Jesus was. The fleshly mind of a man trying to comprehend God is like an ant trying to understand the universe.

Romans 8:22

22 For we know that the whole creation groaneth and travaileth in pain together until now.

Here Paul is talking about the process of being reborn by the Spirit. It is like giving birth to a living creature living within you. Waking up and then going back to sleep again. All the trials and tribulations you go through. You can lose family and friends because of your beliefs. It can feel painful, and it can feel like you are alone at times. But let me make this very clear as I can to you. You are never alone, even when you think you are. God is closer to you at these times than you can imagine. The groaning is also undergoing the metamorphosis.

Romans 8:23

23 And not only they, but ourselves also, which have the first fruits of the Spirit, even we ourselves groan within ourselves, waiting for the adoption, to wit, the redemption of our body.

As someone that God has been waking up for over 30 years now. I understand the waiting for adoption and what the redemption of the body means. But more people are waking up now than ever before. It is a sight and a blessing for my heart to see. I have been groaning inside myself for years. There is a travail or giving birth to the Spirit. And there are a lot of pains during that birth. Such as not knowing who you are half the time. Losing those friends and family members who think you are a nut job. The waking up and falling back to sleep in the Spirit. As a tree grows in a specific season, so does the Soul have a season of growth. I pray that these books I write might help provide many a shortcut and comfort. I have found many pitfalls over the years and waited for many a distance for a ladder to be dropped down to me that I might climb out. But God has always been there with a helping hand, and he lifts me out of that pit. Then points me in the right direction to head in again.

Romans 8:24

24 For we are saved by hope: but hope that is seen is not hope: for what a man seeth, why doth he yet hope for?

People do not see the Spirit in this world. We must put our hope in another world, A world of our "Father", which is Spirit, a world of things unseen.

Romans 8:25

25 But if we hope for that we see not, then do we, with patience, wait for it.

Live in faith as if all has happened already as if you are waiting for everyone else to catch up to the truth. The truth is, everything is already done; it just needs to play out. God will call those that need to be called by God. God will justify those that need to be justified by God. God will glorify those that God wants to be glorified. It is in God's distance that all things happen, not yours or mine.

Romans 8:26

26 Likewise the Spirit also helpeth our infirmities: for we know not what we should pray for as we ought: but the Spirit itself maketh intercession for us with groanings which cannot be uttered.

If Christ came back today, he would be as you and me. And he might be in a guy named Steve, Miguel, or Huber, who knows. But make no mistake; it would be Christ a Spirit, the Son of God. We must also understand that Christ comes back in every one of us whenever we speak the Word of the truth of God. There is Christ because Christ is the Word of God in the body of God. Man thinks in the limitations of the flesh when it comes to God. God is in every one of us. That is what omnipresent means. Christ is in every one of us. He and the "Father" are one. If God is omni-present, and there is nowhere where God is not. Then God is all things, it can be no other way. Just because someone cannot understand it does not make it untrue.

We must get out of our shallow thinking boxes and see that the Spirit is all-powerful. People must stop waiting for a man called Jesus to return to the flesh. Jesus was a man of the flesh, and Christ is a man of the Spirit. You can thank the Roman Catholic Church for the deception on this one. The Spirit itself works for our understanding and enlightenment. The Spirit of the "Father" calls us out of the darkness. When we do not see or understand, we are in the dark.

The reason is the "Father" loves us when we do not know how to love ourselves.

Romans 8:27

27 And he that searcheth the hearts knoweth what is the mind of the Spirit because he maketh intercession for the saints according to the will of God.

In the heart is where the dwelling place of John resides. John's name means love. The person that searches for love understands the mind of the "Father". God does not dwell in the flesh of people. The fleshly man is the man of corruption. When I say fleshly man, you can be either male or female to have the fleshly man. It is that which looks after the things of this world, and it is not that which is you. We have a spirit that dwells in us, that helps us even when we do not know how to be supported. That Spirit is the Spirit of truth. That Spirit of truth dwells within you. Some people call it a conscience. It is always trying to guide you into the light of being awakened. Love happens when we stop seeing each other as men and women, as blue or green, as this religion or that religion, as from this country or that country, as old or young, or whatever other limited minds can think of to divide the people into boxes. The truth has always been this simple: only one body, one Spirit, and many members. When people get lost trying to judge the diversity of God's creation and do not see there is more than one kind of flower. That God made more than one kind of cat and dog, more kinds of planets and fish. Then you can see the big picture in life. Man is no different than the rest of God's creation. It is no less diverse than the rest of the design. The only difference is how man interacts with God's creation. The fleshly man acts in imperfection in God's creation. But the dog acts perfectly in God's creation. Once man surpasses the dog in consciousness and learns to put off the imperfect self. Then we can work with God's creation and not against it. Then we can see ourselves as one with all things in the body of God.

John 16:13

13 Howbeit when he, the Spirit of truth, is come, he will guide you into all truth: for he shall not speak of himself; but whatsoever he shall

hear, that shall he speak: and he will shew you things to come.

Where do you find this Spirit of truth that will guide you? You will find it in the Spirit that dwells within you. That Spirit which you are, that Spirit which all things are.

Romans 8:28

28 And we know that all things work together for good to them that love God, to them who are the called according to his purpose.

God calls his body together for his purposes. Suppose you are waking up to Spirit. It is because God is waking you up to Spirit. Now is the time to find out what your purpose is. If you need to know what your purpose is. Then starting a relationship with your "Father" would be a good way of discovering that purpose.

Romans 4:4

4 Now to him that worketh is the reward not reckoned of grace, but of debt.

We need to rest from all our works in the heart, mind, and Soul, and let go, let God. It all hinges on a thing called faith. If you are still working in the realm of repentance. You are not working in the realm of Spirit. Repentance is in the lower realms of vibration.

Hebrews 6:1

1 Therefore leaving the principles of the doctrine of Christ, let us go on unto perfection, not laying again the foundation of repentance from dead works and of faith toward God.

Let all hear there is a time when all must put aside these false beliefs of the doctrines of the synagogues of Satan. That teaches nothing but the repentance of the flesh and imperfection. It is the flesh that will never get the job done. It is the flesh that will never please God. Never-ending repentance has always been the dead works (deeds) in the flesh. It is time to move into faith in Spirit. It is time to become one with your "Father" rather than this world of sin. Put your trust in the "Father" of Spirit. And not the god of flesh and this world.

Romans 8:29

29 For whom he did foreknow, he also did predestinate to be conformed to the image of his Son, that he might be the firstborn among many brethren.

We are to be conformed to the image of the Word of God. All as one speaking the same language, we are to be brothers and sisters with Christ. How many of you would worship your brother or sister? How many of you want your brother or sister to worship you? Christ does not want you to worship him, either. He wants you to worship the "Father", the All in All.

Romans 8:30

30 Moreover whom he did predestinate, them he also called: and whom he called, them he also justified: and whom he justified, them he also glorified.

Learn to quote this verse, then quit working for something that is already given to you. Pray to the "Father" to be called, pray to the "Father" to be justified, pray to the "Father" to be glorified. Then add faith, then move in that direction, believing the "Father" is in the middle of doing it. Then wait for it to play out in God's distance of travel. Come out of sin and be not part of it.

Romans 8:31

31 What shall we then say to these things? If God be for us, who can be against us?

You might have heard the expression of late. That nothing can stop what is coming. There is nothing more genuine than this statement. Getting out of the "Father's" way would be best. Have faith he is working on it at all times. I know this world is in chaos, and chaos seems to rule the day. And I am afraid for some of my brothers and sisters. Now I know you will make it to where you are going. It is just the distance you will need to travel that makes me concerned. Today people trust one or more men to fix these problems on earth. That is not our concern but the concern of the higher Spirit. Do you think God needs any person's help? We need not judge this world while living in the flesh. It is a trap by Satan; Satan knows what measure you give judgment, and that judgment will be returned to you by your hand. Judge not at all; let the perfect Law of Cause and Effect do all judgment. God designed this law in his perfection to do that job. Do not look for any man or put your trust in any man on this earth to fix the world's problems. Look for God's Kingdom and leave this world to Satan if Satan is the god of this earth. Then who made him the god of this earth? If God made Satan the God of this earth. Then are you fighting with Satan or God? The war inside you is big enough.

Romans 8:32

32 He that spared not his own Son, but delivered him up for us all, how shall he not with him also freely give us all things?

We are looking for all things different from what this world offers.

Romans 8:33

33 Who shall lay anything to the charge of God's elect? It is God that justifieth.

God justifies, God judges, God does all things. Quit working in the world and enter into God's rest. We must stop all 6 days of work in our hearts, minds, and souls. 6 days for the heart, 6 days for the mind, and 6 days for the Soul = 666. We must enter into the 7th day, the day of rest, where we become free from our work and the works of this world. We must **"Let Go and Let God".** The mark on your forehead is thinking and dwelling in your mind (Adam) on the things of this world, in your heart (6 days), mind (6 days), and Soul (6 days). The mark on your hand is reaching forth your hand and partaking of the things of the world with the desire (Eve) with your heart (6 days), mind (6 days), and Soul (6 days) for the things you lust (desire). It is putting forth your hand and partaking of the Tree of Good and Evil. All these things are on a spiritual level to understand. Whether there will be a mark of the beast in the flesh or not. It does not concern me and should not interest you. Because when you are looking without, you are not looking within.

Romans 8:34

34 Who is he that condemneth? It is Christ that died, yea rather, that is risen again, who is even at the right hand of God, who also maketh intercession for us.

The Word of God is what Judges all things in life. If you are not in the Word or Christ is not one with you, you should not judge; it is a grave trap for all that do. Remember the perfect law of cause-and-effect judges just because you don't see it happening immediately. It does not mean anyone is getting away with anything. Sometimes it can take lifetimes for the effect. But to think that someone will get away with something is to believe that God's law is not perfect. That somehow God needs your help in judging someone in his creation. That shows a lack of faith in God's ability to handle his creation. God's creation is perfect and runs on autopilot. When we intervene, it only creates chaos and confusion within his design.

Galatians 6:7

7 Be not deceived; God is not mocked: for whatsoever a man soweth, that shall he also reap.

Here it shows how the perfect law is in action for all. No one escapes the ideal Law of Cause and Effect. Distance is the only reason people do not see it in action. No one should want anyone to come to judgment; rather, to understand the consequences of the law.

Romans 8:35-37

35 Who shall separate us from the love of Christ? Shall tribulation, or distress, or persecution, or famine, or nakedness, or peril, or sword?

36 As it is written, for thy sake, we are killed all the day long; we are accounted as sheep for the slaughter.

37 Nay, in all these things we are more than conquerors through him that loved us.

There is nothing anyone on this earth can do to separate you from the body of God. The only one that can do that is yourself. Only your lack of faith in who you are and what God can do for you and in you.

Romans 8:38-39

38 For I am persuaded, that neither Death, nor life, nor angels, nor principalities, nor powers, nor things present, nor things to come,

39 Nor height, nor depth, nor any other creature, shall be able to separate us from the love of God, which is in Christ Jesus our Lord.

Just remember that God is the God of the living, not those dead in sin, living after the flesh. Nothing can separate you from God's love when living in Christ (the Word of God).

Mark 12:26-27

26 And as touching the dead, that they rise: have ye not read in the book of Moses, how in the bush God spake unto him, saying, I am the God of Abraham, and the God of Isaac, and the God of Jacob?

27 He is not the God of the dead, but the God of the living: ye, therefore, do greatly err.

So, those living in the flesh, thinking God is their God, greatly err because they are dead in sin. Unless, of course, you have been resurrected from that Death of sin in the flesh. God is Spirit and must be worshipped in the Spirit. That does not mean you jump around on a stage and say I am full with the Spirit of the Holy Ghost or the Lord. The "Father" has nothing to do with those living in sin and are dead in sin. Satan uses many Churches today to show many wonders through people and deceive the masses. I have heard it said, "they want a one-world religion", and that is true, but it is another deception because they already have one. After all, all religions worship the flesh of one god or another today. They do not realize they are gods themselves. They are living in the body of the big 'G' god.

1 John 3:9

9 Whosoever is born of God doth not commit sin; for his seed remaineth in him: and he cannot sin, because he is born of God.

When the true rebirth of being reborn or resurrection of the Soul happens, sin has been burned, and you cannot sin anymore because you have placed it on the Altar of God. For evil does not exist in the temple any longer. And you are that temple of God—where God the "Father" dwells. So, God does not dwell in those. That are dead in sin, living in the fleshly man (lower vibration). No matter how much someone thinks, he is. Suppose they are feeling full of the spirit. They should ask themselves whose spirit it is.

1 Corinthians 3:17

17 If any man defile the temple of God, him shall God destroy; for the temple of God is holy, which temple ye are.

When you sin, you are defiling the temple of God. The actions of those sins are destroying the life force of the fleshly being themselves. In turn, destroying your experience in this world. That is, you, which is a seed or Soul. You lose your opportunity to manifest the Spiritual light being that you can become. By now, you must see you are not just a mere mortal, just a weak sinner with no control or help in this life. We have all been lied to forever by demons. It is time to wake up from this nightmare created for us. It is time to cast off these shackles of darkness, return home to light, and become one with the "Father" again. Nowhere in the Bible does it say to continue in sin. Yes, all have sinned, and this is a good thing. We have learned the differences between good and evil through our sins. Now is the time to exercise our God-given right to choose the Tree of Life over the Tree of Good over Evil.

ROMANS 9

1 I say the truth in Christ, I lie not, my conscience also bearing me witness in the Holy Ghost.

What Paul is saying is we all have a conscience that bears us witness to all things. That calm voice tells us when we should not and when we should do something. People, in general, have just stopped listening to it. But it is there waiting for you to recognize it again. Here Paul's conscience is no longer in the fleshly man but in the Holy Ghost.

Romans 9:2-3

2 That I have great heaviness and continual sorrow in my heart.

3 For I could wish that myself were accursed from Christ for my brethren, my kinsman according to the flesh.

Notice Paul references, accursed in the flesh and not after the Spirit.

Romans 9:4-5

4 Who are Israelites; to whom pertaineth the adoption, and the glory, and the covenants, and the giving of the law, and the service of God, and the promises.

5 Whose are the fathers, and of whom as concerning the flesh Christ came, who is over all, God blessed forever. Amen.

Christ came to show the children of the flesh that they were so much more than flesh. We are all Spirit and have been taught that we are only a coat of skin less than they indeed are. Christ comes back within us now to show us a way out of this hell of deception. The Word of God leads us to the "Father". When the Word of God is sent to us by the "Father".

John 14:20

20 At that day ye shall know that I am in my "Father", and ye in me,

and I in you.

Within is where all things happen and take place. It is where you will find the fountain of youth and everlasting life in this world of death.

Romans 9:6

6 Not as though the Word of God hath taken none effect. For they are not all Israel, which are of Israel.

Gods' seeds (souls) have been scattered all over the earth in many races (different flesh)—the same old souls in other bodies and nationalities.

Romans 9:7

7 Neither, because they are the seed of Abraham, are they all children: but, in Isaac shall thy seed be called.

Just as today's society is a melting pot of people, all races scattered abroad and mingled. So are the souls of God scattered in different races of flesh. So, nobody knows who is who anymore. The plot seems always to be to kill the firstborn at the end of a reset. Probably because they know their time is short and want to extend it. Nonetheless, their efforts are in vain, as always. Because they cannot match the frequency of Spirit, it is not of a realm they can reach, even with the CERN Hadron Collider.

Romans 9:8

8 That is, they which are the children of the flesh, these are not the children of God: but the children of the promise are counted for the seed.

Ok, so here it is, God is not of those after the seed of the flesh. These are considered the son of man. Jesus referred to himself many times as the son of man. Remember, there is no respect for persons with God. God made the soul (seed) in humanity for the promise of life. That is the seed that dwells within the flesh. That is the seed that can grow into a quickened spirit. This seed or soul can grow into a Christ-like being or son of God, much more than the son of a man, or seed of the flesh.

Romans 9:9-13

9 For this is the word of promise, at this time will I come, and Sarah shall have a son.

10 And not only this; but when Rebecca also had conceived by one, even by our father, Isaac;

11 (For the children being not yet born, neither having done any good or evil, that the purpose of God according to election might stand, not of works, but of him that calleth);

12 It was said unto her, the elder shall serve the younger.

13 As it is written, Jacob have I loved, but Esau have I hated.

The only way we can understand and make sense of this verse. Is to understand we have lived many lives. How could God love and hate one another before they are born? Especially when there is no respect for a person with God. God loved Jacob for the deeds in the past lives that he lived. His causes lined up with the effects of his past lives. He hated the deeds of Esau for the causes and effects he had done in his past lives. As I said earlier, no one escapes the perfect Law of Cause and Effect. No matter how many lifetimes they live. God does not forget anything you and I have done, but he will forgive all that you have done. All your lives are recorded as if on a USB drive. I know this to be true because God has shown me videos from my past and things also that will happen to me in the future in this manner. It was like watching a video of an old program on TV. It comes with a power and vibration unknown to man. But before Esau or Jacob were planted in the womb, God knew them and predestined them to do what they would do. You have to come to understand God knows all things. That includes the past, present, and future. God knows what you are going to do before you do it. Who is it that made and gave you your heart? All things were made for God's pleasure, Amen. Amen, because for the grace of God go I.

Romans 9:14

14 What shall we say then? Is there unrighteousness with God? God

forbid.

God is righteous because we all are who we are because of the perfect Law of Cause and Effect. God does not need to judge you; you need not judge anyone else. Everyone does an excellent job of that on their own. What God does is what we all should do, that is, show love and mercy.

Romans 9:15

15 For he saith to Moses, I will have mercy on whom I will have mercy, and I will have compassion on whom I will have compassion.

God looks at your heart, not the deeds of your flesh, and the flesh cannot please him. God decides to have mercy on those he chooses to have mercy on. And God has lifetimes of you living lives to look at your heart's honesty. Have you ever seen a young person sing so beautifully? And someone says that person has an old soul, well they do. Some people are drawn to music and have perfected it over many lifetimes. How can a five-year-old play the piano like a seasoned master without instruction? They have a very old soul that has been doing it for lifetimes.

Romans 9:16

16 So then it is not of him that willeth, nor of him that runneth, but of God that sheweth mercy.

These are critical words by Paul. You cannot buy your way into heaven. Or purchase the gifts of God for your use. Was not this world given to Satan? Is he not the god of this world? Christ never tried changing this world. He came here to save those given to him by the "Father". It is the "Father" that offers grace to whom he will offer it.

John 12:47

47 And if any man hear my words, and believe not, I judge him not: for I came not to judge the world, but to save the world.

John 17:9

9 I pray for them: I pray not for the world, but for them which thou has given me; for they are thine.

John 14:3

3 And if I go and prepare a place for you, I will come again, and receive you unto myself; that where I am, there ye may be also.

Christ is Spirit, one with the "Father". We are not of this world; we are of a world much more Holy than this one—a world of Spirit and righteousness. Come out of this world and have nothing to do with it. It is full of nothing but traps and illusions. I will give a couple of verses to ponder below.

Acts 8:18

18 And when Simon saw that through laying on of the apostles' hands the Holy Ghost was given, he offered them money.

The gift of God or Holy Spirit (whole eye Spirit) is accessible to all that would have faith and do the works at the Altar of God. There are no shortcuts to acquiring the Holy Spirit.

Acts 8:19-21

19 Saying, give me also this power, that on whomsoever I lay hands, he may receive the Holy Ghost.

20 But Peter said unto him, thy money perish with thee because thou hast thought that the gift of God may be purchased with money.

21 Thou hast neither part nor lot in this matter: for thy heart is not right in the sight of God.

Notice the heart must be right with God. Science has recently discovered that the heart has neurons that fire like the brain. The heart can and does send out messages through the body. Unlike the brain (masculine), it does not do it through thought as the mind does. But the heart (the feminine) does it through feeling and intuition. We express the heart (empathy) externally, and the mind is of more internal reasoning. When someone can tell something is wrong with you without you saying anything. They are feeling it coming from the heart. It is indeed troubling that person. It is not when a person wants to hear something like, don't be a baby, or suck it up, buttercup. They are feeling it in their soul. But no one should expect genuine compassion from someone living in the flesh. The truth is they don't understand genuine compassion. If they have not understood it by the "Father".

2 Corinthians 6:14

14 Be ye not unequally yoked together with unbelievers: for what fellowship hath righteousness with unrighteousness? And what communion hath light with darkness?

It does not say to get in the middle of evil and try to change it. Darkness cannot exist in the same room as light. No matter if that light is only candlelight. How can anyone of God be friends with those of this world? The children of God are wasting their time trying to exist in this world. Satan has his own rules in place, which are put in place to imprison your mind. You will never get a fair shake from Satan or his army of demons. They distract you from God's actual prize, the union with the Father and Christ (The Word of God), the Apostles, and the whole body. Make yourself ready for the wedding to the Spirit. Oneness with God and all his power is obtained through the Holy Spirit (Whole eye Spirit).

1 John 4:13

13 Hereby know we that we dwell in him, and he in us, because he hath given us of his Spirit.

Notice the words in us, not with us. God is Spirit, that 99.9999999999996% energetic space or energy that dwells within an Atom. And that 99.9999999999996% empty space or energy that dwells outside of an Atom. God is all there is because God is also that small fraction of a percent of the Atom that can be seen. Otherwise, he would not be omnipresent. God is all things vibrating at different frequencies. You are a soul or an awaking spirit or living Spirit. You and me borrow this thing called the 'coat of skin' from God. We should all make the best use of it while on earth. Maybe even coming to the understanding that we may be able to redeem the coat of skin. Even as we seek to be redeemed from the coat of skin.

2 Corinthians 6:15

15 And what concord hath Christ with Belial? Or what part hath he that believeth with an infidel?

The world today worships Baal or Satan. He goes by many names. Baal worship has never gone away; it just went underground. *"840,000 children go missing in the USA a year alone,"* ***according to*** **<u>Google</u>**. *"8,000,000 go missing worldwide a year",* also according to **<u>Google</u>.** We don't like to ask ourselves hard questions. What happens to Eight million plus children a year that go missing? We feel more comfortable not thinking about these kinds of things. But the truth is that children are still abused as they have constantly been abused. As enslaved people for many purposes and on an altar to their god. Then some people will ask, "why does God let this happen to the children"? The mistake is looking at the flesh as it is the only reality instead of the perfect Law of Cause and Effect. If you sacrifice a child in this life, you may be sacrificed as a child in the next life. "As you plant, so shall you reap". You must understand that the Law of Cause and Effect is perfect. The flesh is an instrument of expression of the soul. The flesh has an expiration date unless redeemed, and the soul does not. It all comes down to where you want to spend your time as the soul that you are. We must stop with the importance we put on the flesh. And put the significance on God the "Father". The "Father" is Spirit, and we can manifest that Spirit. When you see a newborn baby, try not to see the baby's flesh. But an old soul traveling to and through its causes and effects. All babies' purposes are in God's hands as well as all souls. God knows the lives they have lived and will live.

2 Corinthians 6:16

16 And what agreement hath the temple of God with idols? For ye are the temple of the living God; as God hath said, I will dwell in them, and walk in them; and I will be their God, and they shall be my people.

We are the Temple of the living God. Notice that little word IN again just as God walked in Christ and Christ in Jesus. You do not belong to this world. We all have a soul (seed) in us, just like the flowers of the field. There are so many different kinds of flowers. God has made each soul as it pleases him to do. Who are we to fight against God's creation and God himself? The idols are any false beliefs we have set up in our minds. We have polluted the Temple of God by doing so.

Isaiah 45:7

7 I form the light, and create darkness: I make peace, and create evil: I, the Lord, do all these things.

God makes all things; he makes the light and the darkness, and he even creates evil. The Lord does all things. It's one of those inconvenient truths that religion does not like looking at or addressing in conversation. Everything in life is in balance, whether we know it or not.

2 Corinthians 6:17

17 Wherefore come out from among them, and be ye separate, saith the Lord, and touch not the unclean thing; and I will receive you.

Our job is to get away from these distractions. Not to get entangled in them and not to try and change them. We need to come out of the world altogether. We are Spirit and must return to worship God in Spirit and truth. All things in this world are lies, distractions, and deceptions.

2 Corinthians 6:18

18 And will be a "Father" unto you, and ye shall be my sons and daughters, saith the Lord Almighty.

So, as the "Father" says, come out of this world. I promise you there is nothing here for you but distractions. Distractions from the truth of who and what you are—a god living in the flesh of a fleshly being. Vibrate yourself and flesh into the realm of heaven. Free yourself from believing you are only a mortal. See yourself in the likeness you were created in.

John 15-19

19 If ye were of the world, the world would love his own: but because ye are not of the world, but I have chosen you out of the world, therefore the world hateth you.

Have you ever felt unloved by this world? I have, and thank God that this world has hated me. God is not the God of this world that you see before you. He gave it over to Satan. Christ is asking us all the same question. ***"Simon Peter, Simon, son of Jonas, lovest thou me more than these"?***

Matthew 10:37

37 He who loves father or mother more than me is not worthy of me. And he who loves son or daughter more than me is not worthy of me.

God's first commandment is not written as a suggestion, nor was it written in vain. We must love God with all our hearts, minds, and souls. When we marry our husbands or wives, we become one in the flesh with them. When we marry into the body of our "Father", we become one Spirit. We will not be reunited with our husbands or wives after death. But as the angels of heaven, we are neither given nor taken in marriage as in the flesh. But are married into the body of Christ, the Word of God.

Matthew 22:30

30 For in the resurrection they neither marry, nor are given in marriage, but are as the angels of God in heaven.

We are so much more than we think we are.

Matthew 10:38

38 And he who does not take his cross and follow after Me is not worthy of Me.

To take up your cross is to crucify the old man of the flesh and his ways. To be found worthy, you must put off the old man by putting your faith in God and resurrecting the new man. If you do not love God above all that there is, you are not fulfilling the first commandment. To love God with all your heart, mind, and soul. We must thank God for his mercy and for calling us out of our deep sleep. The cross represents the dying of the old false beliefs. That we acquired over our lifetimes.

Matthew 10:39

39 He who finds his life will lose it, and he who loses his life for My sake will find it.

He finds he is a soul waking up. Losing the life of the old man he was. And when the old man of the flesh is done away with, you will find your new life in Spirit.

Romans 9:17-18

17 For the scripture saith unto Pharaoh, even for this same purpose have I raised thee, up that I might show my power in thee, and that my name might be declared throughout all the earth.

18 Therefore hath he mercy on whom he will have mercy, and whom he will he hardeneth.

Suppose you see the truth and harden your heart; your heart will become hardened. Just like Pharaoh, after seeing the works and power of God, he could not let the people go. Some people will know this truth and not be able to give up on this world. They will convince themselves that none of it is true. That is when the heart becomes hardened. They need more time in this realm to learn more from their experiences. Before coming to the knowledge of the "Father". For some, it is easier to live a lie than to change into something new.

Romans 9:19-20

19 Thou wilt say then unto me, why doth he yet find fault? For who hath resisted his will?

20 Nay but, O man, who art thou that repliest against God? Shall the thing formed say to him that formed it, why hast though made me thus?

We are all made for God's pleasure and have a role to play. That's why it is not good to judge anything in creation. It is God's creation; who are we to judge it? All are on a path to awakening, either to the darkness or light; who are we to change that path? As if you or I could do more than God could. If God wants someone awake, who can keep them asleep? If God wants someone asleep, who can awaken them from their sleep

Romans 9:21

21 Hath not the potter power over the clay, of the same lump to make one vessel unto honor, and another unto dishonor?

Paul sums it up by saying God has the power to make all things as he sees fit. We must be able to understand good as well as evil play a role in life. Seeing bad things happen helps us understand and appreciate the good stuff. Being hated and loved by others helps us understand love and all its mercy. But you must be able to see that hate without judging. Just see the hate for what it is, no more or less than hate. Adam and Eve were created perfectly and could not appreciate it, not having something to compare their perfection with, but they do now.

Romans 9:22-23

22 What if God, willing to shew his wrath and to make his power known, endured with much longsuffering the vessels of wrath fitted to destruction?

23 And that he might make known the riches of his glory on the vessels of mercy, which he had afore prepared unto glory.

God is the only one that saves souls. And God can save to the utmost. No one has a right to judge God's creation. He has set in place the perfect law to do that. Paul was consenting to the death of the Apostles. Yet he was brought back from the pit of destruction. So, God can call even outer darkness to the light. Let's take a look at what 2 Peter 3:8 says about it all.

2 Peter 3:8

8 But, beloved, be not ignorant of this one thing, that one day is with the Lord as a thousand years and a thousand years as one day.

God does not see time as humans see time. In Spirit it is distance traveled between cause and effect. You can learn the lessons you need in this lifetime or the next. Man, in his arrogance, thinks God is like himself. And limited to this thing called the illusion of time. Restricting God, and tying his hands, believing that God gives man but one life to learn all there is to know and experience. There is so much to learn about God and all the distance he gives us to do it in. One lifetime is not enough to learn all there is to know about God. We could have started as evil to understand what evil was. But if all are dead in sin, are they not evil now? Could it not be just a different degree of evil? But to God, unrighteousness is unrighteousness to any degree. Any degree will keep you out of Spirit. So, who will justify their degree before God? All is damnation. Time is an illusion, just like the days of the week—all distractions from the head of Satan. Our old friend Emperor Constantine adopted the seven-day of the week for official use in AD 321. Sunday was named Sunday because of Sun worship, and Friday was named Friday for the goddess Freyja, where Easter originated. They would take eggs, dip them in the blood of sacrificed children and offer them as offerings to Freyja. And that is where dying easter eggs came about. Don't you love the Pagan traditions set up in Christianity? All days of the week are named after planets and represent a different pagan god. Odin, also known as Woden, is where we get the name for Wednesday. It goes on and on etc. etc. etc. The point is humanity has been lied to for a very long time. Spirit does not see time as mortals do. When you live forever, why would you see time? Why would you ever hurry to get somewhere other than here?

2 Peter 3:9

9 The Lord is not slack concerning his promise, as some men count slackness; but is longsuffering to us-ward, not willing that any should perish, but that all should come to repentance.

God does not wish that any be lost at all. He wants all to understand what and who they indeed are. No matter how lost someone is, there is still hope in

God's mercy, and all means all. Some people have told me that God will never save some people, and I don't see it that way. But I know not, but God does. So, I will leave it to him and wish for the best. I remember how far lost I was, yet I stand here today by the grace of my "Father". Fulfilling the purpose, he has set before me now as I write this.

Romans 9:24

24 Even us, whom he hath called, not of the Jews only, but also of the Gentiles?

It does not matter if you are a Jew (Spiritually minded person), one inward. Or a gentile (man of the flesh) who is outward. There is hope for all if Christ's name is manifested (the Word of God) within us.

Romans 9:25

25 As he saith also in Osee, I will call them my people, which were not my people; and her beloved, which was not beloved.

There is hope for the Gentiles, or the ones living after the fleshly man.

Romans 9:26-28

26 And it shall come to pass, that in the place where it was said unto them, ye are not my people; there shall they be called the children of the living God.

27 Esaias also crieth concerning Israel, Though the number of the children of Israel be as the sand of the sea, a remnant shall be saved.

28 For he will finish the work, and cut it short in righteousness: because a short work will the Lord make upon the earth.

The short work we see is righteousness (right-use-ness of the law), not sin. Anyone that continues in sin is not finishing the work of God—notice also the short work that is to be completed on earth. We do not die and then go to heaven. Because the work still needs to be completed, the work must be done here and now, on earth. We must put on the whole armor of God now.

Hebrews 4:12

12 For the word of God is quick, powerful, and sharper than any two-edged sword, piercing even to the dividing asunder of soul and Spirit, and of the joints and marrow, and is a discerner of the thoughts and intents of the heart.

Notice the Word discerns your thoughts and intentions of the heart—that of the masculine and feminine parts of the soul. Here is a small example of what a little power in the Word can do. Have you ever been caught in a lie by anyone? Then that person called you out on it in front of many people. Then your cheeks turned red, and you became embarrassed and humiliated because everyone had seen your lie, and you could do nothing to hide from it. That is the word working in the lowest vibration that it works in. Imagine if you were in the Spirit using those exact words. That is why learning what love is and manifesting love is so important because of how much damage you can do with the Words (Christ). You would never give your children a gun and say here, play with this. You would be right by their side and give them instructions on using it safely. Just as your "Father" is beside you, showing you how to manifest love. So, you might use the Word (the Sword and Word of God) and all his gifts in love.

Romans 9:29-32

29 And as Esaias said before, Except the Lord of Sabaoth had left us a seed, we had been as Sodoma, and been made like unto Gomorrha.

30 What shall we say then? That the Gentiles, which followed not after righteousness, have attained to righteousness, even the righteousness which is of faith.

31 But Israel, which followed after the law of righteousness, hath not attained to the law of righteousness.

32 Wherefore? Because they sought it not by faith but as it were by the works of the law. For they stumbled at that stumbling stone.

The stumbling block is the same today as it has always been. People think the flesh pleases God. And by doing works in the flesh, they will earn their way into God's grace or heaven, and it will never happen; the flesh cannot please God. And the "Father" and Christ already did all the work for us. The only work we need to do is walk in the direction of faith. That God will do the works that he said he would. Again, look at Romans 8:30

Romans 8:30

30 Moreover whom he did predestinate, them he also called: and whom he called, them he also justified: and whom he justified, them he also glorified.

We do not choose our destination, we do not call ourselves, we do not justify ourselves, and we do not glorify ourselves. God does all things, and we have faith in God. That God will do all things that he promised us he would do.

Romans 9:33

33 As it is written, Behold, I lay in Sion a stumbling stone and rock of offence: and whosoever believeth on him shall not be ashamed.

The old traditions of the churches are the stumbling block. To think that you can sin the same sin over and over. Then come to a church for 2 hours on Sunday. Then have a sinful man forgive you for the same things he is doing. Then to expect forgiveness from God, I don't have the words. It is making a mockery of God and his Holy Word. It is spitting on the blood of Christ and his sacrifice for us. But Satan is happier than you will ever know when people do all these things.

ROMANS 10

1 Brethren, my heart's desire and prayer to God for Israel is that they might be saved.

2 For I bear them record that they have a zeal of God, but not according to knowledge.

There are a lot of decent people that go to different Churches, Synagogues. Mosques, Temples, and any other place called a place of worship. They have what they consider to be a knowledge of God. But have been denied the absolute truth and knowledge about God. These are the ones Paul is talking about here. They go out into communities and help with the homeless and volunteer time to help others. They do not understand the ones needing to be clothed are themselves. Because they are naked in sin before God, they do not know that the fatherless and widows are themselves. Because the "Father" is not their God. Again, the "Father" is the God of the Living, not the dead. And they are widows because they are dead in sin and have died in the Spirit. They need to be married into the body of Christ.

Romans 10:3

3 For they being ignorant of God's righteousness, and going about to establish their own righteousness, have not submitted themselves unto the righteousness of God.

When you live by the Tree of Good and Evil, you believe you are doing good because you compare the deeds that you are doing to those deeds that someone else is doing. When you are doing the same things, but to different degrees, the evil side of the Tree is where evil deeds take place. The Good side of that same Tree is a person comparing the wrong that they have done to another person's wrong that they had done. You are justifying your wrong doing because, in your eyes, it was not as bad as what they did. So, in your eyes, you are more righteous than them. When in fact, you were both wrong to different degrees. God does not care about who is more or less wrong, no matter the degree of it. The only way to bypass this is to eat from the Tree of Life. You can read about this in my book. **"Atom and Eve's walk in the Garden**

<u>of Eden</u>". We cannot go about trying to justify our way into heaven, and we must let go and let God. You must submit yourself before the altar.

Romans 10:4

4 For Christ is the end of the law for righteousness to everyone that believeth.

Christ, the Word of God is the end of the law. The Word leads you into righteousness through faith in the "Father". That God will do what he has promised through his Word.

Romans 10:5

5 For Moses describeth the righteousness which is of the law, That the man which doeth those things shall live by them.

The problem in the time of Moses was that they could not do the law. They would try to do the law through the fleshly man. But their way of thinking (mind), that being the inside of the cup, was polluted. By all the evil things, they would think on day to day.

Romans 10:6

6 But the righteousness which is of faith speaketh on this wise, say not in thine heart, who shall ascend into heaven? (That is, to bring Christ down from above.)

You are one with Christ and the body of God. If you cannot see yourself ascending into the Spirit. You have brought down the Word of God (Christ) that dwells in you. That is where humankind is today. People see themselves as well, as humanity as mortals. In this case, that is what they are. You are no longer a spiritual being in your mind. But you live in the illusion you created for yourself; it is all a question of faith—faith in fantasy or reality. Right now, the delusion is powerful and seems so natural. It is hard to break away from its hold on the people. It is a hard thing to admit to yourself. Your whole life and all you ever believed in is a lie. Once you start down the rabbit hole, it is a long distance before you see the light from an emergency exit at the other end of that hole. You are a creator in the "Father's" image. As a creator, this life is what you have created for yourself. Well done, you have created a reality so good you fooled yourself into the illusion that you are not a god.

Romans 10:7

7 Or, who shall descend into the deep? (That is, to bring up Christ again from the dead.)

So, if you will descend into the depths of that rabbit hole. And obtain knowledge of the Word of God and the "Father". That knowledge will awaken the Christ (Word) within you, which will lead you into the everlasting life of the birth of that seed that dwell within you and the resurrection of the soul from the dead.

Romans 10:8

8 But what saith it? The Word is nigh thee, even in thy mouth, and in thy heart: that is, the Word of faith, which we preach.

Faith is the key to opening or closing the kingdom of God's body. All must have faith that God will do the works within them. All you must do is put yourself on the Altar and trust God will accept your offer of yourself that he will clean you in the fire.

Galatians 2:20

20 I am crucified with Christ: nevertheless, I live; yet not I, but Christ liveth in me: and the life which I now live in the flesh I live by the faith of the Son of God, who loved me and gave himself for me.

We must all undergo being crucified in like manner with Christ. We must all pick up our cross and die daily. We find our faith in the Word, sent by the "Father". It was Christ (the Word) that lived in Paul.

Luke 9:23

23 And he said to them all, if any man will come after me, let him deny himself, and take up his cross daily, and follow me.

You must deny the old man of sin, and he must be put to death on the cross so that you (soul) might live.

Job 23:10

10 But he knoweth the way that I take: when he hath tried me, I shall come forth as Gold.

Here Job is talking about the trying process. The trials and tribulations of humankind. But never tempt the forces within yourself. By saying I would love God even if I lost this or that. That also gives life to Satan (negative thoughts) that dwell within humanity. To them, that, overcome the trials and tribulations they come out as pure Gold as if tried in a fire.

Revelation 3:18

18 I counsel thee to buy of me Gold tried in the fire, that thou mayest be rich; and white raiment, that thou mayest be clothed, and that the shame of thy nakedness does not appear; and anoint thine eyes with eyesalve, that thou mayest see.

The Gold tried in the fire is you; the fire is burning out all the sin within you by putting it on the Altar of God. We are all naked in sin, and the more corruption God burns out of you, the more you become clothed in light. The eye salve is your prayers to God.

Matthew 16:18

18 And I say also unto thee, that thou art Peter, and upon this rock, I will build my church; and the gates of hell shall not prevail against it.

Peter is the rock that dwells in all of us; that rock is faith. Faith is what the true church of God is built on, not in ourselves but in God. That church is not of this world but the world of Spirit.

Matthew 16:19

19 And I will give unto thee the keys of the kingdom of heaven: and whatsoever thou shalt bind on earth shall be bound in heaven: and

whatsoever thou shalt loose on earth shall be loosed in heaven.

We all have the keys to the kingdom of heaven. Whatever you believe is impossible for God to do for you in heaven, it will not be done for you on earth because of your lack of faith in God. If you have faith in God of heaven, anything is possible on earth. Then you can have anything of God you seek. Remember what you are seeking, though. Are you asking for the riches of this world? Or, are you looking for the prosperity of a world unseen, a world of Spirit? Remember what it says in James.

James 4:4

4 Ye adulterers and adulteresses, know ye not that the friendship of the world is enmity with God? Whosoever, therefore, will be a friend of the world is the enemy of God.

It is better not to seek the things of this world. And seek the riches of the invisible world within you. And express that world through yourself to the outer world.

James 1:5-6

5 If any of you lack wisdom, let him ask of God, that giveth to all men liberally, and upbraideth not; and it shall be given him.

6 But let him ask in faith, nothing wavering. For he that wavereth is like a wave of the sea driven with the wind and tossed.

Faith is not a thing asked for today, and you forget about tomorrow. When you pray, you must put all your heart, mind, and soul into what you are praying for nothing wavering when you place your heart into what you are asking. You are putting your consciousness and emotions into what you are asking for from God. See what you are asking for as if it is already yours as if you have received it from God already. If you ask for rain to come, see the rain within yourself, visualize the rain, smell the rain, feel the rain coming down on you, and stand in the shower within your mind. Feel it in your soul and become one with the rain you ask God to bring about. Then say thank you, knowing God heard you and it is on its way.

I live in Oklahoma, and a few years ago, we were going through a bad drought. So bad people were selling off their cattle because the ponds had dried up. As far as you could see, there was no rain in the forecast. I remember praying for rain in the middle of summer. And knowing it was going to come from God. If you know anything about small-town life. You would know that all the ranchers and old-timers meet in the small-town coffee shops in the morning. Well, I am one of those small-town people. So, I started going to the coffee shop in the middle of summer with no rain in the forecast, with an umbrella. I remember one of my friends asking me, "what was I doing carrying that umbrella all the time"? He told me"; that there was no rain in the forecast and we were in a drought". I looked right at him and told him. "I understand that, but it is going to rain soon." I told my friend, "If he was smart, he should get an umbrella so he didn't get wet". Now, I probably looked and sounded out of my mind. But the truth is, I am not trying to please this world. My faith is that God is manifesting the Word of God within me. I know that faith without works is dead. And that works without faith are dead. You must walk in the direction of your faith; that is the works.

It was knowing that God has heard you and you are getting the package in the mail that you ordered online. It is just a matter of the distance between ordering and receiving the item. I was expecting rain and did not want to get caught without an umbrella. And yes, we received a lot of rain. It rained until this year, 2022. Just as people thought Christ and Paul were crazy back in their time. Let people see your crazy side today, and do everything in faith in God. Have faith in things unseen.

Acts 26:24

24 And as he thus spake for himself, Festus said with a loud voice, Paul, thou art beside thyself; much learning doth make thee mad.

You could not imagine how many people would have come to believe you have gone mad when God starts manifesting the Word of God within you. People will see you coming and start to cringe a little. Afraid you might say something about God. And you will because you can't help yourself because it is who you are becoming. You can't help it because you are becoming one with your "Father". Christ did not talk about anything but the Spirit. When you move into Spirit, nothing of this world matters. Your life becomes about Spirit and spiritual things. When you love God with all your mind, guess what is always on your mind? Now imagine what the topic of the day is going to be. So, yes, the closer you get to God, the further from the world you will get. It's like a bee trying to be an ant in front of other bees. The bees will always see it for what it truly is, a bee. You will find the more God gives you growth in Spirit. That light starts to shine in the darkness, and the darkness understands it not. But you will never be alone and always have the Word and "Father" to talk with twenty-four-seven. And they are not far away but very close.

James 1:7-8

7 For let not that man think that he shall receive any thing of the Lord.

8 A double minded man is unstable in all his ways.

All things happen according to faith. How fast something happens is according with your faith and the work you put into your faith. How much are you living in the perfect law? As well as your understanding of that perfect law. Remember the first commandment: love God with all your heart, mind, and soul. One with doubts in their mind and no work can expect nothing.

Romans 10:9

9 That if thou shalt confess with thy mouth the Lord Jesus, and shalt believe in thine heart that God hath raised him from the dead, thou shalt be saved.

This verse has been another tool of Satan's. Once you study for yourself, and understand the deception of the Romans and the Roman Catholic Church. You will see how the Romans worshipped planets and men and women as Gods. It becomes easier to understand how and why they turned Jesus, a man of flesh, into a god at the conclave. The pagan Roman citizens had to buy into the new religion. It also entrapped the true Christians into worshiping a man as God. Christ is the Word of God, and Christ is Spirit. To confess the Word, you must manifest the Word. Notice Paul also says you must believe in your heart. He is telling you to feel the Word of God in every member of your body. If you are to believe in Christ, you must believe in his words. He spoke nothing of himself but what the Father gave him to speak. Then they were not only Christ's words but God's commandments from God himself.

John 1:1

1 In the beginning was the Word, and the Word was with God, and the Word was God.

Revelation 19:13

13 And he was clothed with a vesture dipped in blood: and his name is called the Word of God.

Here it states the actual name of Christ. Christ was God's words manifested here on earth in the form of a man of flesh called Jesus. Just as you have a voice that comes out of your body. God has a voice that comes out of his body. That voice is Christ, and he is perfect knowledge, wisdom, and understanding at expression. God is perfect knowledge, wisdom, and understanding at conception. Our jobs as children of the living God are to learn how to express God perfectly. That is why all of us are here on this earth. It is a training ground for the gods to become like their "Father".

John 12:49

49 For I have not spoken of myself; but the "Father" which sent me, he gave me a commandment, what I should say, and what I should speak.

Again, Christ expressed the Father perfectly. If we are to confess Christ as souls in our bodies of flesh. God raises our souls from the dead, which souls' dwell within the bodies of flesh—moving from mortal to immortal to complete the process.

1 Corinthians 15:53

53 For this corruptible must put on incorruption, and this mortal must put on immortality.

Paul is talking about rebirth or being reborn anew into Spirit.

Romans 10:10

10 For with the heart man believeth unto righteousness, and with the mouth, confession is made unto salvation.

It is not enough to use your mouth and confess the name of Jesus. Then to think you somehow have eternal life. You must put off Satan and his works from yourself. And look to the true Son of God, the one the only Christ. Christ was an accurate image of the "Father" in the flesh. We must feel it in our hearts, minds, and voice. Because our mouths indeed confess what the mind and heart are thinking.

Romans 10:11

11 For the scripture saith, whosoever believeth on him shall not be ashamed.

If you believe in Christ, you accept his words and do them. They were never suggestions; they were commandments.

Matthew 5:48

48 Be ye therefore perfect, even as your Father which is in heaven is perfect.

Christ did not misspeak if he was perfect. Christ would not ask you to do something you could not do if it were understood you could not do it. Yet here is another commandment that he spoke. And since he spoke not of himself, but what the "Father" gave him to speak. Then this is not a commandment from Christ, but from God himself.

Romans 10:12

12 For there is no difference between the Jew and the Greek: for the same Lord over all is rich unto all that call upon him.

There is no respect for persons with God. Anyone can receive God's grace and mercy. All you need to do is go into the closet (within you). Shut the door to the outside world, and call upon God. Place your free will offering on the Altar of

God's mercy seat, and believe, have faith. Walk in that new direction that God shows you. Then watch the magic happen in and around you.

Hebrews 4:16

16 Let us, therefore, come boldly unto the throne of grace, that we may obtain mercy, and find grace to help in time of need.

We are like a nugget of Gold, full of impurities. When we present offerings to God, God burns out that dross from within us. When God's firing process is complete, we become pure refined Gold or Holy to God. Then God has a purified Temple that he can dwell in to make his abode. That is when you can say, "I and the "Father" are one."

Romans 10:13

13 For whosoever shall call upon the name of the Lord shall be saved.

That name of the Lord is "The Word of God". Call on and in the Word and you shall be saved. You must call on the "Father" through and in the true Word to be saved, not just say I believe in the name of Jesus, and believe you will receive eternal life. That is an illusion of Satan to keep you in this realm and at a lower vibration. If Satan can't go to a higher vibration, he does not want you to go.

Romans 10:14-16

14 How then shall they call on him in whom they have not believed? And how shall they believe in him of whom they have not heard? And how shall they hear without a preacher?

15 And how shall they preach, except they be sent? As it is written, how beautiful are the feet of them that preach the gospel of peace, and bring glad tidings of good things!

16 But they have not all obeyed the gospel. For Esaias saith, Lord, who hath believed our report?

Still today, it can be said by Esaias, "Lord, who has believed our report".

Because as long as the world believes it is impossible to put on perfection. The report of all the prophets has gone unheeded.

We have millions of preachers in this world. Unfortunately, they have not been called by God to preach his Word. Men have trained preachers of today to preach what they believe. Other men have trained their preachers and so on. Until you get to the point that Satan and his demons trained those that trained them. God's Word was lost to the world just as it was foretold by God to happen in the book of Acts. But it is time to believe the Word of God again. It is time for the great awakening of God's children, and I believe this in my heart. Indeed, all things happen in God's distance of travel, not beholden to a clock hanging on a wall.

Acts 2:20

20 The sun shall be turned into darkness, and the moon into blood, before that great and notable day of the Lord come.

Christ is the Son (Sun bright shining one); the Apostles are the Moon (those that reflect the light) of the Son (Sun). The Word of Christ was going to be lost. And the Apostles, the fruit (deeds), or the twelve foundations would be polluted as they are today. There is no religion that I know of today speaking the truth about God. I know that it is going to be hard for a lot of people to accept and wrap their heads around. I had to go through some of that within myself. It is hard to believe we have been lied to our whole lives. But other people are only teaching what other people have taught them.

Romans 10:17

17 Faith cometh by hearing and hearing by the Word of God.

Ok, so our faith comes from the Word (Christ) by hearing the Word (Christ). Christ Lives in the temple of God. So where is this temple to receive this Word?

1 Corinthians 3:16

16 Know ye not that ye are the temple of God, and that the Spirit of God dwelleth in you?

Your soul is the temple of God. God the "Father" and Christ (the Word) live in the temple when it is built, reborn, or resurrected.

John 14:18-20

18 I will not leave you comfortless: I will come to you.

19 Yet a little while, and the world seeth me no more, but ye see me: because I live, ye shall live also.

20 At that day ye shall know that I am in my "Father", and ye in me, and I in you.

You become part of one big family of Spirit. One Spirit with many members, all within yourself. You can travel without traveling. Notice the words again in you; what does that mean? It means what it says; they shall be in you. Look at what Christ says in verse 21.

John 14:21

21 He that hath my commandments, and keepeth them, he it is that loveth me: and he that loveth me shall be loved of my Father, and I will love him and will manifest myself to him.

I shall manifest myself to him or you. There is genuinely only one body and many, many, many members. Suppose I tell you to find a place where you could be alone. You would not be able to find a place to do so. If you went 500 miles into space by yourself, you still would not be alone. You would still be surrounded by the space that encompasses all of us. We are one giant organism with many members to it. The matter world is Spirit vibrating at a very slow vibration. Some parts of God vibrate at a low vibration and frequency, and some at a much higher one. But it is all one great big body of God. Shrink the universe down to the size of a snow globe as the existence of it all. Picture all things in the snow globe as you and me as all things. Then look at the snow globe, as God is the snow globe and the fluid in the globe that holds all things within himself, and we have our movement within the globe and God. And all things Vibrate at different frequencies to make them what they are. Now there are just a couple more things. First, God is all things outside the snow globe as well. Second, God is also inside all things that dwell within the snow globe. Third, God is in the middle of the things living inside the snow globe because God is omnipresent. It is much easier to say God is All and in All and All is All.

1 Corinthians 12:12

12 For as the body is one and hath many members, and all the members of the one body, being many, are one body: so also, is Christ.

Christ is Spirit; he and the "Father" are one. We are Spirit and members of that one body. The only question is, where is your vibration within the body? If you are at a lower vibration, you are a gentile, living after the flesh. If you are a Jew, you live in a higher vibration of Spirit.

1 Corinthians 12:13

13 For by one Spirit are we all baptized into one body, whether we be Jews or Gentiles, whether we be bond or free; and have been all made to drink into one Spirit.

Again, "there is only one Spirit and not two". You and I are Adams (Atoms) in that body. No matter if you live to the flesh or the Spirit. Whether you are bound to do the Word of God as Paul was, it does not matter; you are free to make whatever choice you want. But your choices determine the rate of vibration at which you vibrate. There is only one Spirit that makes up the whole of existence. And to try to see yourself existing outside of God is lunacy. All is All, and the only thing that separates anything from anything is not God but deeds the deeds from one Tree or another Tree. You are a Tree in the garden of Eden. And your fruit (Deeds) are either pleasing to God or not.

Ezekiel 31:16

16 I made the nations to shake at the sound of his fall when I cast him down to hell with them that descend into the pit: and all the trees of Eden, the choice and best of Lebanon, all that drink water, shall be comforted in the nether part of the earth.

The choice trees of Lebanon were souls put into coats of skin, and God sent those souls to the nether parts of the earth. The water that comforts is the Living Water, The Word of God Christ.

Definitions of the Word Nether from **Oxford Languages:**

"Nether"

lower in position.

To be in a carnal state of mind in a lower vibration than heaven. Or to be one in the Garden of Eden. Hell is where you and I are right now. To be carnally minded and be a god is hell; trust me on this one.

Ezekiel 31:17

17 They also went down into hell with him unto them that be slain with the sword; and they that were his arm, that dwelt under his shadow in the midst of the heathen.

Pharaoh and his army are being talked about here. They were cast down to the vibration in consciousness, where we are today.

Ezekiel 31:18

18 To whom art thou thus like in glory and in greatness among the trees of Eden? Yet shalt thou be brought down with the trees of Eden unto the nether parts of the earth: thou shalt lie in the midst of the uncircumcised with them that be slain by the sword. This is Pharaoh and all his multitude, saith the Lord God.

It is one of the most revealing verses in the Bible if the people would just read it for themselves. God is talking to Pharaoh, telling Pharaoh he was one of the greatest trees in the garden of Eden. What people need to realize when reading the Bible. It was not written for the coat of skin or man of flesh but for the soul's benefit. It speaks in a language of Spirit, not flesh. It uses things of this world to explain something of the Spirit. **Thoth** uses the expression: **"As above so below, as below so above".** Thoth was saying that things of this world and heaven mirror each other. So, you can use something of this world to explain things of the Spirit. And the Bible does just that indeed. Suppose God is talking about an eagle, for example. He is talking about a soul very high in Spirit. One that can rise above the carnal realm into Spirit and see all things. An eagle flies higher than any other bird and has the best eyesight. Compared to, say, a sparrow that does not get very high off the ground.

Nonetheless, they still do get off the ground. So, they would be someone just getting into spirit. Not as powerful as an eagle, but still in spirit. A snake is always in the lowest realm, seeing it crawls on its belly. It is even below the cattle, which walk on all four hooves. When you understand God's language, the Bible becomes a different book.

John 5:39

39 Search the scriptures; for in them ye think ye have eternal life: and they are they which testify of me.

So many people read the scriptures thinking they have found life in Jesus, not knowing how they have been led down the wrong road. Because the scriptures testify about Christ the son of God. And Christ testifies of the "Father", not himself.

John 5:40

40 And ye will not come to me, that ye might have life.

It would be best to come to the Word of Spirit to have life. The word of the flesh will profit you nothing.

John 5:41

41 I receive not honour from men.

Christ tells you here he receives no honor from men. And he was the Christ, the son, the Word of God. And yet all honor is given to a man of flesh, Jesus. These are the words of Christ and not mine. So, if you are trying to give honor to Jesus, it will let you know he is not receiving it from anyone.

John 5:42

42 But I know you, that ye have not the love of God in you.

You must love God with all your heart, mind, and soul to have a love of God in you.

John 5:43

43 I am come in my "Father's" name, and ye receive me not: if another shall come in his own name, him ye will receive.

Christ is talking about the people who always denied the Spirit. And how the people were always looking for a man of flesh to worship and solve their problems. They are always looking for another man to have a relationship with God for them. Not knowing all must have their own relationship with God. That's why they looked to Jesus back then and still today. Not knowing Christ came in the "Fathers" name, The Word of God.

John 5:44

44 How can ye believe, which receive honour one of another, and seek not the honour that cometh from God only?

In other words, how can you believe a person of sin about God? When that sinner has not overcome the flesh himself. When you can get the knowledge, you need yourself from God, one on one. Also, notice Christ is saying not to receive honor from each other. And yet honor is given to Jesus daily. Is God a respecter of people? Did not Christ say in verse 41 that he receives honor from no man?

1 Corinthians 12:14

14 For the body is not one member, but many.

There are many members of the body of God. All is God, and God is all. God is the All in All, and the All is in All; this is the mystery of God. You cannot create something from nothing. And God is all that there is and ever was or could be God created us from himself. That is why we were made in God's image and likeness. Blessed be God the Almighty, forever and ever and evermore.

Roman 10:18-19

18 But I say, have they not heard? Yes, verily, their sound went into all the earth, and their words unto the ends of the world.

19 But I say, did not Israel know? First, Moses saith, I will provoke you to jealousy by them that are no people, and by a foolish nation, I will anger you.

All happened just as it was supposed to, believe it or not. And it is going according to plan today. Nothing escapes God, not for a moment. And I thank God I am from a foolish Nation.

Roman 10:20-21

20 But Esaias is very bold, and saith, I was found of them that sought me not; I was made manifest unto them that asked not after me.

21 But to Israel he saith, all day long I have stretched forth my hands unto a disobedient and gainsaying people.

Israel's rebellious nature has opened the door of grace and mercy to all souls in all nations. It does not matter your race, what country you live in, or if you are rich or poor. If you would but have faith in God and do the works. The grace and mercy of God will save you.

ROMANS 11

1 I say then, Hath God cast away his people? God forbid. For I also am an Israelite, of the seed of Abraham, of the tribe of Benjamin.

2 God hath not cast away his people which he foreknew. Wot ye not what the scripture saith of Elias? How he maketh intercession to God against Israel, saying,

3 Lord, they have killed thy prophets and digged down thine altars, and I am left alone, and they seek my life

4 But what saith the answer of God unto him? I have reserved to myself seven thousand men who have not bowed the knee to the image of Baal.

Seven thousand people are not very many. So, if only 7,000 have not bowed down their knee to Baal. Out of all the people back then. How many people do you think are left today? Who do you think people are worshipping today? There seem to be many more people in the different churches than 7,000. Whether we see it or not, Baal is still revered today, knowingly and unknowingly. Suppose you worship the creation and not the beloved Creator. Then you are a worshiper of Baal. It is a false idol sat up in front of God the Almighty. To worship the lower vibration that was and is a creation of God is worshiping the creation of God. We saw this earlier in Romans. We must all worship God in Spirit. God is the whole creation of All; you are a soul who can become part of that entire creation instead of being dead as most souls are now. Christ is our brother in the Spirit. To worship Jesus is like the mind of man worshiping an Atom. But the things of this world (Jesus) are upon their lips. But the "Father" (Spirit) is far from their thoughts.

Matthew 12:50

50 For whosoever shall do the will of my "Father" which is in heaven, the same is my brother, and sister, and mother.

We must stop looking at Jesus or any other fleshly man as being the son of

God. He was the son of Mary; he was the son of man. Christ is the son of God and did not wish to be worshiped, nor did Jesus.

Isaiah 42:8

8 I am the LORD: that is my name: and my Glory will I not give to another, neither my praise to graven images.

You cannot make an engraved image of Spirit. And God is not sharing his Glory with anyone else. Back then, they made gods out of statues of gold and brass. Today people also use gold, brass, silver, and canvas. The highest vibrations are Spirit and cannot be seen on earth except in the deeds of humanity. You can make an engraved image of things seen on this earth and worship those things. That would be the creation of the living God. That would include men of the flesh. For example, Buda, Mahammad, Jesus, Hermes, Zeus, Freya, etc. These are people of the flesh, and God is Spirit. That is not to say that these persons did not have an awakened Spirit. I am only showing you a clear separation of things seen (flesh) and unseen (Spirit). And only God, the "Father" of us all, must be worshiped by all. And that must be done in Spirit and not in the flesh. Whether you call him God, the "Father", the Great Spirit, or Allah, it does not matter. God is Spirit and, therefore, must be worshipped in Spirit. There is only one God, and the people have divided God up into boxes for their own purposes. All are saying the same thing that their God is the greatest. God has nothing to do with any of them for just that reason. As if God needs any man to fight for him or God needs to prove anything to mortal men. God teaches love, and where is the love in any of these things? Whether they are Christian, Jew, or Muslim. The answer will be the same for all of them from God. ***"I counsel thee to buy me gold tried in the fire".***

Romans 1:25

25 Who changed the truth of God into a lie and worshipped and served the creature more than the Creator, who is blessed forever. Amen.

The creature is the flesh, and this is putting Jesus or any other fleshly person in front of God the Creator. Whenever someone prays and says through Jesus, Jesus Christ, or any other person or image, you put the creation in front of the

Creator. Becoming anti-Christ (anti-Spirit) and pro flesh, this is done unknowingly every day. It is yet another tool of Satan's arsenal. He took over governments, schools, and churches long ago. And why would he not do that? If he owns this world. And he is the god of this world to do with it as he pleases. Again, I know I have shown this earlier. But it helps to see it again.

2 Corinthians 4:4

4 In whom the god of this world hath blinded the minds of them which believe not, lest the light of the glorious gospel of Christ, who is the image of God, should shine unto them.

Does it make sense now? How many people have lost their way to the truth? How many will harden their hearts and wax hard their ears? I understand this is hard for some to comprehend. You might be saying, "how is this possible the whole world has been deceived"? But if you will not harden your heart and wax hard your ears. And let the "Father" and Christ (the Word of truth) in, and ask God for the truth on this matter; you will not be sorry. You will begin an adventure of a lifetime.

Revelation 12:9

9 And the great dragon was cast out, that old serpent, called the Devil, and Satan, which deceiveth the whole world: he was cast out into the earth, and his angels were cast out with him.

What does this say here? It says that Satan would deceive the whole world. Well, guess what? That has happened. The entire world has been deceived. Now, it is time to wake up from that deception. It is time to join the living and be reborn and resurrected from the dead deeds of the flesh. It is time to be reborn into a new creation of the "Father". A design of Spirit, one Spirit, in one body, with many members. It is time to leave the Atom (flesh) world and join the Adam (Spirit) world.

Romans 11:5

5 Even so then, at this present time, also there is a remnant according to the election of Grace.

A remnant in Christ's time was twelve souls to start. But it grew like wildfire once it began when people started to hear and understand the truth.

Romans 11:6

6 And if by Grace, then is it no more of works: otherwise, Grace is no more grace. But if it be of works, then it is no more Grace: otherwise, work is no more work.

It is all about the will offerings to God. That is the only thing God has ever wanted. It is not about your works but the works of God within you. God's gifts are Grace and love. We know now that the flesh cannot please God. You cannot work your way into heaven through the flesh. If you could do that, it would not be Grace but works. Paul is giving us an example here.

Romans 11:7-8

7 What, then? Israel hath not obtained that which he seeketh for, but the election hath obtained it, and the rest were blinded.

8 (According as it is written, God hath given them the Spirit of slumber, eyes that they should not see, and ears that they should not hear); unto this day.

Yes, until this very day, does the whole world sleep. It was only time to see the truth, once everything could be fulfilled, God wrote. The Sun (Son or bright shining one, Christ) had to be darkened as we all are in the knowledge of the truth. But every person will come in their order, as written below, as all things are fulfilled in this life cycle. Just as all things are born, grow old, and die, so do this earth's and humankind's processes.

2 Peter 3:13

13 Nevertheless, we, according to his promise, look for new heavens and a new earth, wherein dwelleth righteousness.

Notice the wording of new heavens.

1 Corinthians 15:23

23 But every man in his own order: Christ the first fruits; afterward they that are Christ's at his coming.

God numbers every hair on your head and has an order for everything. Why would it not be that way? God created the end in the beginning. People ask whether we are predestined to be who we will be. In God's eyes, yes, because God made us and knows what we will do before we know what we will do. If God did not know what we would do, God would not know everything.

Jeremiah 1:5

5 Before I formed thee in the belly, I knew thee, and before thou camest forth out of the womb, I sanctified thee, and I ordained thee a prophet unto the nations.

Nothing escapes God because God is all things.

Luke 12:7

7 But even the very hairs of your head are all numbered. Fear not, therefore: ye are of more value than many sparrows.

All is in God's hands, and nothing will stop a ball, once that ball starts rolling down a steep hill.

Romans 11:9-11

9 And David saith, let their table be made a snare, and a trap, and a stumbling block, and a recompense unto them.

10 Let their eyes be darkened, that they may not see, and bow down their back always.

11 I say then, have they stumbled that they should fall? God forbid: but rather through their fall salvation is come unto the Gentiles, for to provoke them to jealousy.

From the beginning of time, this has been God's plan. That all might be able to come to the Glory and mercy of his pleasure. Not just those that were able to see the truth. But those also who were not able to see. Their eyes were darkened because of a lack of faith in God. But now those who live after the flesh and those who live after the Spirit have an opportunity. Now all have a chance to enter the kingdom of heaven, Spirit. Love is the fulfillment of the law. The only proper way to obtain love is to understand everything and why they are the way they are. That comes through knowledge, wisdom, and understanding. And that comes from the Word of God (Christ), and that comes from the "Father".

John 6:44

44 No man can come to me, except the "Father" which hath sent me draw him: and I will raise him up at the last day.

All things start with the "Father." The "Father" sends you Christ, the Word of God. Then the words of the Word (Christ) lead you into the "Father" (Spirit).

Romans 11:12-13

12 Now if the fall of them be the riches of the world, and the diminishing of them the riches of the Gentiles; how much more their fulness?

13 For I speak to you Gentiles, inasmuch as I am the apostle of the Gentiles, I magnify mine office.

Paul's office was over the gentiles or those living after the flesh. As Peter was over the Jews or Spiritually minded ones. When you read Paul's writings in the Bible, it is for a guide to begin the awaking process of the soul. Peters is more for those that are advanced or awake in the Spirit. Notice Paul is calling himself an apostle at this time as well. He is no longer considered a disciple needing to be taught by the Word. He is now one with the "Father" and has become a law unto himself.

Romans 11:14

14 If by any means I may provoke to emulation them which are my flesh, and might save some of them.

The Word emulation, according to a word search on **Bing**, is.

"Emulation"

"Effort to match or surpass a person or achievement, typically by imitation.".

Looking closely here, we can see that the gentiles were of the flesh. But Paul was also a Jew of the tribe of Benjamin. But Paul was over the gentiles, as seen in verse 14. Paul says those of them which are of my flesh. Paul is talking about the fleshly body of men as being one body. He is not saying those of them which are of my Spirit. Paul was a Roman citizen as well. Paul was trying to provoke those that were of the flesh. To imitate those at a higher degree than those living after the flesh. At the same time, it would encourage the ones called Jews. To see the gentiles growing in Spirit while standing still in the unfoldment process.

Romans 11:15

15 For if the casting away of them be the reconciling of the world, what shall the receiving of them be, but life from the dead?

All have entered into sin not willingly. We are here to learn to be kind and manifest love to one another. In the end, we wait for God's resurrection from the dead. Let's look at what Paul was talking about in

Romans 8:20

20 For the creature was made subject to vanity, not willingly, but by reason of him who hath subjected the same in hope

Romans 11:16

16 For if the first fruit be holy, the lump is also holy: and if the root be holy, so are the branches.

God has his own language, one of Spirit. Satan also has a language all his own. We are seen and referred to more than once as trees in God's Garden. Paul is talking about bringing in the gentiles to the body of Spirit. That there is only one Holy body or one Holy Tree. Let's look at a couple of other times God referred humanity to trees in the Bible for examples.

Luke 3:9

9 And now also the axe is laid unto the root of the trees: every tree therefore which bringeth not forth good fruit is hewn down, and cast into the fire.

He is talking about those that do not bring forth spiritual deeds. They would be brought down to a carnal state of mind or a gentile state of consciousness. And then be cast out into the darkness, not having God's proper knowledge. The fire is where people are today. Burning in a never-ending judgment of consciousness. Constantly feeling as if we have something to do and a purpose. But not being able to find out what it is.

John 15:1

1 I am the true vine, and my "Father" is the husbandman.

Here Christ is talking about us needing to be in the true vine. Which he is, and the true vine is the Word of God. He is also saying that the "Father" is the one that takes care of the Garden and does the work. A tree does not care for itself and cannot prune its own branches. Just as we cannot earn our way into the vine. We must be grafted into the vine. This little verse says so much, as many of these little verses do.

John 15:2

2 Every branch in me that beareth not fruit he taketh away: and every branch that beareth fruit, he purgeth it, that it may bring forth more fruit.

If you do not do the deeds of the Spirit. You are lowered down to a lower state of vibration into the realm of carnal men. Where you see the world as most people do today. Looking in the mirror and beholding an image that is not you, thinking it is you. All those that go to the Altar and make an offering to the "Father" and move in the direction knowing God will purify them. Bring forth fruit or do the deeds or manifest the foundations perfectly. Again, you can learn more about the foundations in my book: ***"Atom and Eve's walk in the Garden".*** Also, notice Christ is saying the "Father" is doing the taking away when he is speaking. He uses the word (he). It is the "Father" that does the work.

John 15:3

3 Now ye are clean through the word which I have spoken unto you.

Look closely because this little verse shows you one of the biggest mysteries. Christ is the Word of God. It is the words that he has spoken that bring you to God. And the "Father" sends you those words. The Word shows the way to the light. It is not by saying I confess the name of Jesus and expecting to enter heaven. Again, I tell you the truth; it will never happen. People have been kept at a low vibration for so long by Satan. Satan laughs all the way to the bank of your grave, with the souls that go to the grave with the flesh. Where the soul never fulfills its true calling: entering into the one body and one Spirit.

John 15:4

4 Abide in me, and I in you. As the branch cannot bear fruit of itself, except it abide in the vine; no more can ye, except ye abide in me.

Abide in me (The Word of God), and the Word of God will abide in you. You cannot do the deeds of the Spirit without the Word being one with you and you being one with the Word. You must abide in Christ (the Word of God) to abide in Spirit.

John 15:5

5 I am the vine, ye are the branches: He that abideth in me, and I in him, the same bringeth forth much fruit: for without me ye can do nothing.

You can do nothing unless you are one with the one body of Spirit if you do not have the Christ (Word of God) living in you. There is no hope of bringing forth good fruit (deeds of Spirit). Imagine, for a minute, you could live a billion or more experiences simultaneously. If you can imagine that, you can start to understand the "Father", the Word, the Spirit, the Apostles, all things, and even yourself. Notice again the word abides in me. The "much fruits" he is talking about in this verse are the bringing forth of the new deeds that we do. Then by doing these deeds and not talking about acts. Other people come to the truth through your actions, not words. But first, you must abide in Christ (the Word), and Christ (the Word) must abide in you.

John 15:6

6 If a man abides not in me, he is cast forth as a branch, and is withered; and men gather them, and cast them into the fire, and they are burned.

You are cast into outer darkness if you are not one with the Spirit. You are walking around in this world with no purpose. Speaking to yourself, saying there must be something more, and not finding out what it is. You burn in a world of chaos, in darkness, groping around on all fours, as a beast of the field does. Not seeing you are gods in the one beautiful body of Spirit. You are thinking and believing in whatever fantasy comes your way. If you are not one with Christ and him with you. You go through the burning process. Of putting sacrifices on the Altar. And having God purify you until you get to that place. Where you become one with the Christ (Word) and the "Father". Until then, we should wait to teach others. Which we will be going over in Chapter 12 in more detail.

Romans 1:28

28 And even as they did not like to retain God in their knowledge, God gave them over to a reprobate mind to do those things which are not convenient.

According to **Bing word search**, the definition of the word

"**Reprobate**"

"A sinner who is not of the elect and is predestined to damnation".

He says they have been lowered in vibration to a gentile or a carnal man's state of mind. This mind in humankind is where the world is today.

Revelation 22:16

16 I Jesus have sent mine angel to testify unto you these things in the churches. I am the root and the offspring of David and bright and morning star.

Here Jesus, the son of man, is saying after the flesh, he comes from the line of David. But also, he is Christ talking in Jesus saying he is the bright and morning star (bright shining one of God); he is Spirit in the flesh. It was Christ sending his angel to testify through Jesus. This is the Word being made flesh. Jesus was not in the beginning Christ was in the beginning. This is what is meant by John in.

John 1:5

5 And the light shineth in darkness; and the darkness comprehended it not.

This light was the Words of Christ shining into the darkness of people's consciousness. But they being of a lower vibration, or dead in sin. Could not understand the words that Christ spoke. They could not see the awakened Christ (Spirit) living in Jesus. All they could see was the fleshly man Jesus. Even today people are still dead in sin, not believing that they can move into perfection. Not believing the words that Christ spoke when he said: "Be ye therefore perfect even as your "Father" which is in heaven is perfect". They still dwell in darkness or the lower vibrations unable to see the light. They still look to the flesh for redemption or Jesus. Worshipping an image put in place by Satan. Flesh is of the lower vibrations; Spirit is the highest vibration. This goes back to what Paul was saying in:

Romans 1:25

25 Who changed the truth of God into a lie, and worshipped and served the creature more than the Creator, who is blessed forever.

Amen

There is no vibration higher than God because he is all vibrations. You cannot take the lowest form of vibration and put it in front of God and worship it. Christ was in the beginning with God. You will not find the name Jesus anywhere in the Old Testament. But we know that the Word of God (Christ the Son of God) was in the beginning.

Romans 11:17

17 And if some of the branches be broken off, and thou, being a wild olive tree, wert grafted in among them, and with them partakes of the root and fatness of the olive tree.

The Jews of that time were not adhering to the Word of God. It allowed the gentiles or those of a carnal mind to be grafted into the Tree (the Word). Becoming one with the one body of Spirit, with all it has to offer.

Romans 11:18

18 Boast not against the branches. But if thou boast, thou bearest not the root, but the root thee.

If you boast or use the ego of the carnal man. It is not the Spirit doing the boasting but the ego. It is the root (the Word) that you should be one with. And the two of you do all things in the same Mind (Father) and Word (Son).

Romans 11:19

19 Thou wilt say then, the branches were broken off, that I might be grafted in.

Again, Paul is saying to do away with the ego of the fleshly man.

Romans 11:20

20 Well, because of unbelief, they were broken off, and thou standest by faith. Be not high-minded, but fear.

Paul is saying this is a gift from God. You have not done any work to deserve this gift. They should stand in front of God in faith and fear having no ego in front of God.

Romans 11:21

21 For if God spared not the natural branches, take heed lest he also spare not thee.

They stood because of God's mercy and not because of anything they had done to get there.

Romans 11:22

22 Behold, therefore, the goodness and severity of God: on them which fell, severity; but toward thee, goodness, if thou continue in his goodness: otherwise, thou also shalt be cut off.

Paul's words are self-explanatory here. But no one should ever think of themselves as higher than anyone else. We are all part of the same body. We are all just different members of that body. It is like hating your hand and loving your foot. That would not make much sense. Plus, God created all things; who are we to judge his creation as it is? Also, we all stand or fall by our faith in God, not in ourselves or anyone else. Even those who do evil teach us why we should hate sin and love good. All things have a purpose in this world of matter. Just remember the perfect law because no one escapes the law. So, as a Gentile, we get to God by faith in God to do what he promised through the Word, as a Jew, or one of the inner heart or Spirit. We exercise our faith in God through the Word.

Jude 1:9

9 Yet Michael the archangel, when contending with the Devil he disputed about the body of Moses, durst not bring against him a railing accusation, but said, The Lord rebuke thee.

Michael was an archangel of God. He would not allow himself to judge the Devil. But put the judgment to God. We should understand the Law of Cause and Effect to see we need not judge anyone. It becomes an entrapment to judge another. For by doing so, you are judging God's creation, thereby bringing judgment upon yourself. The next time you think about judging someone. Just believe that God is omnipresent, watching you judge his creation. And if you continue to judge his creation, make sure you do it in righteousness because it will return to you in one form or another. But we all decide the distance we want to travel in this life of death. Satan loves it when people judge because he understands the law. He does not judge but says to do whatever feels good to you. Satan and his followers understand the law. Better than the children of light right now. And they use that law to their advantage in holding you down in Spirit. Be in the now, the consciousness of all God's creation. Observe it with no judgment at all. I try and picture all things as a play. I looked into my friends eyes the other day, and said to him bravo. You play the part of a mortal very well. Then he looked at me as if I was crazy. It made it all the more believable to me. But I know he is a god playing a part in this beautiful thing called life, as we all are.

Romans 11:23

23 And they also, if they abide not still in unbelief, shall be grafted in: for God is able to graft them in again.

Those old souls of the Jews did not adhere to the Word of God. They can be brought back into the spiritual body. If they abide in the belief and faith in and of the "Father".

Romans 11:24

24 For if thou wert cut out of the olive tree which is wild by nature, and wert grafted contrary to nature into a good olive tree: how much more shall these, which be the natural branches, be grafted into their own olive tree?

Again, Paul is stating that either Jew (Spiritually-minded) or Gentile (worldly-minded) can enter into life. Being wild in nature at first can now be made clean in the Word of God. Then be welcomed into the one body of Spirit.

Romans 11:25

25 For I would not, brethren, that ye should be ignorant of this mystery, lest ye should be wise in your own conceits; that blindness in part is happening to Israel, until the fulness of the Gentiles be come in.

God, in his loving nature, wanted all to join the one body of Spirit. We should all help one another when climbing into the Spirit and lifting each other when a hand is needed. If it is all about ourselves, then where is love? By loving your neighbor as yourself, you love yourself. Because you are all one body, your neighbor is yourself. And by not helping your neighbor or not loving your neighbor, you do not love yourself. Those of old in Israel were held back in Spirit, so all others had a chance to enter into the body of God. So now those that be last (gentiles) shall be first (to enter in). And those which be first (Jews) shall be last to enter in. But will they not all enter? Notice the word mystery again.

Romans 11:26

26 And so all Israel shall be saved: as it is written, there shall come out of Sion the deliverer, and shall turn away ungodliness from Jacob.

Through God's Word, all ungodliness is done away for both the Jews and the Gentiles.

Romans 11:27

27 For this is my covenant unto them when I shall take away their sins.

It is God that takes away our sins and desires. How many people have said I will lose weight, get in shape, and stop smoking? Or a million other things in this life. Putting it on the Altar and walking in that direction is much easier than to try and do the job yourself. It is better to have that desire taken away from you forever. And that desire exists no more at all than to have that desire come back again and again. (**It is better to let go and let God),** than to say, look what I have done God. I think I can safely say God owes no one anything.

Romans 11:28

28 As concerning the gospel, they are enemies for your sakes: but as touching the election, they are beloved for the father's sakes.

I wonder why they are your enemies concerning the gospel? Could it be because of what people are taught about God in today's churches? Preachers teach about the traditions of old when it comes to religion. God could care less about these traditions. You either are a doer of God's law, or you are not a doer of God's law. The middle ground never has and will never work. With them of old, they believed in doing that law and keeping it by the letter of the law. We must get to God by faith in God. They get there by exercising their faith in the deeds done. So, if you are being instructed in the traditions of Old Testament of the Bible, you are working your way into the kingdom of God. Through deeds that are done in the flesh.

Romans 11:29

29 For the gifts and calling of God are without repentance.

How many preachers have preached repentance is the way to God? All churches that I know of are built on repentance. Here it clearly states that it is not the way to God. If you are living in repentance, you are living in the past. You are not that past; it is just an experience you have had in your body. You can do nothing about that past experience except learn from it. You can only use the past to see what you have done wrong before and learn from it—noticing what you want to experience again and what you do not want to experience again. Spirit is a gift from God that needs only to be accepted by us. Anoint your head with oil (prayer) and go to the Altar, accept God's blessing by becoming a living sacrifice. Let God do his job to purify you and enter into his rest. Quit working in the six days of creation and partaking of the Tree of Good and Evil.

Romans 11:30

30 For as ye in times past have not believed God, yet have now obtained mercy through their unbelief.

People still do not believe in God or put their faith in him today and try to establish their righteousness by themselves. And repeatedly repenting for something they will never be able to overcome by themselves. And will likely do it again tomorrow or the next day. Because it has not been overcome in them by the flames on the Altar of God.

Ezekiel 22:18

18 Son of man, the house of Israel is to me become dross: all they are brass, and tin, and iron, and lead, in the midst of the furnace; they are even the dross of silver.

The dross is the impurities of sin that dwell within us. These are the things that defile the Temple which you are—the improper thoughts and deeds in the fleshly man.

Ezekiel 22:19

19 Therefore thus saith the Lord God; Because ye are all become dross, behold; therefore, I will gather you into the midst of Jerusalem.

Here is the purification process that all are going to go through.

Ezekiel 22:20

20 As they gather silver, and brass, and iron, and lead, and tin, into the midst of the furnace, to blow the fire upon it, to melt it; so, will I gather you in mine anger and in my fury, and I will leave you there, and melt you.

Today all are burning in consciousness. All have been left in this fire of God's furnace, burning day and night.

Ezekiel 22:21

21 Yea, I will gather you, and blow upon you in the fire of my wrath, and ye shall be melted in the midst thereof.

Gold has to be heated until a melting point before it can be separated from the dross or impurities.

Let's take a look further down in Ezekiel 24:11.

Ezekiel 24:11

11 Then set it empty upon the coals thereof, that the brass of it may be hot, and may burn, and that the filthiness of it may be molten in it, that the scum of it may be consumed.

Now, purification is taking place. The dross or sins of humankind are burning out of us for good. But it is essential to see who is doing the work and who is not.

Ezekiel 24:12

12 She hath wearied herself with lies, and her great scum went not forth out of her: her scum shall be in the fire.

God's process of burning out sin from within all is beautiful. This is a blessing from God and not a punishment.

Ezekiel 24:13

13 In thy filthiness is lewdness: because I have purged thee, and thou wast not purged, thou shalt not be purged from thy filthiness any more, till I have caused my fury to rest upon thee.

It is God that does the purging, not we ourselves. It is better to ask for God's mercy than to burn day and night. You're not just praying for your sins in this lifetime but many lifetimes.

Ezekiel 24:14

14 I the Lord have spoken it: it shall come to pass, and I will do it; I will not go back, neither will I spare, neither will I repent; according to thy ways, and according to thy doings, shall they judge thee, saith the Lord God.

Nothing can stop or hinder what is going to take place and what is taking place. This world cannot vibrate at the frequency of God's Spirit.

Ezekiel 24:15-16

15 Also the word of the Lord came unto me, saying,

16 Son of man, behold, I take away from thee the desire of thine eyes with a stroke: yet neither shalt thou mourn nor weep, neither shall thy tears run down.

It is God that takes desire from us, not ourselves. There is no need to mourn when you understand the truth; we are all here to learn. Those souls that die in the flesh will be back again until they overcome this world through God. Until then, it is nothing more or less than an experience. In the training ground of the gods. It is God that takes away our tears. There is no need for tears when you have understanding. Understanding why things are happening the way they are.

Romans 11:31

31 Even so, have these also now not believed, that through your mercy they also may obtain mercy.

Oh, that beautiful Law of Cause and Effect, better known as what goes around, comes around. Or the first shall be last, and the last shall be first. Because the last will be the ones that wake up first and help those that did not believe at first.

Romans 11:32

32 For God hath concluded them all in unbelief, that he might have mercy upon all.

Again, God has mercy on all, but we can have mercy on others as God has compassion on us. And that is our duty, to do. But do it with a willful and loving heart.

Romans 11:33

33 O the depth of the riches both of the wisdom and knowledge of God! How unsearchable are his judgements and his ways past finding out!

Just think how many times men have spit on the sacrifice of God's son. And yet God still has his hand out and will show us mercy.

Isaiah 9:17

17 Therefore the Lord shall have no joy in their young men, neither shall have mercy on their fatherless and widows: for everyone is a hypocrite and an evildoer, and every mouth speaketh folly. For all this, his anger is not turned away, but his hand is stretched out still.

All that the people have done and still are doing today. Yet the hands of God are still stretched out as they have always been. Waiting for us to come to the Altar. With a will offering from the heart. He is waiting, and that is where he will receive you back into his body of Spirit. He is waiting for you to get tired of working in this world. The question is, are you tired of working yet? Have you had enough of playing in the Devil's playground? Are you ready to rest from all your work? These are questions only you can answer. I aim to show you that there is something more than the world of flesh and blood.

Romans 11:34-35

34 For who hath known the mind of the Lord? Or who hath been his counsellor?

35 Or who hath first given to him, and it shall be recompensed unto him again?

Paul was probably speaking as a man here. Because no one has ever given God anything, God is All and owns all things, but Paul was making a point. That you cannot work for the gift. You cannot buy your way in with deeds of flesh or money.

Romans 11:36

36 For of him, and through him, and to him, are all things: to whom be Glory forever. Amen.

All things belong to God, and all things are God.

<u>Nikola Tesla</u> said:

"If you wish to understand the universe, think of energy, frequency, and vibration".

I say it a little differently:

"If you wish to understand God, think of energy, frequency, vibration, and rhythm".

God is All that there is in a nutshell. Everything is Spirit, and there is only one Spirit, not two. It is just running at different speeds of vibration. Rhythm is the music that is given for the dance!

I say, ***"Enjoy the dance, my friends, enjoy the dance".***

ROMANS 12

1 I Beseech you therefore, brethren, by the mercies of God, that ye present your bodies a living sacrifice, holy, acceptable unto God, which is your reasonable service.

Paul is not saying to continue in sin. Paul is not saying: "don't worry about sin; all is good". Paul is telling us to present our bodies as living sacrifices. He is saying to be Holy, and it is a reasonable service for us to do so. The Temple must be cleaned out and purged of all sin. What is a sacrifice? According to **Oxford Languages**, the definition of the word

"Sacrifice"

"An act of slaughtering an animal or person or surrendering a possession as an offering to God or to a divine or supernatural figure".

Paul is telling you to put yourself as that offering on that Altar. Your soul, which you are, can become a quickened Spirit and must be presented as a pure and clothed offering to the Living God. And God the "Father" is the God of the living. God is not the God of the dead. All that are dead in sin are dead. That offering must take place at an Altar, and that Altar is in the Temple, which you are. That Altar is where you must have that personal relationship, which no other person on earth can have for you. It would be like growing up and never talking to your father and mother, but talking to a third person all the time to interact with them for you. That does not make much sense. Satan has removed everybody so far from the "Father". It has all been by design from the beginning. If you genuinely want to see a master at work in his craft. Look no further than the fallen one and his legion of demons.

Romans 12:2

2 And be not conformed to this world: but be ye transformed by the renewing of your mind, that ye may prove what is that good, and acceptable, and perfect, will of God.

I wish Paul would have used the word metamorphosis instead of transformation. But Paul is showing us to come out of the world's way of doing things. That God will do that through the reprogramming of our minds. Because of old false thoughts which Satan has fed us throughout our lives. And the only way to do that is to have God do it in you. It is becoming children again, learning all things over and anew. Notice Paul using that little word perfect again? How often the Bible says to be perfect and not sin always amazes me. How many people bought into the deception of non-perfection is a much larger amazement to me.

Romans 12:3

3 For I say, through the grace given unto me, to every man that is among you, not to think of himself more highly than he ought to think, but to think soberly, according to God hath dealt to every man the measure of faith.

When we enter the Spirit at a higher vibration by God's grace, we become servants to all below us in knowledge. We do not Lord it over others and govern ourselves with ego by ruling over the lower vibrations. Satan and the spiritually wicked people and entities are the ones that are masters at that in the world today. Yes, there are other lifeforms other than ours; why would there not be? Just ask yourself what you would do if you were God, the Creator of earth and mortals and all things. What would you honestly do if you had no limitations?

1 Corinthians 15:40

40 There are also celestial bodies, and bodies terrestrial: but the glory of the celestial is one, and the glory of the terrestrial is another.

Yes, there is so much more to this life than a god living as a mortal can comprehend.

1 Corinthians 15:41

41 There is one glory of the sun and another glory of the moon, and another glory of the stars: for one-star differeth from another star in glory.

Christ, the Apostles, and one soul to the next in Spirit. Yes, more suns and other moons and more stars as well. But we know by now that the Bible was written for the edification of the soul.

1 Corinthians 15:42

42 So also is the resurrection of the dead. It is sown in corruption; it is raised in incorruption.

The soul is sown in corruptible flesh and then resurrected into an incorruptible Spirit within the flesh.

1 Corinthians 15:43

43 It is sown in dishonour; it is raised in glory: it is sown in weakness; it is raised in power.

The soul is placed in a dishonorable and weak body and then raised in the glory of the "Father's" body (Spirit).

1 Corinthians 15:44

44 It is sown a natural body; it is raised a spiritual body. There is a natural body, and there is a spiritual body.

There is a body of man (flesh-matter) and a body of soul (Spirit). The problem is that people of today only know of one body, flesh. Just as long as they see that they are that body. They will never come to understand the other side of themselves. It is like living in a split family and only living with one parent. You never come to know anything about your other parent except bits and pieces. You will have to do some digging to find out anything. About the other side of who you are and where you came from, to make yourself whole again.

1 Corinthians 15:45

45 And so it is written, the first man Adam was made a living soul; the last Adam was made a quickening spirit.

Religion has gotten it wrong so often. It makes me wonder how churches still have an audience. God made the first man Adam, a living soul, not a living flesh. In other words, he was not dead in sin as we are today but alive in Soul. The last Adam, Christ is the Spirit that lived in Jesus (man of the flesh). That first man Adam, a living soul, transformed into a quickened spirit. How long did it take Adam to get to redemption? We all go through this redemption process or purification process.

1 Corinthians 15:46

46 Howbeit that was not first which is spiritual, but that which is natural; and afterward that which is spiritual.

It is natural; if people would look around them, all things come from seeds. Even science is starting to understand that planets form seeds from dust. Why would God make the soul-spirit any different? First comes soul (seed) in matter (shell,) then comes Spirit from soul. Look at the butterfly again. It starts out crawling on the ground, eating bitter leaves. Then it goes within itself and undergoes a metamorphosis and becomes a butterfly. Flying in the heavens eating the nectar from God.

1 Corinthians 15:47

47 The first man is of the earth, earthy; the second man is the Lord from heaven.

The first human is of matter, lower vibration. The second person is the soul able to become like its "Father". Giving life to the lower vibration (flesh) to redeem it, or raise the dead. The man of the flesh is from this earth and of this earth. The second man is a spiritual being, a Lord from heaven. Suppose people would stop worshiping Jesus, the man of flesh. And start seeing Christ as their brother, as he always wanted. Then we can begin to see our potential and not our limitations.

1 Corinthians 15:48

48 As is the earthy, such are they also that are earthy: and as is the heavenly, such are they also that are heavenly.

The matter is matter, and Spirit is Spirit. Those from the world of matter are matter. Those that are Spirit are Spirit.

1 Corinthians 15:49

49 And as we have borne the image of the earthy, we shall also bear the image of the heavenly.

We have borne the image of the person we see in the mirror. We shall also take the image of the Spirit when we awaken to the truth. As a soul, we have lived in the flesh. We shall also live in Spirit when we manifest the "Father".

1 Corinthians 15:50

50 Now this I say, brethren, that flesh and blood cannot inherit the kingdom of God; neither doth corruption inherit incorruption.

It is good that we are not only flesh and blood, or we could never enter heaven if we remained in the lower vibration. But if we do not go through the purification process, neither does the soul because it remains corrupt. Flesh nor sin can enter heaven. A corrupted person of the flesh does not inherit incorruption. Satan has fooled all into coming back to hell over and over again. So, you might serve him here in the lower vibration. You are a god living in the lowest vibration. Do you not think that you are in hell now? As long as you keep looking for an afterlife instead of living life. You will keep coming back over and over again.

1 Corinthians 15:51

51 Behold, I shew you a mystery; We shall not all sleep, but we shall all be changed.

Behold, I reveal a mystery to you. What will you do with the information you now have? Will you start the change with your "Father"? Or will you still sleep within the matrix created for you by yourself and the god of this world?

1 Corinthians 15:52

52 In a moment, in the twinkling of an eye, at the last trump: for the

trumpet shall sound, and the dead shall be raised incorruptible, and we shall be changed.

People are dead in sin, but they will awaken. God will change us into the image of himself. Not later, not after you die, but now we shall be changed.

1 Corinthians 15:53

53 For this corruptible must put on incorruption, and this mortal must put on immortality.

Paul is telling you here you have a job to do. It does not say God is going to do this after you die. But you, as a mortal, must put on immortality. The resurrection has happened, you have been reborn into a new creature a quickened Spirit.

1 Corinthians 15:54

54 So when this corruptible shall have put on incorruption, and this mortal shall have put on immortality, then shall be brought to pass the saying that is written, Death is swallowed up in victory.

When you have put on the "Father", then and only then is there no more death.

1 Corinthians 15:55

55 O death, where is thy sting? O grave, where is thy victory?

You no longer have to return to the land of trials and tribulations (hell). The redemption has taken place. You have been crucified as Christ was on the cross. You have raised the lower vibration of the flesh, to the higher vibrations of Spirit. You will not see the grave; it has no dominion over you.

1 Corinthians 15:56

56 The sting of Death is sin; the strength of sin is the law.

If this place is a place that people love. Then they should stay in this world and serve Satan. Some people make their living taking advantage of other people, and they are of their father, the devil. They put their faith in their father, as we put our faith in our "Father".

John 13:12-13

12 So after he had washed their feet, and had taken his garments, and was set down again, he said unto them, know ye what I have done to you?

13 Ye call me Master and Lord: and ye say well; for so I am.

Christ is the Son of God, the bright, shining one. He took the form of a man and washed their feet. That is showing authentic leadership by example.

John 13:14-15

14 If I then, your Lord and Master, have washed your feet, ye also ought to wash one another's feet.

15 For I have given you an example, that ye should do as I have done to you.

I don't know if you have ever had the chance to wash someone's feet. I have been blessed to wash two women's and two gentlemen's feet. One had a tumor in her brain, from which she recovered. The other one was someone I consider to be a member of my family. She had cancer, and she passed away. The one that recovered wanted to stay longer here on earth. The other was ready for a new experience, and I am happy for both. I pull these memories from the library of my mind from time to time and find joy. It is a humbling experience to ask someone if you can wash their feet, then do the act itself. I think everyone should seek someone that they do not know too well. And ask them if you can wash their feet and pray over them. It will let you know how Christ felt—being the Word of God and humbling himself to do the same.

Romans 12:4

4 For as we have many members in one body, and all members have

not the same office.

Paul and I are alike in one way; we go over things more than once, as my wife has told me on more than one occasion. We are all different according to how God has chosen to make us. We are all different, but we are members of the one body and of the one Spirit, and not two.

Romans 12:5

5 So we, being many, are one body in Christ, and every one members one of another.

Like the atoms of your fleshly body are to you, is how we, as Adams are to God. We all have our movement within God, as God has his movement within us.

Romans 12:6

6 Having then gifts differing according to the grace that is given to us, whether prophecy, let us prophesy according to the proportion of faith.

As Paul would say, "I speak as a man here" Unless you and the Word and the "Father" are one, you should not prophesy. Nonetheless, let it be with the faith given by God doing the works within you. There is nothing worse than a false prophet. What they have done over the years is only forgivable by God. And Satan uses many to deceive God's children into the great sleep they find themselves. Ask yourself these questions. How can someone be dead in sin and speak for the God of the living? Do those that be in the graves of the ground speak for you? Many people prophesy, heal the sick, and do great signs in the father's name. It just happens not to be the father they are thinking of. The dead do not speak for the living. It is the living that speaks to and for the dead.

John 5:19

19 Then answered Jesus and said unto them, Verily, verily, I say unto you, The Son can do nothing of himself, but what he seeth the Father do: for what things soever he doeth, these also doeth the Son likewise.

The "Father" will show you what to do and when. Because it is the "Father" telling you what to do and when to do it when you become one. Satan works many miracles through those who believe they are doing God's works, leading many into hell.

Matthew 7:22-23

22 Many will say to me in that day, Lord, Lord, have we not prophesied in thy name? and in thy name have cast out devils? And in thy name done many wonderful works?

23 And then will I profess unto them, I never knew you: depart from me, ye that work iniquity.

If someone is not perfected in God's works, and God is not living in the Temple of their soul. Then this is who Christ will not know. People living in the flesh and the carnal state of man being dead in sin have nothing to do with God. And God has nothing to do with them. God is not working in or through them, even if they believe he is. But Satan works in the dead, deceiving the dead. God is the God of the living.

Romans 12:7

7 Or ministry, let us wait on our ministering: or he that teacheth, on teaching.

Paul is explaining to those just starting to wake up, to wait to teach anyone. The reason for this is when you first begin to wake up in the Spirit. You see in part and half-truths. If you wait and keep looking, the complete insight into the question will become clear. But people start mixing the half-truth they get from God with their intellect instead of waiting for the entire truth. They begin to reason and fabricate something that sounds good to themselves but is not correct. It becomes a mixture of this world and the Spirit world. Many religions have been started in this manner. These half-truths have deceived many people.

I tell everyone I talk to, not to take everything I say to be true. I am not trying to start a new religion, I do not like religions at all. I see all religions as synagogues of Satan. God is not a religion or in a house made with man's hands; God is All. Take everything I say or have written to God and ask God if it is true. You do not need me or any other man to teach you anything about the "Father". God loves you as much as he does me or any other soul that seeks him. I am trying to show how to get to the "Father" and have a relationship with him and the Word. Also, I tell people to fulfill the commandments in love. And to open your eyes to the mass deception plaguing our world today. And as far as religions go, I have been told I should go to church to fellowship with others. If I wanted to live in the land of the dead, that would be true. But I am looking for the land of the living to have a relationship.

1 John 2:27

27 But the anointing which ye have received of him abideth in you, and ye need not that any man teach you: but as the same anointing teacheth you of all things, and is truth, and is no lie, and even as it hath taught you, ye shall abide in him.

Seek to find the Gold, which is God in his purest form.

Romans 12:8

8 Or he that exhorteth, on exhortation: he that giveth, let him do it with simplicity; he that ruleth, with diligence; he that sheweth mercy, with cheerfulness.

Everything Paul talked about back then was simplicity. Paul was over the gentiles, those of the flesh. This is all the information I am talking about in this book. This lets you know just how far the world is lost today. These words I write today are Paul's words, and they are simple. Peter was of the Jews (spiritual ones). Peter's words are more considered meat. Paul's words were the milk of the gospels. People should love God with all their hearts, mind, and soul. And to love one another as God loves you. Because in the end, All is All, and in All. As it says in the **Kybalion**:

"While All is in the ALL, it is equally true that the ALL is in ALL. To him, that understands this truth hath come great knowledge."

Romans 12:9

9 Let love be without dissimulation. Abhor that which is evil; cleave to that which is good.

Love should govern our hearts, minds, and souls. Love should govern our lives. Love is the fulfillment of the law.

Romans 12:10

10 Be kindly affectioned one to another with brotherly love; in honour preferring one another.

Keep company with those that lift you in Spirit. Those that are there for you and seek your well-being in Spirit. You will find there is no more significant task than that.

Romans 12:11-12

11 Not slothful in business; fervent in Spirit; serving the Lord.

12 Rejoicing in hope; patient in tribulation; continuing instant in prayer.

Remember it takes time to eat the harvest you have planted. You have been cultivating for years. Do not get discouraged when things go wrong. Keep moving in a forward motion. And plant perfect causes to receive the perfect effect. What is the perfect cause to plant? God called me, and God will justify me and God will glorify me. The result will be God calling you, justifying you, and glorifying you. Mix in a full cup of faith and mix well into this recipe.

Romans 12:13

13 Distributing to the necessity of saints; given to hospitality.

Suppose you meet those genuinely doing God's work. That would be those looking after your spiritual well-being and growth—those who seek your soul's growth (seed), those trying to cover your sins. Most likely, God has already taken care of them. But if they have a family, while looking after your family.

Make sure their family does not go without and any need that they have, if it is within your power to help. But above all, do it from a place of a loving heart. If it is not from a loving heart. It is better to withhold from helping, and that is ok. Do everything in life with a clean and clear conscience and a loving heart.

Romans 12:14

14 Bless them which persecute you: bless and curse not.

We want to bless all remembering with whatever measure you dish it out, it will return to you. Judgment is a trap that we should avoid at all costs.

Romans 12:15

15 Rejoice with them that do rejoice, and weep with them that weep.

In which world was Paul living? It sure is not in the world we are living in today. But this is the world I am looking for, the one I want to live in and have my being. How about you? It all starts with you and me and the cause we chose today. All we need to do is, awaken from this Death of sin.

Romans 12:16

16 Be of the same mind one toward another. Mind not high things, but condescend to men of low estate. Be not wise in your own conceits.

Someone is always higher and lower than you on the road to enlightenment. Always remember that you want help seeing a higher state of consciousness from brothers or sisters you might run across on your path. You should be just as eager to help others that need it. It's a fine line to balance when helping others. I use the rule if someone asks me for help, I give it. If they do not, I let them enjoy their journey to self-enlightenment. I will be honest; I have difficulty holding in my love for the "Father". It is hard not talking about what's on your mind. When you start to love God with all your mind, that is all that is on your mind. So, I let it all out in my books. If a book or two never get published. I know that it has at least saved my wife's ear from me chewing on it all the time.

Romans 12:17

17 Recompense to no man evil for evil. Provide things honest in the sight of all men.

Again, you do not need to pass any judgment upon the deeds of anyone when you understand the perfect Law of Cause and Effect. Nobody, and I mean nobody, gets away with anything. What a person does to themselves in the perfect law that God created. Is ten times worse than whatever you could think about doing to them. The deeds hold them in the hell of a carnal state of mind. And when you see in truth that they are a god lost in flesh. What more can you do to them that they have not already done to themselves?

Romans 12:18

18 If it be possible, as much as lieth in you, live peaceably with all men.

When you understand the perfect Law of Cause and Effect, you understand the more love you manifest, the more love comes back to you. You see the boomerang effect of creation. It is better to love and receive love, than it is to be hateful and receive hate. But in the end, free will belongs to all, to do as they will.

Romans 12:19

19 Dearly beloved, avenge not yourselves, but rather give place unto wrath: for it is written, Vengeance is mine, I will repay, saith the Lord.

The more that you can learn from God to forgive. The more you are forgiven for the things that you do. Indeed, all are lost in this land of illusions created by Satan and his demons. And all can be saved by the grace of God. Who are you and I to judge another's creation? Look below at a couple of verses for insight.

2 Peter 3:9

9 The Lord is not slack concerning his promise, as some men count slackness; but is longsuffering to us-ward, not willing that any should

perish, but that all should come to repentance.

All means All, and it does not imply a few. Remember also what it said in Romans.

Romans 9:21-23

21 Hath not the potter power over the clay, of the same lump to make one vessel unto honour, and another unto dishonour?

22 What if God, willing to shew his wrath and to make his power known, endured with much longsuffering the vessels of wrath fitted to destruction:

23 And that he might make known the riches of his glory on the vessels of mercy, which he had afore prepared unto glory.

God knows all things. Only God knows who is prepared for his glory? Be careful judging God's creation. Remember, we are all living in clay that the will of God can reform.

Romans 12:20

20 Therefore if thine enemy hunger, feed him; if he thirsts, give him drink: for in so doing thou shalt heap coals on fire on his head.

I have found nothing makes a person more confused. When they happen to be upset with you, if you humble yourself, it will shut down the ego quicker than an argument with them.

Romans 12:21

21 Be not overcome of evil but overcome evil with good.

The problem is in truth, we do not want coals of fire, put on anyone's head. When we understand we are all one body. And we were once lost, but stand only by God's grace. Some of our body is just more lost than others. Remember: **"by the grace of God go I"** It could be you who is lost far within the land of illusions. But by God's grace, it is not you; if you judge that person, it could be you. Do good to those that are lost in this world. I am reminded of a beautiful story by a man named **Alan Watts**. I want to share it with you. If you have yet to have the opportunity to read any of Alan's work. I suggest them to you. Alan had a very different look on life and was an enlightened soul. I have taken many of his works within myself and made them a part of who I am.

Alan Watts ***via*** **The Archaic Revival**

"So then, when you're in the way of waking up and finding out who you are, you meet a character called a guru, as the Hindus say, 'the teacher,' 'the awakener.' And what is the function of a guru? He's the man that looks you in the eye and says, 'Oh, come off it. I know who you are.' You come to the guru and say, 'Sir, I have a problem. I'm unhappy, and I want to get one up on the universe. I want to become enlightened. I want spiritual wisdom.' The guru looks at you and says, 'Who are you?' You know Sri-Ramana-Maharshi, that great Hindu sage of modern times? People used to come to him and say, 'Master, who was I in my last incarnation?' As if that mattered. And he would say, 'Who is asking the question?' And he'd look at you and say, go right down to it, 'You're looking at me, you're looking out, and you're unaware of what's behind your eyes. Go back in and find out who you are, where the question comes from, why you ask.' And if you've looked at a photograph of that man--I have a gorgeous photograph of him; I look by it every time I go out the front door. And I look at those eyes, and the humor in them; the lilting laugh that says 'Oh come off it. Shiva, I recognize you. When you come to my door and say `I'm so-and-so,' I say `Ha-ha, what a funny way God has come on today". **~Alan Watts...**

We are many members of one body and one Spirit, and there are not two. That soul that played **Alan Watts** has moved on, but I hope to run into that soul someday. I think our conversations would be more fun than a barrel of monkeys.

Matthew 10:16

16 Behold, I send you forth as sheep in the midst of wolves: be ye therefore wise as serpents and harmless as doves.

We do not allow ourselves to be used by the wolves or serpents of this world. But we must be as wise as they are without harming those lost. If God made both the good and the evil ones. What do you have to fear if they come after you for any reason? Remember, let go; let God. Trust me; they do not want the sword of God (The Word). The serpent wants you and I to judge them and ourselves. They know it will not be harmful if you are not strong in the "Father" when your judgment comes. What they fear is the judgment of God. Darkness cannot exist in light or around light. Darkness will run from you as the moon runs from the sun across the sky. If wicked people can hang around you. You must ask yourself, how great is your darkness if they are not fleeing from you?

Luke 17:2

2 It were better for him that a millstone was hanged about his neck, and he cast into the sea, than that he should offend one of these little ones.

The judgment that the serpent's fear is this, not yours or mine. Free yourself from your burdens, lay them on the Altar as a will offering to God. Then walk in that direction as they melt away.

ROMANS 13

1 Let every soul be subject unto the higher powers. For there is no power but of God: the powers that be are ordained of God.

Yet another tool of Satan's that plays on the masses of today's people, is to become subject to government and countries. People are dying in wars for those wicked individuals. Killing any person that government tells them to kill. Let me be clear here; God has nothing to do with it. God wants nothing to do with the world of flesh. Notice Christ said: "Let every soul be subject to the higher power." God is Spirit and the higher power; every soul must worship in Spirit. There is no killing in the name of God, for God and Country. Paul is not calling for the men of the flesh to be subject to the higher power of government. Paul calls for every soul to be subject to the higher power of God and the Word of God (Christ). There is but one higher power, and that is not of the god of this world or any country, but the "Father" and the body of his Spirit. We are not of this world if you be one of God's children. The matter world is subject to the Spirit. The Spirit (high vibration) is not subjected to matter (low vibration). Just look at what Christ had to say about the matter in Matthew.

Matthew 22:20-21

20 And he saith unto them whose is this image and superscription?

21 They say unto him, Caesar's. Then saith he unto them, Render therefore unto Caesar the things which are Caesar's; and unto God the things that are God's.

That which belongs to Caesar (this world) is of matter and chaos, all of the lower vibration. It can never belong to God's world of heaven or the body of God. They are saying to render unto the lower vibration the things of the lower vibration. Render unto the higher vibration the things of the higher vibration. The higher vibration is love, peace, compassion, mercy, etc. You will not find that in the killing of men. For one country to be able to take another country's oil, minerals, or whatever the case may be. One day the 99% will awaken to the 1% deception. Whether it be republican or democrat, as Puerto Rican poet and journalist **Lola Rodríguez de Tió** said;

"<u>As two wings of the same bird</u>". No human being of flesh will ever save you and is never coming to protect you. Only the Spirit of the "Father" can do that when you become one with him.

Romans 13:2

2 Whosoever, therefore, resisteth the power, resisteth the ordinance of God: and they that resist shall receive to themselves damnation.

I would say almost all have resisted the true higher power of God. And nearly all are living that damnation Paul is talking about right now. Suppose you could see how far you have fallen from your higher state of being, as a god. You could see with clarity the damnation you are living in today.

Romans 13:3

3 For rulers are not a terror to good works, but to the evil. Wilt thou then not be afraid of the power? Do that which is good, and thou shalt have praise of the same.

If you are doing the will of the Spirit of God, as Christ did back then. Christ knew he could speak truths to the masses. He did not need to judge anyone. Let's look at what Christ did in the book of John for a minute.

John 8:6

6 This they said, tempting him, that they might have to accuse him. But Jesus stooped down and, with his finger, wrote on the ground as though he heard them not.

People are always looking to find fault with people because they are always looking at a faulty image of flesh that cannot please God. God is Spirit, and Christ worshipped God in Spirit, not flesh. So, the people were trying to judge Jesus and did not see the perfected Christ within him. Christ knows all things being one with the "Father" began to write in the sand.

John 8:7

7 So when they continued asking him, he lifted up himself, and said unto them, He that is without sin among you, let him first cast a stone at her.

Christ pricked their hearts and made them think with their hearts and souls. Christ woke up; their conscience within them.

John 8:8

8 And again he stooped down and wrote on the ground.

I am assuming Christ was writing in the ground all the sins that each one had done without calling them out in public. He could have and would have if he was a man after the flesh and not Spirit.

John 8:9

9 And they which heard it, being convicted by their own conscience, went out one by one, beginning at the eldest, even unto the last: and Jesus was left alone, and the woman standing in the midst.

Consciousness is what we should all live by in life. It will always look after the things of God. It is a very soft voice that is hard to hear for those not listening. But the "Father" made it heard within them that day. They could not stand against the Spirit of truth and they left one by one.

John 8:10-11

10 When Jesus had lifted up himself and saw none but the Woman, he said unto her, Woman, where are those thine accusers? Hath no man condemned thee?

11 She said, No man, Lord. And Jesus said unto her, neither do I condemn thee: go, and sin no more.

No man can stand against the truth, the sword of the Word. One more thing to notice here is that Christ told the Woman to "sin no more." Why would Christ ask her to do something she could not do? The answer is that he did not; we can all be without sin when we move into Spirit instead of flesh.

Christ understood the perfect Law of Cause and Effect. If you are living on earth trying to be perfect through God in all you do, what law could you or would you break? We do not follow man's law if it conflicts with the law of Spirit. You must live to your conscience and let it be your guide in all things.

Romans 13:4

4 For he is the minister of God to thee for good. But if thou do that which is evil, be afraid; for he beareth not the sword in vain: for he is the minister of God, a revenger to execute wrath upon him that doeth evil.

Christ is the Word of God. When Christ or the Word of God is spoken, that becomes the sword Paul talks about here. The truth is so sharp it can cut between the flesh and soul. A good example is to think back to when you were younger when someone had caught you in a lie in front of a group of people, and there was nothing you could do about it. And there was no way you could escape it because you knew that the words spoken were valid. You felt like you were on fire inside; your face turned red because you were so embarrassed about being caught; this is cutting by the sword of truth on a small scale. The higher you are in the Spirit, the sharper the blade is when used. You should never use the sword on the lost sheep; it is reserved for the spiritually wicked. God uses the rod upon the lost children to bring someone back into the fold, doing no damage to the soul. But I can attest that you will know when you have done wrong and must change.

Proverbs 13:24

24 He that spareth his rod hateth his Son: but he that loveth him chasteneth him betimes.

God is our "Father" and loves us. God wants us to come back into line with the Spirit. That is why the children of God get the rod. To nudge us back into line when we go off track.

Romans 13:5

5 Wherefore ye must needs be subject, not only for wrath but also for conscience's sake.

There it is again; conscience is the rule of our life. That compass tells you that you are on the right or wrong path in your unfoldment. And some people's unfoldment is different. So, everyone's consciousness is going to be different. That's why we judge not others in the things that they do. Suppose you have a rare earth magnet that is 3" long. It is a powerful magnet at both ends of the poles. But where is the fight between those poles? The world is full of different degrees of right and wrong. But it is the conscience that must always be your guide. And you must do all things in faith in God. Know that what you are doing is just and proper. But if later you find out that you were wrong. Just lay it down and move on without Judgement. Knowing that you thought you were correct at the time. All things are experiences to learn to overcome the flesh. Pick up what you know is true and make it who you are. Lay down what you find wrong as you would lay down a piece of rotten fruit (deeds). It does no good to eat it because it is not suitable for the body (soul).

Romans 13:6

6 For this cause pay ye tribute also: for they are God's ministers, attending continually upon this very thing.

I have another issue with churches. I met a man from Mexico at a friend's house in Las Vegas, Nevada. He was traveling as a preacher for a local church. I was introduced to him by another gentleman when we were at his house. This gentleman was a co-worker of mine from work. We used to talk about God a lot. He asked me to speak with his family and friends about my beliefs. One night he brought his preacher friend to hear what I was telling his family and friends. When talking to the preacher, I came to find out it was his job to preach at different people's houses by traveling around to other areas. Wherever the church told him to go, he would collect donations from the people present. Then he would have to give that money he collected to the church. That was all this man and his wife with a newborn baby did. They received very little pay from the church. He should have been able to keep all the money donated for his wife and baby. The people thought they were contributing to him and not the church.

We definitely have Jesus, Mohammad, and Buda in the churches, but where is the "Father"? Where is the Son (The Word-the Bright Shining One) of God? It is possible that Christ (Spirit) was the same soul in all three of these people's flesh; wouldn't that be a kicker? We as humans must start thinking outside the box; God is limitless. Let us break down the following two verses closely.

John 10:16

16 And other sheep I have, which are not of this fold: them also I must bring, and they shall hear my voice; there shall be one-fold, and one shepherd.

All sheep or lost souls belong to the "Father," and the Word of God brings them into the fold. Remember what Christ said: "I speak nothing of myself, but what the "Father" gives me, I speak." No matter who or where they are in this world. Of all nations and all people. They belong to God and have heard the Word of God. Nobody is unique, and there is no respect for persons, period. Christ has gone to all and talked to all. Look beyond the flesh, the coat of skin, for the Spirit. Christ could be anyone from the old days telling the people about God. So, yes, Christ was Adam, David, Jesus, and could have been Buda, Mohammad, and many more.

John 10:34

34 Jesus answered them, is it not written in your law, I said, Ye are gods?

Christ is saying that he said we are all gods in the old law, not that David said. If so, it would have said, "Is it not written in your law that David said ye are gods." The same Spirit that was in David was the same Spirit that was in Jesus. Also, again notice the small g in this verse. The All in All, the "Father" is with a capital G.

Psalm 82:6

6 I have said, Ye are gods, and all of you are children of the Most High.

Here it is in the book of Psalms where it was said. Except David was saying it. That's because Christ was the same Spirit in David, the fleshly man or the Son of man. That was in Jesus, the fleshly Son of man. I will give you another example from the bible.

John 1:21

21 And they asked him, What then? Art thou Elias? And he saith, I am not. Art thou that prophet? And he answered, No.

When John the Baptist was asked if he was Elias. John answered no. Because when we are reborn into this life, we have no remembrance of former things. So, John did not see himself as Elias or know he was. He answered the question in good conscience. Because he did not think he was the same soul as Elias, that was in John the Baptist.

Matthew 17:12-13

12 But I say unto you, That Elias is come already, and they knew him not, but have done unto him whatsoever they listed. Likewise, shall also the Son of man suffer of them.

13 Then the disciples understood that he spake unto them of John the Baptist.

But Christ is the Son of God and knows all things, being one with the "Father." He knew that the soul of Elias was the same soul that was in John the Baptist. It is always best to keep an open mind when seeking God. It is easier to learn something about God. Then it is to give up an old belief about God. We must put off these old constraints we have put on God that he has limitations of any kind. God has no boundaries, only the lower vibrations of the fleshly man do, and they are put off in Christ (the Word of God).

Romans 13:7

7 Render, therefore, to all their dues: tribute to whom tribute is due; custom to whom custom; fear to whom fear; honour to whom honour.

Offend no, man, if you can help it. Live peaceably with all people. If you are following the second commandment, these are all easy to do. Love your neighbor as yourself, and if you can't love yourself, love your neighbor. You will have that going for you, at least.

Romans 13:8

8 Owe no man anything, but to love one another: for he that loveth another hath fulfilled the law.

It is never good to owe anyone anything. It can cause fights between very close family members. It can cause thoughts about you consciously or unconsciously, just as bad as words spoken about you. Because all causes and effects come before God. If you love one another, what evil can they talk of you? And love fulfills the law of God. Suppose someone asks you to borrow money. If you have it, give it to them. Do not lend money to people; it is a trap of the mind, thereby becoming a trap to the soul. Remember all you have. God has given you knowingly or unknowingly. If you loan a loan and it becomes unpaid, Judgement will enter your mind. Then you both become imprisoned in your mind thereby tying up your flesh.

Luke 7:40

40 And Jesus answered said unto him, Simon, I have somewhat to say unto thee. And he saith, Master, say on.

Simon was still a disciple at this time. He was not able to discern with his heart. He still thought as a man and in the old letter of the law. Christ was going to teach Simon a lesson in true love.

Luke 7:41-42

41 There was a certain creditor which had two debtors: the one owed five hundred pence, and the other fifty.

42 And when they had nothing to pay, he frankly forgave them both. Tell me, therefore, which of them will love him most?

When God forgives you to the utmost, and you are a person with a dark closet.

We always say why me after all I have done? These kinds of people have a more profound love for God. You may ask me to prove that statement, and I cannot. I am only working off my own experience here. But ask yourself how Paul could not love the "Father" for forgiving him. Even after the consent to killing the other Apostles? But in the end, all are prodigal sons and daughters to some degree.

Luke 7:43-44

43 Simon answered and said, I suppose that he, to whom he forgave most. And he said unto him, thou hast rightly judged.

44 And he turned to the Woman and said unto Simon, seest thou this Woman? I entered into thine house, thou gavest me no water for my feet: but she hath washed my feet with tears and wiped them with the hairs of her head.

It is not the deeds of the flesh that please God; this is what the world does not understand; it is the deeds of the heart that come from the feminine nature of the soul, which comes from a circumcised heart, not a fleshly heart—the actual manifestation of love, not the mere taking care of the needs of the fleshly man.

Luke 7:45-48

45 Thou gavest me no kiss: but this Woman since the time I came in hath not ceased to kiss my feet.

46 My head with oil thou didst not anoint: but this woman hath anointed my feet with ointment.

47 Wherefore I say unto thee, her sins, which are many, are forgiven; for she loved much: but to whom little is forgiven, the same loveth little

48 And he said unto her, thy sins are forgiven.

Now the next Chapter of Luke talks about Christ preaching. And brings up Mary Magdalene being there. More than not, this is the Woman Christ forgives here.

So, giving with a loving heart or not giving at all is better. The same goes for borrowing from someone; it is also a trap. If you need something, ask God and wait for it to come, but ask living in the law and ask in faith, nothing wavering.

Romans 13:9-10

9 For this, thou shalt not commit adultery, thou shalt not kill, thou shalt not steal, thou shalt not bear false witness, thou shalt not covet; and if there be any other commandments, it is briefly comprehended in this saying thou shalt love thy neighbor as thyself.

10 Love worketh no ill to his neighbor: therefore, love is the fulfilling of the law.

How easily we could fulfill the law if we love God and one another. Just ask yourself what you would want to happen to yourself, then do it to that other person. If you can afford it and have two things that someone needs, give them the better item; you have an extra. Did not God bless you with both the items? Will not God give you more if you need it? Count all things of this world as dung. Remembering what you are to inherit.

Matthew 5:20

20 For I say unto you, that except your righteousness shall exceed the righteousness of the scribes and Pharisees, ye shall in no case enter into the kingdom of heaven.

We all must do better than those of the religions of the flesh. If we do not, there is no hope of entering the Kingdom of God.

Romans 13:11

11 And that, knowing the time, that now it is high time to awake out of sleep: for now, is our salvation nearer than when we believed.

Paul is saying the same thing back then. What I am saying now, we must awaken our souls from the sleep of death. It is time for the resurrection of your true self. We must put away the workings of the fleshly man, put on the working of the Spirit, and be clothed in light that God no more sees our sins.

Romans 13:12

12 The night is far spent, the day is at hand: let us therefore cast off the works of darkness, and let us put on the armour of light.

We must put off the workings of the flesh. And put on the Son (Sun), the bright shining one, the illuminated soul. The armor is a way to salvation for those who put it on.

Romans 13:13

13 Let us walk honestly, as in the day; not in rioting and drunkenness, not in chambering and wantonness, not in strife and envying.

Begin walking in honesty of Spirit by putting off the work we have done in the carnal man through the "Father" and altar.

Romans 13:14

14 But put ye on the Lord Jesus Christ, and make not provision for the flesh, to fulfill the lusts thereof.

Putting on the Christ (The Word) of truth. Make no provision for the carnal man. We must envelop our whole being in the Word of truth. We must become love in all its Glory, God the "Father." Remember, while putting on the Word, you are putting on Spirit.

ROMANS 14

1 Him that is weak in the faith receive ye, but not to doubtful disputations.

Who in today's world does not require more faith? We do not need to debate with anyone about the truth of God. It is better to understand that we all are on the path to enlightenment, even those who seem lost without any hope. All belong to God to be judged or enlightened. God numbers every hair on our heads. Do we really think God needs our help? Remember, Paul knew all things were lawful to him. But Paul also learned that not all things were expedient to him. Paul had to decide as well as we all have to decide whether we are willing to travel the distance. We will all have to travel that distance between the cause and effect of our choices.

Even arguing or entering into disharmony with someone at a lower vibration is not suitable for you. Vibrating at that lower state of consciousness will be all you will accomplish. You will not lift someone to a higher state of consciousness; you always move to the lower vibrations. Until you can stay at a higher vibration within the "Father." We do not all see things with the same clarity. I had a brother when I was first growing in the Spirit, and I always tried to prove to him that I was at his level. Now, I realize by doing so, I could never be at the level he was. I was trying to advance my ego when you have to let go of the ego. So, receive a brother or sister but expect them to be somewhere other than where you are in the unfoldment process. Be patient with them; they are going to have growing pains. They have become like children again, learning everything they have ever known has been a lie. They are being reborn in Spirit and need time to grow. The problem is they have an adult mind and the flesh to overcome. Our minds have been programmed by society throughout our lifetime. And to my dear friend and brother in Christ. I want to say I am sorry for all those years of fighting with you, with the ego that dwelt in me. You will be glad to know that I understand it was not me doing the fighting but the old man of the flesh. I look back now and know that the old man of the flesh lived up to his name of certified **shole. And God the "Father" works mightily in you, as he has in me. Looking back, I could have done nothing different; that is where I was in my unfoldment. Just as my friend was at where he was in his unfoldment, and you are in yours right now. We are where we are right now because this is where we need to be. And this is where we have put ourselves now. Right or wrong, the causes and effects that you and I have made. Reading this verse of this book has brought us to the moment where we are right now. And I will take the time right now, in writing this book, to say hello.

Luke 12:7

7 But even the very hairs of your head are all numbered. Fear not, therefore: ye are of more value than many sparrows.

Romans 14:2

2 For one believeth that he may eat all things: another, who is weak, eateth herbs.

The Bible was not written to benefit the flesh of men or the carnal man. We know that because the flesh cannot please God. Paul is talking about spiritual food here. Remember, all is for the soul's benefit to grow into a quickened Spirit. Paul is talking about those that are just starting in the Word. Not to give them meat or things that will blow their minds about God. They should be given simplicity in the Word (milk). You can drive people away and draw people to God through your deeds and words. But it is best to let them see your deeds (fruit). They speak louder than words ever can.

Romans 14:3

3 Let not him that eateth despise him that eateth not; and let not him which eateth not judge him that eateth: for God hath received him.

If you love studying God day and night. And if someone reads once a week about God. Don't judge that person or see yourself as higher or lower than them. We all have our functions in the body. We all have different paths to the same destination. Remember, the new kingdom has twelve gates to enter the kingdom. It also has the twelve foundations; we all have different strengths and functions within the body of God. Let's take a look at 1 Corinthians.

1 Corinthians 12:27

27 Now ye are the body of Christ and members in particular.

When you are lifted in Spirit, you, as a member of the body, have a place in that body. But you may have a different function within the body.

1 Corinthians 12:28

28 And God hath set some in the church, first apostles, secondarily prophets, thirdly teachers, after that miracles, then gifts of healings, helps, governments, diversities of tongues.

In the body of Spirit, we have different functions. You cannot expect everyone to see things as you do. It is like a rocket engineer expecting a plumber to understand how to build a rocket. Or a rocket engineer understanding all there is to plumbing. I would argue that the plumber has the more important job. We all play a part as members of God's body. We have to go to the "Father" to determine our function. It gets better when you continue to read chapter 13.

1 Corinthians 13:1-3

1 Though I speak with the tongue of men and of angels and have not charity, I am become as sounding brass or a tinkling cymbal.

2 And though I have the gift of prophecy, and understand all mysteries, and all knowledge; and though I have all faith so that I could remove mountains, and have not charity, I am nothing.

3 And though I bestow all my goods to feed the poor, and though I give my body to be burned, and have not charity, it profiteth me nothing.

In these verses, Paul shows you the secrets of the mystery of God again. Here Paul shows you that you must put your body on the Altar for the sin to be burned out of yourself. If you do not have love and charity for one another, what does it profit you? Nothing, all roads lead to love.

1 Corinthians 13:4

4 Charity suffereth long, and is kind; charity envieth not; charity vaunteth, not itself, is not puffed up.

The fulfillment of the law is love. And if you do all the works alone, without God doing them in you. You have not fulfilled the law of love because you are doing it for yourself and not for the benefit of the body (others).

Romans 14:4

4 Who art thou that judgest another man's servant? To his own master, he standeth or falleth. Yea, he shall be holden up: for God is able to make him stand.

Paul makes it clear here as well. When a person understands the perfect Law of Cause and Effect. You will see that there is never a reason to judge another person. They do it themselves when they think and speak, just as you and I do. God is the one that holds up all and allows them to stand. Remember what Paul said in Romans 8:30

Romans 8:30

30 Moreover, whom he did predestinate, them he also called: and whom he called, them he also justified: and whom he justified, them he also glorified.

God has every one of us in excellent hands, his. "Now, faith is the substance of all things hoped for."

Romans 14:5

5 One-man esteemeth one day above another: another esteemeth every day alike. Let every man be fully persuaded in his own mind.

It is essential to understand your consciousness. It is what we use as a court within us. We go before the judge of consciousness, the Spirit of truth. We try our case in the fire, debating whether we should or should not do something. And if the law comes down and you feel it is wrong to do what was decided on by the judge of consciousness, you decide to go ahead and do what has been decided on anyway. Then you have sinned within and without yourself. Because you did whatever it was without a clean conscience. The Spirit of truth shall lead you into all truth and eternal life. You can find the Spirit of truth within you.

John 16:13

13 Howbeit when he, the Spirit of truth, is come, he will guide you into all truth: for he shall not speak of himself; but whatsoever he shall hear, that shall he speak: and he will shew you things to come.

There is a magical world inside God's children, in the realm of Spirit. One of the many things that the Spirit of truth will show you, out of the many things, is the effects of your causes. Most people refuse to see the truth up front in the court. So, they see the effect after the cause instead of before the cause.

Romans 14:6

6 He that regardeth the day, regardeth it unto the Lord; and he that regardeth, not the day, to the Lord he doth not regard it. He that eateth, eateth to the Lord, for he giveth God thanks; and he that eateth not, to the Lord he eateth not, and giveth God thanks.

Some people live in traditions, and others do not. For example, some eat wafers on easter or Sundays, and others do not. Paul again is saying; we must live to the consciousness that dwells within us. It will always lead us to the truth. Whether you are an atheist or Christian. We all live in God and have our movement. So, we all do all things in God. That is true whether you acknowledge God or not. Some go to churches, and some do not. Some study the Bible some do not. It is God that calls a person and opens their heart to love. Instead of looking at people as lost souls or even evil souls. It would be best to look at them as young souls in the early stages of their unfoldment. You would never look at a two-year-old expecting them to carry on the conversation of an adult. It would not be possible, so why would you expect righteousness from an unruly young soul? A young soul rebelling going through its teenage years. Trying to learn to stand on its own feet. Not understanding yet, it is ok to let your parents ("Father") help. Try not to look at the flesh of people. There can be a very young soul in an eighty-year-old person. As well as an old soul in a ten-year-old child.

Romans 14:7-8

7 For none of us liveth to himself, and no man dieth to himself.

8 For whether we live, we live unto the Lord; and whether we die, we die unto the Lord: whether we live therefore, or die, we are the Lord's.

We belong to the Lord, whether spiritually alive or dead in sin while living in the flesh, because we all live in life or live in death by the Word of truth. Whether you tell the truth or lie, you still live by the Word of Truth's cause and effect. Whether you believe in God or not. You are still governed by the Word (The Word of God), whether in or out of the body. The Word of truth applies to us all. So, whether you believe in the law or do not believe in it, it makes no difference. You are still governed by that law and cannot escape the perfect law. It is up to you to learn to live in the law. The law will wait; it is going nowhere and does not change; you must change.

Romans 14:9

9 For to this end Christ both died, and rose, and revived, that he might be Lord both of the dead and living.

Christ (The Word) is over those dead in sin and living in Spirit. The Word governs everyone's life, and the Word is true. Both being alive and being dead, walking in the flesh. He is not talking about those fleshly buried in the ground. Their bodies become dust as you (the soul) move on to new experiences. So, whether you are dead in sin or alive in Spirit, The Word of God (Christ) works through you and in you. As that great Law of Cause and Effect, nobody escapes the law. And nobody escapes the Word of God (Christ).

Romans 14:10

10 But why dost thou judge thy brother? Or why dost thou set at nought thy brother? For we shall all stand before the judgement seat of Christ.

All stand at the judgment seat of Christ (The Word) every moment of every day, within the perfect Law of Cause and Effect. And that is decided in the court with the judge of consciousness. You cannot escape cause and effect. And you should use your consciousness (the Spirit of truth) to make your decisions before acting, and you should consult God on everything. It is not that all will stand before the judgment seat, which is a true statement. It's waking up to the fact that you live that judgment here and now. That every move you make is in front of the Word and God's judgment seat.

Romans 14:11

11 For it is written, As I live, saith the Lord, every knee shall bow to me, and every tongue shall confess to God.

Every knee must bow to the "Father" And confess that God's Word is true. Every tongue must speak the truth in all things. That is the proper way to acknowledge God's Word (Christ). We must manifest the "Father" and Word within our being. We must become the Word ourselves. Then we can say as Christ, "I and the "Father" are one," and being one with the Word of God. You become perfect in both conception and expression.

Romans 14:12

12 So then every one of us shall give account of himself to God.

Every one of us gives account for ourselves. Every moment we live, think and talk and act. We shall all look at our past life. Then we will have to change in the now to become creators of a new life and creation. All this starts at the Altar of God.

Romans 14:13

13 Let us not, therefore, judge one another anymore: but judge this rather, that no man put a stumbling block or an occasion to fall in his brother's way.

If you could but just realize that there is only one Spirit and one body. Then you can see yourself in other lost souls. Truth be known, you might have been in worse predicaments than them before. Between Hot and Cold, there are many different degrees of temperature. We all have opinions on where we think hot starts and cold ends. So, if you see a truth different from someone else. It is because you are looking at it from another (degree) in your pole. If you want to know more on this subject. I refer you to **"The Kybalion Hermetic Philosophy"** I have read this book many times and will read it many more times, God willing. But as with all books, take the information to God for what is true. Knowing it's another person's journey you are looking at when reading. We all grow, and we all change as we grow, and that includes knowledge, wisdom, and understanding.

Romans 14:14

14 I know, and am persuaded by the Lord Jesus, that there is nothing unclean of itself: but to him that esteemeth anything to be unclean, to him it is unclean.

Paul saw everything as a learning experience, even when something terrible happened to him. You are learning not to do it again. If you do not realize the lesson, you will repeat it repeatedly. One must live unto their own consciousness. And your understanding is given to you by the Word of God.

Romans 14:15

15 But if thy brother be grieved with thy meat, now walkest thou not charitably. Destroy not him with thy meat, for whom Christ died.

The flesh will fight back against you; it is accustomed to running the show. If another person cannot handle the truth given to you by God. You should never burn them with that truth by using the sword of God on them. Some people need more time to be ready for your reality. They might be traveling the same path but at another mile marker in the journey. If I visit, Hawaii and a friend goes to Paris. Then my friend tells me what I am missing from not seeing Paris. The truth is they don't know what I am experiencing in Hawaii. They are two trips going to the same place, a place called an adventure. But it is the same thing from two different perspectives, just as all go to the one body of Spirit at different travel distances and gates of entry.

Romans 14:16

16 Let not then your good be evil spoken of.

I was in a church talking to a priest one day, years ago. I was showing a man calling himself a bishop, where Christ said it was possible to be perfect in Matthew 5:48. Then he called me a son of Satan for believing I could be perfect as God was—then told me to get out of his blanking church. At that time, I was burning him with the sword of truth. He could not handle hearing that much truth. Because it made him question all he ever had learned and knew. I always felt it was my fault for not knowing that. But how could I? I needed that experience to learn that lesson, and he also required that experience for his path.

Romans 14:17

17 For the kingdom of God is not meat and drink, but righteousness, and peace, and joy in the Holy Ghost.

The kingdom of God is not just what you know. But the deeds that you do. With the knowledge that you have. The knowledge that you are one with all things. And not just to know these words but see the oneness within yourself because of the grace of God. And it is found in a joyous heart.

Romans 14:18

18 For he that in these things serveth Christ is acceptable to God, and approved of men.

So, what is that service to Christ? Or what is that service to the Word? To think, speak and manifest love to all, including yourself, through and in the Word.

Romans 14:19

19 Let us, therefore, follow after the things which make for peace and things wherewith one may edify another.

We should always be there to lift up one another in all things. Doing all things in love, understanding God has things well under control. The joy you will start to feel when you learn peace of soul. That it is ok to let go and not judge. The freedom from stress, knowing all is taking care of itself without your help. To stand back and see the chaos and not have to join in. But see it for what it is, nothing more than a fabricated illusion of chaos.

Romans 14:20

20 For meat destroy not the work of God. All things indeed are pure, but it is evil for that man who eateth with offence.

I am guilty of this with a friend. In my mind, I see him as a vessel of God. So, I tried very hard to wake him up. And he is indeed a vessel of God, and God will use him for his work. It could be in another lifetime for him, and I don't know when. But I understand now God does not need my help to wake him up. So, now I plant seeds in the fields of his mind. Christ will water, and God will give the increase when it is his time. I was trying to force-feed him, and he was getting offended. Because it was going against all, he had learned in the church. When you get close to God in Spirit, you only want to share God with others because God is all there is to you. You live and breathe God; all you want to do is talk about God. Sometimes, we need to stop and remember others are not on our path. Don't make someone hate you and God because they can't handle the meat you are trying to force-feed them. They will come when in God's order.

Romans 14:21

21 It is good neither to eat flesh, nor to drink wine, nor any thing whereby thy brother stumbleth, or is offended or is made weak.

Now, we know by this time, the flesh profits nothing. And these words are spiritual. But if you are going to manifest love, you want to do it on all levels. Suppose you are eating around a vegetarian, for example. Let's say you know it and believe eating meat in your heart is ok. And your friend does not believe it is ok. Suppose you eat the beef thinking nothing of it. You have not sinned and have done nothing wrong if your friend decides to eat the meat. Believing in his heart that it is wrong because he has seen you do it. He has sinned before God and himself because he has done it with an unclean conscience. We don't want that for anyone. So, joining your friend in that meal would be better than eating meat. If you were to talk that person into eating meat when you knew it was a conflict within them. Then you are a partaker of that sin or trap they undertake because you have led your brother or sister into a pit or laid a stumbling block for them. And as long as your friend is in the prison of his mind, you will be as well because you put the stumbling block in his way.

Romans 14:22

22 Hast thou faith? Have it to thyself before God. Happy is he that condemneth, not himself in that thing which he alloweth.

It is better to keep quiet than to lead someone into a trap. That person might take years to climb out if they are in pain because of you. You are in pain because of what you have done. It falls under the Law of Cause and Effect. And the law is perfect on all levels. If you cause someone pain, you will be in pain. It is like a big rubber band you pull back on your leg. It is going to hurt when you let go. Demons always do this, but they suggest making it your idea and not theirs. They know how to play the game of cause and effect very well.

Romans 14:23

23 And he that doubteth is damned if he eat, because he eateth not of faith: for whatsoever is not of faith is sin.

Paul sums it up here by saying. Do all things in good conscience. If you do not do everything with a good conscience, it is of sin because of your lack of faith. But we do not self-justify ourselves when we know it is wrong. It is easy to talk yourself into almost anything. But in truth, we always know what is right and wrong.

ROMANS 15

1 We then that are strong ought to bear the infirmaties of the weak and not to please ourselves.

According **<u>to *Bing on search in* Microsoft Office</u>**: the definition of *"ought"* is defined as:

"<u>Ought</u>"

"Used to indicate duty or correctness, typically when criticizing someone's actions."

Paul is conveying we must bear the weaknesses of others. It is better to manifest love to others than to look after our interests in this life. That would be the definition of love. Not constantly finding fault (evil side of the tree) in others. Or having to defend yourself (the good side of the tree) and your ego when judged by others. Life needs no explanation to anyone. It is a personal journey between you, God, and no one else. When your knee hits the ground before God, you will be alone.

Romans 15:2

2 Let every one of us please his neighbour for his good to edification.

Definition from **<u>Oxford Languages</u>***:*

"<u>Edification</u>"

"The instruction or improvement of a person morally or intellectually."

Most people try to help their neighbors in ways of the flesh. Thinking that, in some way, they are fulfilling the will of God. Paul is talking about looking after the needs of your neighbor's soul—information and things they might need to overcome the fleshly man. One of the best ways to help someone is to pray and meditate for them. They do not need to know you are praying or meditating for them. Then you will know that God made the change and not yourself. We must remember to God goes all Glory.

Romans 15:3

3 For even Christ pleased not himself; but, as it is written, the reproaches of them that reproached thee fell on me.

We all have a perfect example of the manifestation of love: Christ, the Word of God. The problem is that most people worship Jesus, believing it is impossible to be like him by manifesting Christ within themselves, even though the scriptures teach otherwise. The second commandment was to love your neighbor as yourself. It would be a world to see people thinking of others more than themselves. But that is precisely what Paul is talking about here. We all have the power to change this world for the better. And it all starts with a bit of love for one another. That starts with you and me manifesting the "Father" and the Christ (Word). Start by asking yourself, do you love your neighbor as yourself? Or are you loving yourself more? I am not trying to prick anyone's heart. I am opening others up to a new way of thinking, a spiritual way of thinking. Christ had a life that was pretty dang good. And he gave that life up to enter into hell for you and me.

Romans 15:4

4 For whatsoever things were written aforetime were written for our learning, that we through patience and comfort of the scriptures might have hope.

The Bible is for the soul's instructional purposes. It was to help instruct us to move from that man of the flesh (Carnal) to the man of Spirit.

Religious books like the Bible, the Koran, the Vedas, and countless others were to illuminate the soul within humankind's growth. But the man, in all his worldly wisdom, has turned them into weapons of war instead of loving thy neighbor as yourself. They have used all these books to justify killing one's neighbor in the name of God. And God has had nothing to do with it at all. Humanity has always done these things in the name of men's greed and lust for more, more, more. For more money, more gas, more oil, more gold and more diamonds, and more power and control etc. The men and women who have fought are poor and do the bidding of the rich. And in the rich man's eyes, you have always been expendable because they are all children of darkness, evil spirits living in the flesh of human bodies as you are a child of light living in a fleshly body. That is what Paul meant when he said.

Ephesians 6:12

12 For we wrestle not against flesh and blood, but against principalities, against powers, against the rulers of the darkness of this world, against spiritual wickedness in high places.

These are not just words spoken. There is a war going on in this world. Whether you know it or not, believe it or not, you are a part of it. And if you don't know it, you are being deceived by the illusions. If you are starting to see the war, you are waking up and welcome to the battle zone. We will win this war in love with the "Father."

Romans 15:5

5 Now the God of patience and consolation grant you to be likeminded one toward another according to Christ Jesus.

Here it was gotten right, the words "Christ" Jesus. We are putting the Spirit before the flesh. It is the only way to manifest perfect love. We must be likeminded in our true self's Spirit. And manifest that Spiritual love through our fleshly man to others. That is the only way to be perfected in the flesh, truly.

Romans 15:6

6 That ye may with one mind and one mouth glorify God, even the "Father" of our Lord Jesus Christ.

The only way to have one mind is to be one with the "Father." The only way to have one voice is to speak the same Word. And that Word has been the same since the beginning of it all. That Word is Christ, and everything he has ever said has been the words from the "Father" himself, to Glorify the "Father".

John 14:10

10 Believest thou not that I am in the "Father," and the "Father" in me? The words that I speak unto you I speak not of myself: but the

"Father" that dwelleth in me, he doeth the works.

Romans 15:7-8

7 Wherefore receive ye one another, as Christ also received us to the Glory of God.

8 Now I say that Jesus Christ was a minister of the circumcision for the truth of God, to confirm the promises made unto the fathers.

The fleshly man Jesus was one with Christ. As Christ was one with the "Father." Christ was speaking through Jesus. The words that were coming from the "Father." He was preaching to those who had been circumcised in the heart.

Romans 15:9

9 And that the Gentiles might glorify God for his mercy; as it is written, for this cause I will confess to thee among the Gentiles, and sing unto thy name.

The Gentiles live after the flesh and are dead in sin. The Gentiles are the ones waking up today and will be glorifying God. It is only because of God's mercy that it will happen. The only way to enter the kingdom of God is to quit working for it. And put yourself at the feet of God's Altar, and offer yourself up as a free-will offering to him.

Matthew 26:41

41 Watch and pray that ye enter not into temptation: the Spirit indeed is willing, but the flesh is weak.

Even Christ was showing at the time. He, the Son of God, was willing to do everything, but Jesus was weak then.

Matthew 27:46

46 And about the ninth hour, Jesus cried with a loud voice, saying, Eli, Eli, lama sabachthani? That is to say, My God, My God, why hast thou forsaken me?

The flesh has always been the weak side of who we are. Christ knew that his "Father" would never forsake him. But the fleshly man is always looking to doubts and fears. Even Jesus, at the last minute, doubted God. But Christ, the Son of God, never questioned God's power to keep his Word. God is Spirit and must be appropriately worshiped by us in our proper form, Spirit.

Romans 15:10-12

10 And again he saith, Rejoice, ye Gentiles, with his people.

11 And again, Praise the Lord, all ye Gentiles; and laud him, all ye people.

12 And again, Esaias saith, there shall be a root of Jesse, and he that shall rise to reign over the Gentiles; in him shall the Gentiles trust.

All can manifest the "Father" the "Word" and the Holy Ghost within themselves. It does not matter your race or whether you are a man or a woman. It all boils down to your faith in God. No one can give you faith or take it away from you. Faith comes from God when he reveals himself to you. Go within to the Altar, and leave a free-will offering. Then walk in that direction in faith (the works). It is believing in your heart that God will accept your offering. God burns out all the unclean dross from within you, and you become pure Gold to God. Or you become cleansed by God. The problem today is everyone is trying to do the work themselves. That is when it becomes a debt to be paid by God. Suppose you want to clean yourself from sin and do all the work. God will stand by and let you try until the cows come home, until you see that the only way home is by the grace, he has given us. That is the Word of God that God spoke. It is not a laborious burden that God has placed on us. The commandment from God is to love. And no one has seemed to be able to master that yet.

Matthew 22:37-40

37 Jesus said unto him, thou shalt love the Lord thy God with all thy heart, and with all thy soul, and with all thy mind.

38 This is the first and great commandment.

39 And the second is like unto it; thou shalt love thy neighbor as thyself.

40 On these two commandments hang all the law and the prophets.

On these two commandments hang all the laws of the prophets. That is all there is to it, folks; entering the kingdom is easy. Why do we find it so hard to love? Because we try to love with the flesh and a fleshly state of mind. That has nothing to do with God in the least. We have been reading the Bible from a fleshly state of mind, which is in the simplest form in which to read it (seven-seals). We must read the Bible with a Spiritual understanding. And the only way to do that is in the Word (Christ). I will give you an example down below.

James 2:15

15 If a brother or sister be naked and destitute of daily food.

To be naked is to be in sin, one without clothes. The daily food is that which feeds the soul, not the flesh.

James 2:16

16 And one of you say unto them, depart in peace, be ye warmed and filled; notwithstanding ye give them not those things which are needful of the body; what doth it profit?

If you have information that your brother or sister needs. To overcome their weakness, or if you see a trap they might be in and you are not supplying them with any help. You are not providing their body (soul) needs to help them grow. It will not profit them as well as yourself. Where are your fruits? Now, if you see someone that requires food for the need of the flesh, and manifest love to them and give them some food, that is a good thing to do, according to the Law of Cause and Effect. You will not go hungry in the fleshly body. But Spirit is a higher vibration and must be expressed in a higher vibration—cause and effect work on both plains of consciousness, physically and spiritually. The Bible can be read on both a physical and Spiritual level by all. Christ used things of the world to explain something of the Spirit, as did all the Apostles of Christ. Sometimes they did not wholly understand the Spirit during their discipleship. I do not want to beat a dead horse here. But it is essential to realize that the Bible talks on many levels. And the only way to understand it all is in a spiritual mind or God's Word (Christ).

John 6:60

60 Many, therefore, of his disciples, when they had heard this, said, this is an hard saying; who can hear it?

You can see it was hard for some of Christ's disciples to understand the words of the Spirit. Because Christ was using things of this world to express spiritual things. They kept trying to see them from a fleshly state of mind. And they did not make any sense to them. Just as churches do today with the Bible. Looking at the Bible in one dimension. The Bible has seven candle sticks. Which means seven different lights or levels of understanding. The book of Revelations also says it has seven seals.

John 6:61-62

61 When Jesus knew in himself that his disciples murmured at it, he said unto them, Doth this offend you?

62 What and if ye shall see the Son of man ascend up where he was before?

I am sure this blew their minds at the time. Thinking Jesus was going to float off into space. Instead, he was talking about raising his soul within him to become one with the "Father" in Spirit. Raising the vibration of the lower man of flesh into a being of light.

John 6:63

63 It is the Spirit that quickeneth; the flesh profiteth nothing: the words that I speak unto you, they are Spirit, and they are life.

According to **Englishhttps://glosbe.com,** quickeneth definition is.

"**Quickeneth or quickened**."

"Means to bring to life or make alive."

Christ plainly said the Spirit does the work. It brings the soul to life. The flesh does not profit anything at all, and again the flesh cannot please God. Christ plainly says he is speaking in Spirit. That means he is not speaking as a fleshly man or the son of man. He is speaking as the Son of God. So, all religions trying to please God in the flesh or by fleshly deeds or by repentance of the flesh cannot do so. We can go back to Romans for a quick look.

Romans 8:8

8 So, then they that are in the flesh cannot please God.

You will never please God if you are trying to do good deeds in the flesh. Instead of doing them in the Spirit.

Romans 11:29

29 For the gifts and calling of God are without repentance.

You will get lost trying to live in the past and not living in the now. You cannot do anything about what you did yesterday. Because it is only a memory of what has happened. Now, you can learn from that memory so you do not repeat that action in the present. Leave yesterday's memories on the library shelf in your mind unless those memories are needed for a short time for reference. But for the sake of all that is real, do not live in the past. You are no more the past than you are the person you see in the mirror.

John 6:64

64 But there are some of you that believe not, for Jesus knew from the beginning who they were that believed not, and who should betray him.

Talking to someone indoctrinated into mainstream religion about the true Spirit can be challenging. I tried many times until I became blue in the face. You can show some people all the proof in the world about Spirit. And they will refuse to consider that they may be wrong. These are the scribes and Pharisees Christ talked about then and now. They interpret the Bible on the fleshly level, which is the Jesus level. Never wanting to see the Christ (spirit) level. God is Spirit and must be seen and worshiped in Spirit.

Matthew 23:13

13 But woe unto you, scribes and Pharisees, hypocrites! For ye shut up the kingdom of heaven against men: for ye neither go in yourselves, neither suffer ye them that are entering to go in.

They teach doctrines for the fleshly man and the deeds he can or cannot do. For example, they drink wine and eat a cracker. Or whatever other tradition of the fleshly man. It takes away from the soul and what God must accomplish in it. As well as telling people they cannot become perfect. Doing all these things keeps souls from awakening and becoming one with the "Father." Even if someone starts to wake up and question the narrative, they may see where it talks about being perfect and ask someone at church about it. The church tells them they are only sinners and no one is perfect. And that person believes it, and it keeps that person from waking up to the actual spiritual being that they are. Now would you want to be the person waking up and going back to sleep? Or the person that kept that person from waking up because you told them a lie? Because you did not want to study it yourself and ask God to find out the truth. They are both still asleep in Christ the Word. But to who goes the greater damnation?

Matthew 23:14

14 Woe unto you, scribes and Pharisees, hypocrites! For ye devour widow's houses, and for a pretense make long prayer: therefore, ye shall receive the greater damnation.

What is a widow? It is someone whose husband has died. All are dead in sin, looking to be married into the body of Christ. We are the widows; the house is our soul; we are the temple of God. They stand and make long prayers to be seen by others. And the prayers have nothing to do with the building of the souls of humankind. But they say, watch over us today as we drive home. Thank you, God, for all that could make it here today. I am not trying to come down on you if you are one of these preachers. You have earned a degree somewhere. In fact, just the other day, one of my friends told me about another one of our friends. He told me our friend had just received his certificate to start preaching; I believe it was the Baptist. I asked him where he got his degree and who gave it to him. I already knew the answer, and my friend already knew my response. He had obtained a degree from his religious institution to teach what another man led him to teach. What has the world come to when we do not get our degrees from God? When another man can tell me or anyone if we are qualified to teach about God, this vicious circle keeps going round and round. No man of the flesh can ordain anyone to preach the Word of God. You can look back to 1 John 2:27 and see that you don't need anyone to teach you. We all must have our own relationship with God.

Matthew 23:15

15 Woe unto you, scribes and Pharisees, hypocrites! For ye compass sea and land to make one proselyte, and when he is made, ye make him twofold more the child of hell than yourselves.

Definition from ***"Oxford Languages"***

"proselyte"

"a person who has converted from one opinion, religion, or party to another."

Do you know of churches that have crossed an ocean to convert other people to their religion? I would want to ensure I was teaching Spirit if it were me. I have read these verses for a year now. And they put the fear of God in me. It kept me from talking to people for a lot of years. I did not want to be a two-fold child of hell. How can any man that has not overcome sin teach another man to overcome sin if they have not seen how to overcome sin themselves? How can you show someone to put off sin if you do not believe you can? The churches make the matter worse than if they had left these poor people alone. But Satan must have all under his illusion for his plan to work. These poor people have to unlearn this lousy programming they have been taught. Before they can install the new one into their minds, a perfect example would be the Native Indians. They believed in many spirits in the land, air, sky, animals, etc. The Indians thought that all these Spirits made up the one Spirit, and they were right. Many Native Indians have been converted to worshipping one fleshly man as God. The Indians would have been better off if they were left alone, with their Spirits and one "Father." Now they have been deceived as all others to worship the flesh, not the "Father," the one true Spirit.

Matthew 23:16

16 Woe unto you, ye blind guides, which say, whosoever shall swear by the temple, it is nothing; but whosoever shall swear by the Gold of the temple, he is a debtor!

The temple is our soul, which is the house of God. The Gold is our purification of the soul. We start as Gold pulled straight from the earth. It has many impurities of dross within it because it is raw. The more we go to the Altar, the more impurities are burned out of us by God until we are pure Gold and Holy. God is no longer just our God; he is our "Father." No man should swear on anything he does not own, and God owns everything.

Matthew 23:17

17 Ye fools and blind: for whether is greater, the Gold, or the temple that sanctifieth the Gold?

Christ is not only calling them fools which was a lot for Christ. But notice he is calling them blind. Blind for not seeing that they are the temple of the living God. We are the temple that sacrifices the Gold. The old self is put on the Altar to be crucified in like manner with Christ. You can go back and look at Romans 12:1 to see this verse. Or, look at what Paul says here in the book of Galatians.

Galatians 2:20

20 I am crucified with Christ: nevertheless, I live; yet not I, but Christ liveth in me: and the life which I now live in the flesh I live by the faith of the Son of God, who loved me and gave himself for me.

Ok, a lot is going on in this verse. First, we see we need to be crucified with Christ, the putting off of the old man, by putting the old man of sin on the Altar. Second, he is saying even though he is crucified, he still lives. If it were by the flesh, that would not be possible. But it is the soul that is risen from the grave of sin and transforms the body of flesh. Third, Paul says, "well, not I the fleshly man is living anymore." But the Word of God (Christ) lives in me. Fourth, Paul now says he lives by faith in the Word of God (Christ). He no longer has faith in the old man of the flesh, who is being crucified; Paul's theology is now perfected in the Word. If men truly loved Christ, they would fulfill his commandments. But they live after the flesh and worship the flesh of the Son of man, not knowing that Satan has robbed them of their inheritance of all things with God. They have unwillingly and unknowingly become anti-Christ. You could say anti-Words that came from God because they do not believe what has been written by God.

2 Thessalonians 2:10

10 And with all deceivableness of unrighteousness in them that perish; because they received not the love of the truth, they might be saved.

The love of the truth is salvation from the dead. The resurrection from the dead by the Word of God. It is the **"be perfect as your "Father" in heaven is perfect."**

2 Thessalonians 2:11

11 And for this cause God shall send them strong delusion, that they should believe a lie.

This strong delusion is worshipping the flesh and putting it before the "Father" and the Word.

2 Thessalonians 2:12

12 That they all might be damned who believed not the truth but had pleasure in unrighteousness.

In the flesh dwells all the unrighteousness we find today. It is the dwelling place of Satan, this world, and all its lower vibrations. God is not of the lower vibration but, the higher vibration.

My wife asked if God is omnipresent and if God is in the lower and higher vibrations. And I say yes and no to the question. Yes, because God is omnipresent in all places. But no, at the same time, and here is what I mean.

We will have to look at our limited minds for the answer. But remember, we are limited as God is not. We have the Tree of Good and Evil and the Tree of Life within us. Both these Trees are deeds we do. The Deeds we do are the fruit of the two Trees. We can choose to do good in our lives, or we can choose to do evil. God has given us free will to choose to work or rest. So far, man has chosen to work and eat from the Tree of Good and Evil. We were created in the image of our "Father" as small 'g' creators as we choose to do only good and dwell in only goodness in our mind. God is no different. He chooses not to dwell in the lower vibrations in his mind. Even though God is All things, it's like being at a party and sitting alone. And your mind is off in a faraway place, so much so you are not at the party except in body. Hopefully, this helps to explain the question; it is as clear as I see it myself.

Solomon 1:4

4 For into a malicious soul wisdom shall not enter; nor dwell in the body that is subject unto sin.

God is all Knowledge, wisdom, and understanding. God chooses just as we can choose. And God decides not to enter into sin with his mind; the Holy Spirit dwells in perfection. I know it is a complex concept to wrap our heads around. We have to get away from the limitations of the lower frequencies of humankind. Have you ever had a conversation with someone that was talking to you? And you did not hear a word they said. Even though they were right in front of you. Because you were somewhere else in your mind. That's about as close as I can get to explaining it. But I know it is a lot more complicated than that. God is the God of the living Spirit, not the dead. It is the Word that brings you to the "Father." The Word (Christ) is over both the living and the dead.

John 14:6

6 Jesus saith unto him, I am the way, the truth, and the life: no man cometh unto the "Father," but by me.

The only way to the "Father" is the Word of God. But it is the "Father" that sends the Word.

2 Thessalonians 2:13

13 But we are bound to give thanks alway to God for you, brethren beloved of the Lord because God hath from the beginning chosen you to salvation through sanctification of the Spirit and belief of the truth.

According to ***Bing word search on word*** *the word* "sanctification" *means:*

*"**Sanctification**"*

"The action of making or declaring something holy."

By believing the truth about the Word of God, we enter into the acts of being made holy by the Word of God through the "Father" at the Altar.

Matthew 23:18-20

18 And, whosoever shall swear by the Altar, it is nothing; but whosoever sweareth by the gift that is upon it, he is guilty.

19 Ye fools and blind: for whether is greater, the gift, or the Altar that sanctifieth the gift?

20 Whoso, therefore, shall swear by the Altar, sweareth by it, and by all things thereon.

The Altar is a sacred place dwelling within you. It is between the outer court, the land of the carnal man, and the inner court, the place of Spirit. When you swear by yourself, you are swearing at everything God owns. It is also called the Holy of Holies. It was also named the closet by Christ—where you close the door and talk to God.

Matthew 6:6

6 But thou, when thou prayest, enter into thy closet, and when thou hast shut thy door, pray to thy "Father" which is in secret; and thy "Father" which seeth in secret shall reward thee openly.

It is not a closet like in your home; it is a place within the quietness of your mind. A place in silence and peace with no distractions of the world outside, it is a place of meditation. It is not a place in front of other people where you pray. But it is a secret place for you and the "Father."

Psalm 63:6

6 When I remember thee upon my bed and meditate on thee in the night watches.

Meditation has been around for a long time. Many cultures over the centuries have done it.

Psalm 63:7

7 Because thou hast been my help, therefore in the shadow of thy wings will I rejoice.

I know there is only one God to which all Glory goes. And God is never far from me.

Psalm 63:8

8 My soul followeth hard after thee: thy right hand upholdeth me.

You have to seek God with all of who you are. To find the Gold hidden in the streams and caves of yourself. It is not the flesh that seeks God, but the soul.

Psalm 63:9

9 But those that seek my soul, to destroy it, shall go into the lower parts of the earth.

Those who seek your souls to destroy will be cast out into the lowest vibrations of the carnal mind. Then there will be weeping and gnashing of teeth. God also takes no pleasure in those that stand in the churches and street corners, making long prayers that go nowhere.

Matthew 6:5

5 And when thou prayest, thou shalt not be as the hypocrites are: for they love to pray standing in the synagogues and in the corners of the streets, that they may be seen of men. Verily I say unto you; they have their reward.

You cannot pray to God while living in the sins of the flesh and make God happy. There is only one way to make yourself and God happy. That is to pray to God in the oneness of your essence. Manifest the Word and be part of the one Spirit.

Matthew 23:21

21 And whoso shall swear by the temple, sweareth by it, and by him that dwelleth therein.

By using the words, I swear, we are swearing on ourselves and by God. We must consider the things we are vowing to do. It would be best not to do it in the first place. How can you swear on anything? When all you have is borrowed from God, and you own nothing at all.

Matthew 23:22

22 And he that shall swear by heaven, sweareth by the throne of God, and by him that sitteth thereon.

23 Woe unto you, scribes and Pharisees, hypocrites! For ye pay tithe of mint and anise and cummin, and have omitted the weightier matters of the law, judgement, mercy, and faith: these ought ye to have done, and not to leave the other undone.

They have looked to the things of the outer manifestation, this world. They have looked after all the needs of the fleshly man. You cannot smell the law, you cannot touch judgment, you cannot hear mercy, and you cannot taste faith. These are all things that come forth from the heart and soul. These are the things left aside, and these are the things of God.

A friend of mine was going to preach for the first time at his church. And he asked me to come to hear his sermon. I have a deep brotherly love for my friend, so I went. And I tell you, I cannot stand, nor do I like going to churches. I could not listen to my friends talk. I was distracted the whole time by two blackboards. They both occupied my mind the entire time. One was on stage to the left of my friend, and one was on his right. The one on the left had written on it all the money the church raised from its members the last month. The one on the right showed how much money needed to be submitted by the members to meet or surpass the previous month's earnings. I concluded that the church was in it for money, not God. I could not get past the two chalkboards to hear my friend's message if the churches could muster just a little faith in God. They would not have to ask people to give them money. God would provide the funds for them to give to their members.

Matthew 23:24

24 Ye blind guides, which strain at a gnat and swallow a camel.

Living by man's laws is much more complicated than living by God's. With God, you turn them over to him on the Altar. With man, your pains and burdens never go away. Humanity still strains at the words, "Be perfect as your "Father" is perfect." Is it easier to sin and ask for forgiveness over and over, or just become righteous by God's grace? At the end of the day, what profit is there in all the sins that humankind has done?

Sin is constantly passing from the now to the past, with no more feelings remaining of what happened while doing the sin. Only the memories of the act of sin are left. If you die in the flesh, what can you take with you? While your (souls) are in your bodies, you collect Knowledge, wisdom, understanding, and karma. What kind of Knowledge, wisdom, understanding, and karma do you want to take with you?

Matthew 23:25

25 Woe unto you, scribes and Pharisees, hypocrites! For ye make clean the outside of the cup and of the platter, but within they are full of extortion and excess.

They present themselves as Holy men of God in the Flesh (Outside cup). But in their minds have the same sinful thought that other men have. They live like other men six days a week. They are professing themselves to be holy on the seventh. Saying listen to what I have to say about God. Yet they know nothing about God. You cannot honestly know God if you are living in sin. No one in the flesh can please God. God is not the God of the dead, only the living. You must be in the Spirit to be living. And if you are in the Spirit, you have been made free from sin. And if the soul is waking up. You are walking in faith and grace.

Matthew 23:26

26 Thou blind Pharisee, cleanse first that which is within the cup and platter, that the outside of them may be clean also.

We must become children again, as Christ said. You must realize all we have ever been told or learned is a lie. Satan has been working in this world for a long time. We must Cleanse the inside of the mind (cup). When your soul and mind have renewed, the body will fall in line (outside of the cup). Anyone else saying God lives in the flesh is of those Christ called the dead, burying the dead.

Matthew 18:3

3 And said, Verily I say unto you, except ye be converted, and become as little children, ye shall not enter into the kingdom of heaven.

Little children know nothing as they ought to; they learn everything from their parents. We must learn from the "Father" all things anew. It is the only way to enter the kingdom of God.

Matthew 23:27

27 Woe unto you, scribes and Pharisees, hypocrites! For ye are like unto whited sepulchres, which indeed appear beautiful outward, but are within full of dead men's bones, and of all uncleanness.

Christ is not holding anything back here. He is saying the preachers and people of the flesh are make themselves look holy on the outside of the body on Sunday when they preach and are seen. But inside, their souls are dead in sin and full of unrighteous deeds and thoughts.

Matthew 23:28

28 Even so, ye also outwardly appear righteous unto men, but within ye are full of hypocrisy and iniquity.

They have the appearance of holy men of God outwardly. But they are dead in sin, and the soul has no life within them. God is omnipresent. The Word of God dwells in each one of us. But if someone was to preach for God and if they were called to preach by God. They would be well on their way in their resurrection process within God. And God would say something like this below to them.

Ezekiel 3:4

4 And he said unto me, Son of man, go, get thee unto the house of Israel, and speak with my words unto them.

God would be one with you in mind and voice.

Romans 8:30

30 Moreover whom he did predestinate, them he also called: and whom he called, them he also justified: and whom he justified, them he also glorified.

According to "**Dictionary.com**" the meaning of predestinate is.

"**Predestinate**"

Theology. to foreordain by divine decree or purpose.

Obsolete. to foreordain; predetermine.

Adjective

predestined; foreordained.

God knows what is going to happen to all. God had destined us before we were put in our mothers' wombs to have the experience we will have. God does all the work when God's creation is working perfectly. Our job is to praise God and thank God through (IN) the Word. We do not see the future now. But God wrote the story that is unfolding now. You and I are just now catching up with the script.

Jeremiah 1:5

5 Before I formed thee in the belly, I knew thee, and before thou camest forth out of the womb, I sanctified thee, and I ordained thee a prophet unto the nations.

God knows every one of us. The problem is not that God does not know us but that the people do not know God. People want to work for something that is a gift. And it does not work that way—the old ***Frank Sinatra*** song. ***"I did it my way"*** does not work with God. It must be done his way and should be.

John 6:65

65 And he said, therefore said I unto you, that no man can come unto me, except it were given unto him of my "Father."

No man can come to Christ (The Word of God) except the "Father" leads them to the Word. The Words of Christ are the waters that lead to life. Remember that the "Father" calls, justifies, and glorifies you.

John 6:66

66 From that time many of his disciples went back and walked no more with him.

They could not comprehend the words of the Spirit. People were too caught up in doing the traditions and deeds of their fathers. Like today, if you tell people they need to be holy and perfect. They would be more comfortable living in the lie they have constructed for themselves. Their will is perfected in this world and not perfected in the realm of Spirit.

Galatians 5:17

17 For the flesh lusteth against the Spirit, and the Spirit against the flesh: and these are contrary the one to the other: so that ye cannot do the things that ye would

Most people do not even know this war is going on within every one of us—the battle of Spirit and flesh. People have been living by the flesh for so long. They don't even see the Spiritual side of the war anymore. They have lost the battle and become mere mortals. Because that is what their faith tells them they are.

Galatians 5:18

18 But if ye be led of the Spirit, ye are not under the law.

You are free from all the laws of the Bible. When the Spirit leads you, you become the law and one with the "Father."

Galatians 5:19-21

19 Now the works of the flesh are manifest, which are these; Adultery, fornication, uncleanness, lasciviousness,

20 Idolatry, witchcraft, hatred, variance, emulations, wrath, strife, seditions, heresies,

21 Envyings, murders, drunkenness, revellings, and such like: of the which I tell you before, as I have also told you in time past, that they which do such things shall not inherit the kingdom of God.

Where does it say here you will be forgiven when you die, as religions teach? I read, "they will not inherit the kingdom of God." Where does it say to use the secret password "Jesus" when you get there?

Galatians 5:22

22 But the fruit of the Spirit is love, joy, peace, longsuffering, gentleness, goodness, faith.

Here is part of the secret password, but it must be manifested before it is too late because heaven is within you.

Galatians 5:23

23 Meekness, temperance: against such there is no law.

The commandment of God is easy, summoned up in one word, love.

Galatians 5:24

24 And they that are Christ's have crucified the flesh with the affections and lusts.

The flesh and all its doings must be put on the cross and crucified with Christ (The Word) of God, or God's Word. That old person must die and make way for the new one to live. By raising its vibration along with the soul, to a quickened Spirit.

Romans 12:1

1 I beseech you therefore, brethren, by the mercies of God, that ye present your bodies a living sacrifice, holy, acceptable unto God, which is your reasonable service.

To become a living sacrifice is to put your old man of sin on the Altar of God. The only way to manifest God (Spirit) is to present yourself to God as a living sacrifice. Then and only then can it be said that this mortal has put on immortality.

Galatians 5:25

25 If we live in the Spirit, let us also walk in the Spirit.

We must live, breathe, walk, and talk Spirit. There is no part-time spirit or lukewarm.

Galatians 5:26

26 Let us not be desirous of vain Glory, provoking one another, envying one another.

There is no envy or jealousy in Spirit. The ego of the fleshly man will become crucified on the cross and no longer exist.

John 6:67-68

67 Then said Jesus unto the twelve, Will ye also go away?

68 Then Simon Peter answered him, Lord, to whom shall we go? Thou hast the words of eternal life.

Peter (Faith) says you have the WORDS of life. To believe in Christ is to believe in his Words. That was quite a detour, but I hope it was worth it. Let's get back to verse 13.

Romans 15:13

13 Now the God of hope fill you with all joy and peace in believing, that ye may abound in hope through the power of the Holy Ghost.

The Holy Ghost is the opened pineal gland, and seeing things as the "Father" sees with all the powers of the Godhead when God opens it for you. It is not something we do ourselves. I have seen many videos on opening the pineal gland. I am here to tell you that you cannot do this yourself. And it is funny how you can watch a video on how to open the pineal gland. When the person doing the video has not opened the pineal gland. It would be robbing your way into heaven if God did not cleanse you first. You have to become a spiritual member of the body. It is a gift from God, not something you earn or can achieve alone.

Romans 15:14-16

14 And I myself also am persuaded of you, my brethren, that ye also are full of goodness, filled with all Knowledge, able also to admonish one another.

15 Nevertheless, brethren, I have written the more boldly unto you in some sort, as putting you in mind, because of the grace that is given to me of God,

16 That I should be the minister of Jesus Christ to the Gentiles, ministering the gospel of God, that the offering up of the Gentiles might be acceptable, being sanctified by the Holy Ghost.

Paul is trying to present all our souls as a living sacrifice to God. But notice in verse 16 that the Holy Spirit does the sanctifying, not something we do on our own.

Romans 15:17-20

17 I have therefore whereof I may glory through Jesus Christ in those things which pertain to God.

18 For I will not dare to speak of any of those things which Christ hath not wrought by me, to make the Gentiles obedient, by word and deed.

19 Through mighty signs and wonders, by the power of the Spirit of God; so that from Jerusalem, and round about unto Illyricum, I have fully preached the gospel of Christ.

20 Yea, so have I strived to preach the gospel, not where Christ was named, lest I should build upon another man's foundation.

Christ preached to the twelve Disciples; they were his foundation. Paul was not over the Spiritual minded but of those of a carnal state of mind. Paul preached to the gentiles explaining to the gentiles the path of the Spirit was from within. He was preparing them to receive faith (Peter) in the Word (Christ) from within themselves. Christ (The Word) from within leads you into the Spirit and awakens you. But how can you look for something you have never heard about? Enter Paul. Today, as back in his time, people did not understand the difference between flesh, soul, and Spirit. How can you see something if you need to know what you are looking for or where to look for it? How can you become part of the Spirit if you only see yourself as a mortal of flesh? How can you believe the Word of God if the Word dwells within you? If you only see the Jesus that lives without in the flesh? Paul came to answer all these questions for humankind, which is why the book of Romans is the essential book in the Bible. It is an instruction to put off the old man and put on the new man. For now, the world is full of Gentiles, those with the hearts of men. But we need a world with Jews, those with the nature of God. Whether you be black, white, brown, Russian, American, or Chinese, it does not matter. Spirit is not an expression of the flesh. The flesh is an expression of the Spirit. What kind of Spirit are you? Well, that's up to you and God.

One of the most important things to remember is something I have said over and over again in this book. And I am sorry, but I do it a lot on purpose. Because we need to reprogram the mind to get rid of the old man. But THERE IS ONLY ONE BODY, ONE SPIRIT, WITH MANY MEMBERS. To look at a race of people as different from yourself is just another trap of Satan's to keep the body divided. We must not try to unite as one Nation or a World. We must come together as one body of Spirit. Remember, Christ had many sheep of different flocks.

Romans 15:21

21 But as it is written, to whom he was not spoken of, they shall see: and they that have not heard shall understand.

Paul is talking about the awaking of the Gentiles. How the Gentiles would see and understand the Words of Christ come from within. That all should worship the "Father" and him alone.

Romans 15:22

22 For which cause also I have been much hindered from coming to you.

Paul is talking about the unenlightened ones of flesh or those of the carnal mind, coming after him for speaking the words of truth. A lot of sons of darkness do not like the truth getting out.

Romans 15:23

23 But now having no more place in these parts, and having a great desire these many years to come unto you.

They came after Paul so mightily that he had nowhere safe to go. It will be no different this time around.

Romans 15:24

24 Whensoever I take my journey into Spain, I will come to you: for I trust to see you in my journey, and to be brought on my way thitherward by you if first I be somewhat filled with your company.

The gospel was preached in all the world back then by the disciples. Paul shows this by going to Spain at the time. There are a lot of Gentiles in this world for the moment, but that is set to change soon.

Romans 15:25-27

25 But now I go unto Jerusalem to minister unto the saints.

26 For it hath pleased them of Macedonia and Achaia to make a certain contribution for the poor saints which are at Jerusalem.

27 It hath pleased them verily; and their debtors they are. For if the Gentiles have been made partakers of their spiritual things, their duty is also to minister unto them in carnal things.

Notice here that Paul is saying some of the gentiles had overcome and been partakers of the Spirit. Now they could preach and show how to overcome the carnal things of the fleshly man. To those that were of more a spiritual mind. Because even in the Spirit, mistakes have been made.

Galatians 2:11-14

11 But when Peter was come to Antioch, I withstood him to the face, because he was to be blamed.

12 For before that certain came from James, he did eat with the Gentiles: but when they were come, he withdrew and separated himself, fearing them which were of the circumcision.

13 And the other Jews dissembled likewise with him; insomuch that Barnabas also was carried away with their dissimulation.

14 But when I saw that they walked not uprightly according to the truth of the gospel, I said unto Peter before them all, if thou, being a Jew, livest after the manner of Gentiles, and not as do the Jews, why compellest thou the Gentiles to live as do the Jews?

The difference is when you learn in the Spirit, you do not justify the wrong. I am sure Peter told Paul, "You are right, Paul; thank you for showing me that." In which case God would not even see it. Because you are still eating from the Tree of Life and not the Tree of Good and Evil. Because of the deeds you were doing and where your heart was.

Romans 15:28

28 When therefore I have performed this, and have sealed to them this fruit, I will come by you into Spain

Paul was going to impart some knowledge (Fruit.)

Romans 15:29-31

29 And I am sure that, when I come unto you, I shall come in the fulness of the blessing of the gospel of Christ.

30 Now I beseech you, brethren, for the Lord Jesus Christ's sake, and for the love of the Spirit, that ye strive together with me in your prayers to God for me.

31 That I may be delivered from them that do not believe in Judaea; and that my service which I have for Jerusalem may be accepted of the saints.

Back then, it was a difficult time for true believers. Satan is the god of this world, then and now. Satan does not want souls to wake up to the truth. I know it will be no different in today's world. Life cycles have a way of repeating themselves. But I will let you in on a little secret I know, God wins God always wins.

Ecclesiastes 1:9-10

9 The thing that hath been, it is that which shall be, and that which is done is that which shall be done: and there is no new thing under the sun.

10 Is there anything whereof it may be said, see, this is new? It hath been already of old time, which was before us.

All things have been written down for all to see. But all had been given eyes to see (flesh) and not see (Spirit). And ears to hear (flesh) and not hear (Spirit). The Sun (The Word) was darkened, the Moon (the Foundations, the Apostles) turned to blood or the Knowledge was polluted. God has foretold all things, and all things come true.

Matthew 24:29

29 Immediately after the tribulation of those days shall the sun be darkened, and the Moon shall not give her light, and the stars shall fall from heaven, and the powers of the heavens shall be shaken.

Who do you think the stars are that fell from heaven? And if they fell from heaven, they are no longer in heaven. So, they would need to find their way back into heaven.

Romans 15:32

32 That I may come unto you with joy by the will of God, and may with you be refreshed.

Side note: Matthew's name means Will he is one of the Twelve Foundations in The New Jerusalem. Will is one of the Foundations that God will build within you. That you may have that perfect will to do everything perfectly.

Romans 15:33

33 Now, the God of peace be with you all. Amen.

Paul's works are stunning to read in the Spirit. They are instructions for us all to enter into eternal life. Not after we die, but right here and right now. By understanding, God does all the work. We need to stop working in the flesh to please God. The fleshly man is never going to please God in any lifetime. If you don't believe me, there are many lifetimes for you to look at for examples. Look out into the world today and pick any one of them you like to look at.

ROMANS 16

1 I commend unto you Phebe our sister, which is a servant of the church which is at Cenchrea:

2 That ye receive her in the Lord, as becometh saints, and that ye assist her in whatsoever business she hath need of you: for she hath been a succourer of many, and of myself also.

3 Greet Priscilla and Aquila, my helpers in Christ Jesus.

Women and the deception played on the world by the Roman Catholic Church. Satan does not want men and women coming together. The Church went so far as burning women alive and calling them witches back in the day. Women were property in the days of old. Women were a commodity and nothing more. Women are a help to men when he is climbing in the Spirit. As well as, men are a help to women when they are climbing into the Spirit. It is tough to climb into Spirit when fighting with a loved one. Not only are you fighting with your flesh, but your partner's flesh as well.

Women teach men about the aspect of the heart, the emotions, and how to use them in the perfected ways of God. Adam (masculine) and Eve (feminine) learn together what perfect desire is in Spirit from God. Men help women discern the matters of consciousness coming from the conscious mind. The mind, as well as the heart; both can think. The reason shows it in thought, the heart in feelings. We both have our different strengths in the soul while in the flesh. Men and women become one flesh with each other. And we already know the flesh does not please God. So, we help each other in matters of overcoming the flesh. Thereby both become one in the Spirit of God when manifested. The woman talks to God with the heart, and the man talks to God through conscious thought. Women get more of a feeling or intuition about God, as men get ideas in thought.

Definition from **Oxford Languages***:*

"Intuition"

"The ability to understand something immediately, without the need for

conscious reasoning."

Women use their hearts more to talk to God, as a feminine aspect. And men use the conscious mind to do so as a masculine principle. But at the end of the day, both men and women must use both. But while in the flesh, as **John Gray** would say: *"Men are from mars, women are from Venus."* So, men help guide the desire to more Godly things in Spirit. Women show how to use the feminine side of the heart in Spirit. This is the proper desire for Spirit. And men help to express a more perfect Spirit in masculinity in Spirit (mind). All souls being creators have both masculine and feminine traits. As long as the god of this world, Satan, can keep men and women divided, he wins. Men are not over women, and women are not over the man. When you become one, you are no longer two but one. It is like the hand trying to rule over the foot. The hands and feet work for the body without ever having to think about it, do they not? So, as you both become one in the flesh. Will you not become one in the Spirit? Seeing there is but one Spirit and one body. Suppose we cannot find a way to love our partners enough and humble ourselves to them. The ones we love and that we are one flesh with. How can we humble ourselves to God or anyone else? Love starts at home.

Ephesians 5:25

25 Husbands, love your wives, even as Christ also loved the Church and gave himself for it.

Christ laid down his life for the Church. As husbands, we should lay our lives on the Altar of God for our wives and children. Is that not what true love is supposed to be, to die for someone you love? If women have an unbelieving husband, should she not do the same?

Colossians 3:18

18 Wives, submit yourselves unto your own husbands, as it is fit in the Lord.

Notice that this verse says as, "it is fit in the Lord." Having nothing to do with the fleshly person. The Lord is a spiritual being, the masculine principle relating to Adam. The feminine principle in Spirit is Eve. Just as a magnet has two opposite poles. But just as a magnet has a positive and negative pole. No one can tell you where the negative and positive start within that magnet's positive and negative poles. They are both equal in their respective poles. In any relationship, people are always looking to be correct. Magnets do not work in this manner; they are the same. A magnet will only show resistance when another magnet tries to come at one of its poles or the other half of itself. Just as you should when someone is trying to separate you from your partner. I have found out more than once when my wife and I have come to some impasse about who was right and wrong. That God would show me we were both right and wrong simultaneously. Right in our perspective in looking at it. And wrong for not trying to see it from the other's perspective. To look at it from a different perspective is love for your partner. If we cannot become one with the family that we love. How shall we ever become one with the "Father"? It is against nature for two sides of the same magnet to work against themselves. But when it finds an idea that it is attached to, it slams into it and holds on for dear life. Not knowing which side is which until attraction or conflict comes calling. That is the true love the husband and wife should have in life. And if this is the love you do not have. Try putting the "Father" in both of your lives. If only one of you believes in God it is tough. But with God all things are possible.

There is a lot to learn from Mary Magdalene. Look past the message of the Church of Rome. See the message from the "Father" of Spirit.

John 20:11-14

11 But Mary stood without at the sepulchre weeping: and as she wept, she stooped down, and looked into the sepulchre,

12 And seeth two angels in white sitting, the one at the head, and the other at the feet, where the body of Jesus had lain.

13 And they say unto her, Woman, why weepest thou? She saith unto them, because they have taken away my Lord, and I know not where they have laid him.

14 And when she had thus said, she turned herself back and saw Jesus

standing, and knew not that it was Jesus.

Mary was seeing the faithful Christ, the Son of God. Mary could not tell who she was talking to in the flesh. Jesus was an image of Christ. Reread 14. she knew not that it was Jesus.

John 20:15

15 Jesus saith unto her, Woman, why weepest thou? Whom seekest thou? She, supposing him to be the gardener, saith unto him, Sir, if thou have borne him hence, tell me where thou hast laid him, and I will take him away.

Mary thought it was a gardener and not Jesus. Mary could not recognize the form that Christ had taken. Mary is pleading with the gardener, not knowing it was Christ, the Son of God, which took another flesh. Mary was trying to find out by who and to where Jesus had been taken to. It was not the only time Christ took another form to show up when meeting his followers.

John 20:16

16 Jesus saith unto her, Mary. She turned herself and saith unto him, Rabboni; which is to say, Master.

When Christ spoke Mary's name, she recognized the voice talking to her. It had awakened and stirred the Soul within her. Christ was also called Rabbi by many in the Bible. To be a Rabbi back in that period and not be Married was looked upon as a sin. The law saying to become fruitful and multiply and fill the earth was a commandment from God. So, being an unmarried Rabbi would have been almost unheard of back then. I have read books on Jesus being married to Mary Magdalen. All I know is the Bible has been messed with so much by the Romans it is hard to say. But as Adam had a wife and David had a wife. I do see where Jesus could have been married. It would be best if you remembered the Romans have gone to great lengths to separate the husband from the wife. Why would God deny Jesus the beauty of one of his creations? It is best to keep an open mind to all things. When I do, God reveals to me the truth in proper distance. You will never find the truth if you shut your mind off from any possible reality. It is another excellent tool of Satan's to get you to close your mind from asking a question, keeping you lost in a false belief.

Mark 16:1-3

1 And when the sabbath was past, Mary Magdalene, and Mary the mother of James, and Salome, had bought sweet spices, that they might come and anoint him.

2 And very early in the morning the first day of the week, they came unto the sepulchre at the rising of the sun.

3 And they said among themselves, who shall roll us away the stone from the door of the sepulchre?

For a single woman as Mary Magdalene was thought to be to anoint the body of a dead man, and that man was not her husband. It would have been a big no-no and a giant red flag back then. It was not just coming in contact with a dead man's body. But that she might see his nakedness, the issue itself deserves a lot of questioning.

Matthew 27:55

55 And many women were there beholding afar off, which followed Jesus from Galilee, ministering unto him.

Many women ministered to Jesus. Why was it so important to the churches to turn Women into witches? Satan has always separated the people. If you cannot see it in our society today, you are not looking too hard.

Matthew 27:56

56 Among which was Mary Magdalene, and Mary the mother of James and Joses and the mother of Zebedees children.

Here it states one of those women that ministered to Jesus was Mary Magdalene. Why call out Mary Magdalene here by name in the first place? Why not leave her with the other women in verse 55? We must question everything the Roman Catholic Church has had its hand in. They have been trying to rule the people by keeping them down in Spirit and separated from each other in both flesh and Spirit. There was a reason they wanted to destroy the women's reputation in the churches. The husband and the wife were to be one flesh; why? Husbands and wives today can't even do that.

1 Corinthians 11:8

8 For the man is not of the woman; but the woman of the man.

The woman was indeed of the man. But the man is of the woman by birth.

1 Corinthians 11:9

9 Neither was the man created for the woman, but the woman for the man.

Remember that the Bible was written for our souls' benefit, not our flesh's. I would also ask you to remember that there is no respect for persons with God, that includes men and women. Women have been created to help men (the Soul). So, ask yourself, if Women were created for man's help, what do they have that we need to understand the Spirit? As for the women, the man was also created to help lift women in the Spirit. The man and the woman working together in the "Father" is the only way this happens. The Soul of men governs with their brains; the Soul of women governs with their hearts. Both must be as one to conquer the desires of the flesh and the mindfulness of the fleshly things. Both men and women must do everything in love and the "Father."

1 Corinthians 11:10

10 For this cause ought the woman to have power on her head because of the angels.

I have one question, what power? I am sorry I don't have the answer to this yet. It is power, nonetheless, and all power and authority come from God.

1 Corinthians 11:11

11 Nevertheless, neither is the man without the woman, neither the woman without the man, in the Lord.

In Spirit, we are one because there is only one body and one Spirit. There is no husband and wife in Spirit in a fleshly view. So, the only way to understand this verse is in Spirit. The Soul itself has both masculine and feminine properties. It is saying here—both masculine and feminine properties to create.

1 Corinthians 11:12

12 For as the woman is of the man, even so, is the man also by the woman; but all things of God.

We are equal in Spirit, period. Let's look at Luke.

Luke 20:35

35 But they which shall be accounted worthy to obtain that world, and the resurrection from the dead, neither marry nor are given in marriage.

We are no longer married in Spirit. That is a deed for the fleshly man. Notice he said you shall become one flesh in Mark.

Mark 10:8

8 And they twain shall be one flesh: so, then they are no more twain, but one flesh.

In this world, you are one flesh. In God's Spirit, you become one Spirit.

Luke 20:36

36 Neither can they die any more: for they are equal unto the angels; and are the children of God, being the children of the resurrection.

The reward you receive for helping each other overcome this world is discussed here. But you must work as one in the flesh to help each other receive a resurrection to the Spirit. Look where it says they are equal to the angels. It does not say one is above the other. But another illusion by the Roman Catholic Church. If you research the Roman Conclave, you will understand that Pagans built the Roman Catholic Church's foundations upon pagan doctrines. Then you will see that the Romans built all their religions and philosophies, on the same pagan foundation that the Romans established worldwide. Through the Bible, the Romans put together all the wars they started worldwide—never having anything to do with love. They always came in so-called love but killed and ruled in greed of the flesh. God has never been with them, for they are all dead.

Romans 16:4

4 Who have for my life laid down their own necks: unto whom not only I give thanks, but also all the churches of the Gentiles.

Paul talks about women and men laying down their lives for him and the Word of God. The Romans did their best to scrub women from the history of God and Spirit and made them by words; ask yourself why? Men and Women need to put off this deception by the Roman Catholic Church. And form the new Church of God, as they did back then. So many people came together and came up with churches for the Gentiles. But they knew it was a short stop while their souls were manifesting into the body of God.

Romans 16:5

5 Likewise, greet the Church that is in their house. Salute my well-beloved Epaenetus, who is the firstfruits of Achaia unto Christ.

But Paul also was talking about the Church of the body here. Their house is the temple of God which they are. The first fruits are those who wake up in the Spirit first. They are Paul's fruit from his labor of waking them up in God.

Romans 16:6

6 Greet Mary, who bestowed much labour on us.

Again, the women labored as well as the men. We must all be resurrected from the death of sin while in this world through God. We are all like the angels of heaven when we overcome.

Matthew 22:30

30 For in the resurrection they neither marry, nor are given in marriage, but are as the angels of God in heaven.

Now, what does that look like? We can all use both the masculine and feminine principal in perfection. When we conform to the actual image of our "Father."

Romans 16:7

7 Salute Andronicus and Junia, my kinsman and my fellow prisoners, who are of note among the apostles, who also were in Christ before me.

These two Apostles could have been awake when Paul was still consenting to the Apostle's death back in the day. They may be in other books that never made it in the Bible, and many letters did not make it into the final book. The Vatican has been keeping them from the people as they do a lot of books that have genuine knowledge in them. If these books ever got out, they would no longer be able to control or rob the people of their money and souls. It would not be very good for business. Notice also that others besides the twelve became Apostles, as you can become one as well.

Acts 19:25-26

25 Whom he called together with the workmen of like occupation, and said, Sirs, ye know that by this craft we have our wealth.

26 Moreover ye see and hear, that not alone at Ephesus, but almost throughout all Asia, this Paul hath persuaded and turned away much people, saying that they be no gods, which are made with hands.

Having only one true God is bad for business, for people who live after the flesh.

Acts 19:27

27 So that not only this our craft is in danger to be set at nought; but

also, that the temple of the great goddess Diana should be despised, and her magnificence should be destroyed, whom all Asia and the world worshippeth.

They could not have Paul destroying their way of life and livelihood. Would it be any different today? What if people were turning to the Truth, and there was no need for their business anymore? How would they survive without your money and your slave labor? They have always counted on the children of God sleeping and not waking up.

Acts 19:28

28 And when they heard these sayings, they were full of wrath, and cried out, saying, Great is Diana of the Ephesians.

They cried out with WRATH, for goodness' sake. They were mad because they could no longer enslave the people's minds because of the Truth Paul spoke. They cried out to the false god Diana with no help. Today, they shall call out to the god Baal, and there shall be no help. God wins because God already won. After all, there is nothing outside of God. And no matter how they shall try and get wrath. They cannot vibrate at that frequency of Spirit. That frequency that only God and the children of light can. It is not of this realm, so they cannot match it. And God is frequency, God is energy, God is vibration, and God is rhythm. He is all this world's things and the beautiful realm of Spirit. And the wicked can never and will never match that frequency. No matter how hard they try, and they do try. That is why they have lost in the past, and that is why they will fail now.

Acts 19:29

29 And the whole city was filled with confusion: and having caught Gaius and Aristarchus, men of Macedonia, Paul's companions in travel, they rushed with one accord into the theatre.

And what do we say to this verse here? Well, only one thing can be said.

Matthew 10:28

28 And fear, not them which kill the body, but are not able to kill the soul: but rather fear him which is able to destroy both soul and body in hell.

We are in hell right now, which is a carnal state of mind is hell. The only way out is to rise our vibration to a higher level of Spirit, through the "Father."

Romans 16:8-14

8 Greet Amplias, my beloved in the Lord.

9 Salute Urbane, our helper in Christ, and Stachys my beloved.

10 Salute Apelles approved in Christ. Salut them which are of Aristobulus' household.

11 Salute Herodion, my kinsman. Green them that be of the household of Narcissus, which are in the Lord.

12 Salute Tryphena and Tryphosa, who labour in the Lord. Salute the beloved Persis, which laboured much in the Lord.

13 Salute Rufus chosen in the Lord, and his mother and mine.

14 Salute Asyncritus, Phlegon, Hermas, Patrobas, Hermes, and the brethren which are with them.

In verse 14, could this be Hermes Trismegistus? Thoth the great the philosopher. Probably not, but I love reading all of his writings. There are so many books to read when seeking God. For me, that is the fun in it all, the seeking. It's like playing hide and seek with God. When you read a book, saying to yourself. Will I find you in this book? Then you find out after reading all those books, he was not hiding in any of those books. They were just breadcrumbs that led you to his actual hiding place within you. Then when you find that out, the true game of hide and seek begins.

Romans 16:15

15 Salute Philologus, and Julia, Nereus, and his sister, and Olympas, and all the saints which are with them.

Paul, again, treats the women the same as the men, not as a lord over them. No matter how hard they try to take everything out and add stuff to the Bible, there are always breadcrumbs. There were many that overcame and became saints in that period of history.

Romans 16:16-17

16 Salute one another with a holy kiss. The churches of Christ salute you.

17 Now I beseech you, brethren, mark them which cause divisions and offences contrary to the doctrine which ye have learned; and avoid them.

If anyone preaches anything but love, forgiveness, mercy, perfection, and Holiness. That is a person you should stay far away from having an association with. You must love God with all your heart, mind, and soul. And love all others as yourself. To be perfect as your "Father" in heaven is perfect. It would help if you were careful listening to anyone teaching you repentance and that it is ok to sin. Telling you: ***"after all you are just a human."*** You are so much more than that. And you should see yourself as so much more than that. ***"Do not seek after men to understand God, but seek God to understand yourself and men." Ray Roberts***

Matthew 6:33

33 But seek ye first the kingdom of God, and his righteousness, and all these things shall be added unto you.

You must seek God, not settle for what you have heard from another person.

Romans 16:18

18 For they that are such serve not our Lord Jesus Christ, but their own

belly; and by good words and fair speeches deceive the hearts of the simple.

The Roman Catholic doctrine has deceived many a person. The ideology of most churches is structured on the Roman Catholic Church Pagan beliefs. They have changed some of the Bible to suit their needs to rule the people. And they have hidden many truths in the Vatican from the people. They only did this after some time. Whenever they would conquer a nation, they would take all their knowledge of God, destroy it, or keep it for themselves. Then they would teach them a new religion that imprisoned their minds and souls. One based on paganism, from old Roman and Viking gods. But God knows the hearts and deeds of all people.

Romans 16:19

19 For your obedience is come abroad unto all men. I am glad therefore on your behalf: but yet I would have you wise unto that which is good, and simple concerning evil.

All of the deeds of the flesh are evil to different degrees. That is the "simple concerning evil" Paul is talking about here.

Romans 16:20

20 And the God of peace shall bruise Satan under your feet shortly. The grace of our Lord Jesus Christ be with you. Amen.

Within you is the Tree of Good and Evil. Within you is the Tree of life. Somewhere within you, between you and heaven is the Garden of Eden. Within you is the war between good and evil, a place between unrighteousness and righteousness between God and Satan. It is all in a world within you. So, stay on the path and remain before the Altar of God. Remember, your faith is not in this world but in God. Satan will not be able to stand too much longer before fleeing from before you. Take heart, see what Job endured while climbing, but never tempt God in vain like saying within your thoughts. I would love God so much even if I lost ______. Cause and effect can bring all seeds to life.

Matthew 4:6-7

6 And saith unto him, if thou be the Son of God, cast thyself down: for it is written, He shall give his angels charge concerning thee: and in their hands, they shall bear thee up, lest at any time thou dash thy foot against a stone.

7 Jesus said unto him, it is written again, thou shalt not tempt the Lord thy God.

Your thoughts need to be watched at all times. But realize when you are making this change. That there is a lot of old programming there to delete. That programming is not your true self. But a false programing that did not happen overnight. Also, remember that programming is a memory. And not who you indeed are. You certainly can only be described as the consciousness of the now. It is the past and only an experience from a point in time that no longer exist except in memory.

Genesis 3:15

15 And I will put enmity between thee and the woman, and between thy seed and her seed; it shall bruise thy head, and thou shalt bruise his heel.

Eve was a living soul; her seed was a living soul. The serpent was a soul; I cannot tell you what kind of soul. But this is the war within all of us. Should I do it, or should I not do it? As far as DNA goes, you are 50% of Eve and 50% of the serpent, living in free will. But there is hope if you would just reach forth your hand and partake of the deeds from the Tree of Life. Do the works of your true "Father" and not the false father.

Genesis 3:22

22 And the Lord God said, Behold, the man is become as one of us, to know good and evil: and now, lest he put forth his hand, and take also of the Tree of life, and eat, and live forever.

We must reach forth our hands and seek God. We have always had the power to overcome and live forever. We have been lied to by Satan for a long time. He tells us it is impossible to be perfect when Christ commands us to be perfect.

Matthew 5:48

48 Be ye therefore perfect, even as your Father which is in heaven is perfect.

Being told and believing we are imperfect. Is the very thing that keeps us in the flesh.

1 John 3:9

9 Whosoever is born of God doth not commit sin; for his seed remaineth in him: and he cannot sin, because he is born of God.

Here it says if you are born of God (Spirit), You cannot sin. And that is precisely what Paul is showing us all to do. God's seed remains in us, the un-generated soul in man's body, that seed that must be quickened into a living spirit. Again, in Romans 8:11

Romans 8:11

11 But if the Spirit of him that raised up Jesus from the dead dwell in you, he that raised up Christ from the dead shall also quicken your mortal bodies by his Spirit that dwelleth in you.

It all happens while you live, not after you die. Can you see the deception of Satan yet?

Romans 16:21-22

21 Timotheus, my workfellow, and Lucius, and Jason, and Sosipater, my kinsman, salute you.

22 I Tertius, who wrote this epistle, salute you in the Lord.

I never knew Tertius wrote this epistle for Paul. It never ceases to amaze me how much you can learn—by reading these books repeatedly.

Romans 16:23-25

23 Gaius mine host, and of the whole Church, saluteth you. Erastus, the chamberlain of the city, saluteth you, and Quartus, a brother.

24 The grace of our Lord Jesus Christ be with you all. Amen.

25 Now to him that is of power to stablish you according to my gospel, and the preaching of Jesus Christ, according to the revelation of the mystery, which was kept secret since the world began.

These are the true secrets of secrets that have been kept hidden since the times of old. And I have read many secrets of secrets books over the years, all of them talk about a secret that is so secret it must be kept private from men because men might misuse the knowledge. I say hogwash, anyone can enter in, but you need to do the work in faith. And it must be done perfectly in the perfect law. The true secret everyone should share with the world is that the "Father does the works within you. No one is going to sneak their way into heaven with these words. Because the only way in is through love and the "Father." And you can't fake the act of love before God. The Truth is all you have to do is love. Not the way the world loves but a Spiritual love. It is knowing that we are all one body with many members. We are one atom (Adam) living next to the next atom (Adam) and just vibrating away at our frequency and vibration, dancing to the rhythm of this thing called life. The great mystery is you have to have faith in God and do the works at the Altar. You have to put yourself on the Altar as a free-will offering. You must love God with all your heart, mind, and soul. And your neighbor as yourself. If you want to enter the kingdom of God, you must want the All in All in All of us. Now the cat is out of the bag. And the big secret is revealed, faith in the "Father" and love are the keys that open all doors, and that lock is within you.

Romans 16:26

26 But now is made manifest, and by the scriptures of the prophets, according to the commandment of the everlasting God, made known to all nations for the obedience of faith.

Now is the time for the work to be done by All. All must rise as one, and the ones must increase in the All. All this can only be done with faith in God.

Hebrews 11:1

1 Now faith is the substance of things hopes for, the evidence of things not seen.

Do all things in faith in the "Father," not yourself or others. Some people will tell you to say things over and over to reprogram your mind and self. You should not because you would be working. Stop working and let God do it for you. Put in on the Altar and walk in that direction; that's the work. Faith knows God will get the job done.

Romans 16:27

27 To God only wise, be glory through Jesus Christ forever. Amen.

I hope that this book finds you some peace. Whoever you might be in this world. And in the body of the All in All of Spirit. I have been waiting for my brothers and sisters to talk with me for many years. It does my heart good to see so many people waking up. But be careful my brothers and sisters. Satan will not give up without a fight just because you are waking up. Refrain from trusting any man or politician to save the day. That is also another distraction created by Satan. He has been working on this for a long time. Remember, the flesh cannot please God. So, if someone is in the flesh and not Spirit, they are not pleasing God. If they are in the Spirit, they are without sin before God. Put on the whole armor of God.

1 Peter 5:8

8 Be sober, be vigilant; because your adversary the devil, as a roaring lion, walketh about, seeking whom he may devour.

Already I see so many waking up stumbling at the stumbling block and putting their trust in men to fix the world. The problems the world is having do not concern us. We are not of this world; we are of the body of Christ's Spirit. Everything else is a distraction to keep you in a lower vibration. The world and its problems cannot be fixed until we overcome the world in God.

1 Peter 2:8-9

8 And a stone of stumbling, and a rock of offence, even to them which stumble at the word, being disobedient: whereunto also they were appointed.

9 But ye are a chosen generation, a royal priesthood, an holy nation, a peculiar people; that ye should shew forth the praises of him who hath called you out of darkness into his marvelous light.

No man can fix the problems of this world; only God can.

John 17:16

16 They are not of the world, even as I am not of the world.

We are not of this world if you be of God.

John 15:19

19 If ye were of the world, the world would love his own: but because ye are not of the world, but I have chosen you out of the world, therefore the world hateth you.

This verse is for my daughter and son, as it was for me at their age. They do not understand that I felt the same as they do today about the world. We do not seek the love of this world. But only the love of the "Father" and the Word of God. In which that love flows through. They might not see it today, but they will; this is my faith in God. And my faith will not be shaken. This world is full of hatred and pain. Spirit is a world of love and peace. It is a world of rest from your labors.

I have covered this before, but I will cover it again.

2 Corinthians 6:14-17

14 Be ye not unequally yoked together with unbelievers: for what fellowship hath righteousness with unrighteousness? And what communion hath light with darkness?

15 And what concord hath Christ with Belial? Or what part hath he that believeth with an infidel?

16 And what agreement hath the temple of God with idols? For ye are the temple of the living God; as God hath said, I will dwell in them, and walk in them; and I will be their God, and they shall be my people.

17 Wherefore come out from among them, and be ye separate, saith the Lord, and touch not the unclean thing; and I will receive you.

The fight is not with this world; the war is within you. Trust me, the battle within you is big enough for anyone to fight. But we will overcome with the "Fathers" help in "The Word."

Revelation 19:13

13 And he was clothed with a vesture dipped in blood: and his name is called the Word of God.

For years I have always seen myself. Living in the streets, talking to people to explain all this. I never seen myself in a million years writing books. I do not see myself as being a very intelligent person in the least. You could probably find more than one grammar mistake in this book. That's ok as long as the Word gets across. Isn't God funny, and does he not have a wonderful sense of humor?

FINAL THOUGHT'S

Paul's Book of Romans is a journey from death to life, a quest in one's travel to find oneself in light when lost in a land of darkness. It is a journey from the man of the flesh to the man of the Spirit. Paul teaches us to put off the old man of flesh so that the new man of Spirit might live. Christ said it himself, and Paul was echoing the words of Christ.

John 4:23-24

23 But the hour cometh, and now is, when the true worshippers shall worship the "Father" in spirit and in truth: for the "Father" seeketh such to worship him.

24 God is a spirit: and they that worship him must worship him in spirit and in truth.

The message of the Bible has always been the same. The people need to understand that religion has been a tool of Satan, the same as today's media, schools, and governments. Look around you, see all the deception and lies, and ask yourself these questions. Is the world you know today the same as the one you grew up in when you were younger? Or has this world always been this way? And you are just now waking up to the fact that it is evil? The grandest deception Satan has pulled off is that people believe God does not exist or is some by word. But by far, the most significant con Satan has pulled is to get people to worship false idols, which are many. Satan has brought humanity to worship the image of a man—a white man with long blond hair and blue eyes. Just the image alone should tell you all you need to know. Let's look below for a minute at a couple of verses.

Exodus 20:4

4 Thou shalt not make unto thee any graven image or any likeness of anything that is in heaven above, or that is in the earth beneath, or that is in the water under the earth.

I was looking for the exception where it said it was ok to make an image of

Jesus and worship him, but I could not find it anywhere.

Exodus 20:5

5 Thou shalt not bow down thyself to them, nor serve them: for I the Lord thy God am a jealous God, visiting the iniquity of the fathers upon the children unto the third and fourth generation of them that hate me.

It says that God alone shall be worshipped, and we must worship God in Spirit, not flesh.

Isaiah 53:2

2 For he shall grow up before him as a tender plant, and as a root out of a dry ground: he hath no form nor comeliness; and when we shall see him, there is no beauty that we should desire him.

Here it says that Jesus would not be a handsome man. It says he was going to have no beauty to look upon. It also says he will have no form. Yet they make Jesus in the pictures an attractive person with long flowing hair. The Bible also talks about hair, saying long hair would not have been acceptable then.

1 Corinthians 11:14

14 Doth not even nature itself teach you, that, if a man have long hair, it is a shame unto him?

It would have been a shame for Jesus to have long hair; he would not have done it. But Satan's little helpers needed an image everyone would love and fall down and worship.

According to **The University of South Carolina's website** quote:

"But the all-time most-reproduced image of Jesus comes from another period. It is Warner Sallman's light-eyed, light-haired "Head of Christ" from 1940. Sallman, a former commercial artist who created art for advertising campaigns, successfully marketed this picture worldwide."

"Through Sallman's partnerships with two Christian publishing companies, one Protestant and one Catholic, the Head of Christ came to be included on everything from prayer cards to stained glass, faux oil paintings, calendars, hymnals, and night lights."

The site also states:

"No one knows exactly what Jesus looked like, and there are no known images of him from his lifetime. Art history professor Anna Swartwood House writes in The Conversation about the complicated history of the images of Christ and how historically they have served many purposes."

They talk about the head of Christ as if men can see it. Christ is Spirit as his "Father" is Spirit. I cannot believe that the Catholic Church would be involved in this picture; what a surprise. And don't say they did it for profit so that they could market his image to the masses. Do you see it? That it is not about your soul but your money and control.

Welcome to the image of the beast that all would fall and worship.

Revelation 13:15

15 And he had power to give life unto the image of the beast, that the image of the beast should both speak, and cause that as many as would not worship the image of the beast should be killed.

All that did not go along with the new religion the Romans had established were put to death by the Church. Not to mention that all are dead in sin and have been killed already. Jesus' son of man has spoken to the hearts of many people. And many worship the son of man instead of the "Father." All you have to do is study the Spanish Inquisition. All that would not fall down and worship this newly created image and religion of the Roman Catholic Church were tortured and killed. Just ask the Gnostics; oh yeah, you can't ask them; the Romans destroyed them all. They did not want to follow the new religion and what they were doing to the Bible. Wherever the Romans went with the cross before them, the Church never manifested love, only murder, and destruction.

Revelation 1:14

14 His head and his hairs were white like wool, as white as snow, and his eyes were as a flame of fire.

In Revelations, John describes what he saw as not someone with long blonde hair. It says here the hair was white; also, it was like wool. I do not know too many white men with hair like wool, do you?

Revelations 1:15

15 And his feet like unto fine brass, as if they burned in a furnace; and his voice as the sound of many waters.

If you burn brass without melting it in a fire, it just turns jet black. I know because I have tried it for myself.

The problem with idols is they are hard to put down because people believe in them with all their hearts. Here is an example to look at in Christianity. But you can revise it to anyone's religion. As a Christian, what do you think of someone that kneels to a Buda statue or worships a cow? Please take a second and honestly think about it. If you look to Jesus and the image of a man of flesh that Satan has sat up, the truth is. You are doing the same thing. You have made an image of something on earth and have bowed down to it. The "Father" alone is to be worshiped, and I hate the word worship. Because everyone should love the "Father" for the mercy, he has shown us. Worship, to me, is a word that means you have to do it. Love is something that comes from your heart. Love is something you want to do. We must put off all the illusions that the god of this world has made for us. And through God alone, move into the seventh day of rest.

Ezekiel 44:26

26 And after he is cleansed, they shall reckon unto him seven days.

The seventh day is a day of rest, the day you quit working in this world. You understand you cannot overcome this world no matter how much and how hard you try. You realize the only one that can do that for you is God.

Ezekiel 46:1

1 Thus saith the Lord God; the gate of the inner court that looketh toward the east shall be shut the six working days; but on the sabbath, it shall be opened, and in the day of the new moon it shall be opened.

The east is within the holy of holies as long as you are working and trying to do the job yourself in heart, mind, and soul. The inner courts are closed to you. Only on the seventh day, the day of God's rest, are they opened.

Ezekiel 46:12

12 Now when the prince shall prepare a voluntary burnt offering or peace offerings voluntarily unto the Lord, one shall then open him the gate that looketh toward the east, and he shall prepare his burnt offering and his peace offerings, as he did on the sabbath day: then he shall go forth, and after his going forth one shall shut the gate.

It must be a voluntary offering unto the Lord. Then the gates are opened to you. Then you enter God's rest. The gates shall be shut to all others still working in the six days of creation.

John 6:44

44 No man can come to me, except the "Father" which hath sent me draw him: and I will raise him up at the last day.

Christ (the Word of God) comes to us by way of the "Father." It is not the other way around. The Words of God, or the Word of God, raise us into the dimension of Spirit. Christ is those words, and he and the "Father" are one. The simplest way to see it is God is the cause, and Christ is the effect. To put Jesus or Christ first is to worship the effect before the cause of the effect. Christ is our brother in God.

Matthew 12:50

50 For whosoever shall do the will of my "Father" which is in heaven, the same is my brother, and sister, and mother.

Christ and Jesus never wanted you to worship them. Christ tried to tell us we were the same as him. Look at this verse; we only need to do the will of the "Father."

So, we need to stop trying, **let go, and then let God.** Enter into that seventh day through the purification process. Put all your faith in God to do all things in you. And you walk in the direction of that newness of life. Knowing that God is working in you and doing the work that he said he would. And you do this within 100%, Peter (perfected faith). That is the only way to become a brother, sister, and mother to Christ. The beloved one sent from God the "Father," the All in All. Now back to Ezekiel.

Ezekiel 42:27

27 And in the day that he goeth into the sanctuary, unto the inner court, to minister in the sanctuary, he shall offer his sin offering, saith the Lord God.

Here is the place within yourself where you offer your free will offering to the "Father." It is an offering of the sin that dwells within you that you no longer want to be a part of. Here is where you offer yourself up to be crucified with Christ. You are the Temple of the living God.

Galatians 2:20

20 I am crucified with Christ: nevertheless, I live; yet not I, but Christ liveth in me: and the life which I now live in the flesh I live by the faith of the Son of God, who loved me and gave himself for me.

We must also be crucified with Christ, just as he was. He is also saying that the Word of God (Christ) also lived in him. All this happens when you live by faith in God and nothing else, not yourself. He was living by the faith (Peter) in the Word (Christ) that the "Father" sent to him.

Ezekiel 43:5

5 So the spirit took me up, and brought me into the inner court; and, behold, the glory of the Lord filled the house.

Ezekiel was lifted into the Spirit. Here is where the inner court is, Where the Glory of the Lord dwells, and that place is within you. The inner court is that place. That is on the other side of the veils placed on your eyes.

2 Corinthians 3:16

16 Nevertheless, when it shall turn to the Lord, the veil shall be taken away.

These are the veils it is talking about; when you are purified, they are done away within you, seeing all things as they are in truth and Spirit.

Ezekiel 43:3

3 And it was according to the appearance of the vision which I saw, even according to the vision that I saw when I came to destroy the city: and the visions were like the vision that I saw by the river Chebar; and I fell upon my face.

Heaven is within you, where God lifts you into the Spirit—where you have visions and are lifted into God's spiritual body.

Ezekiel 42:28

28 And it shall be unto them for an inheritance: I am their inheritance: and ye shall give them no possession in Israel: I am their possession.

God is the inheritance, not a piece of land in Israel or any other place on earth. It is a place where God dwells in you, and you in God, and you are one. Just as Christ and the "Father" are one. We live in God, and God lives in us. There is only one body with many members.

God is Spirit, and the whole world needs to ask themselves four little questions. That will start them on a journey down a rabbit hole that will last them a lifetime to seek the answers. What is the fleshly man? What is a soul? What is a spirit? And how do I know which one I am dwelling in?

If the only way to please God is to be in the Spirit 24 hours a day, 7 days a week. We should all want to know what it feels like to be in Spirit. If the flesh cannot please God, are you pleasing God? That would depend. Are you in the flesh?

A lot is riding on these four questions. And I can tell you they lead to a lot more questions. I have spent many nights crying at the Altar of God for these answers. I pray that it keeps you from having to do the same. I know they come to me in God's distance of travel and not mine. I hope God sparks an ember in your soul. And you can genuinely feel the power of Spirit within yourself.

The Altar is where this incredible journey starts. Just knock on the door. If God does not answer right away, keep knocking until God does. Leave a gift of a will offering at the door. Faith is the doorbell for the door within you. Ring it loud for all to hear. Pick up an umbrella in the middle of July when no rain is in the forecast and not expected, and tell other people it is going to rain. When they think you are out of your mind, watch it rain. Remember, see the rain, feel the rain, feel it puddle up in your mind. Stand in it barefoot and feel the mud in between your toes. Then, after all, that, say: "thank you for hearing me "Father." Have faith and stand back because it is going to rain. Now do the same with knowledge, wisdom, and God's understanding. Then stand back because it is going to rain within you. The Water of the Word of God will rush over you. And start your soul growing on a journey upward.

The Bible, as well as all spiritual books written over the years, are all beautiful books with a lot of knowledge. But if you do not have the Spirit to guide you through them. You will need to receive the understanding and wisdom to go along with them. God is that knowledge, understanding, and wisdom that we all need. The flesh and the mind of the fleshly man profit nothing when it comes to the knowledge of the Spirit.

Galatians 5:24

24 And they that are Christ's have crucified the flesh with the affections and lusts.

If you have yet to undergo the crucifixion of the flesh, how can you be in Spirit? And if you have yet to do this, how do you know what Spirit feels like and what Spirit truly is? These are all questions that you must answer for yourself.

I have come to my conclusions, as you must yours. Satan and his demons are alive and well, as they have always been. Satan and his demons are spiritually alive in the flesh of men. They are ruling this world in spiritual wickedness. They know what they are doing and who they are. And they war against all souls waking and sleeping. Then we have the sons of God waking up to the fact that they are not of this world and want nothing to do with this war. You also have those waking up and getting entrapped in the illusion within an illusion of this war. They are both spiritually conscious to some extent. Then you have the people of the flesh. They know nothing of the actual battle or the spiritual beings they are. They go about as serpents on the ground of this earth, eating dust.

Knowing nothing of the war, they are slaves to this earth and their father, the devil. They know not that they are dead in sin. They see themselves as mere mortals instead of the gods they are. Satan sees you as nothing more than someone to do his bidding, knowingly or unknowingly. But make no mistake; he is laughing either way. Remember how Christ cast out the demons back then that lived in men? It is no different today. Remember, God, cast down one out of three hosts of heaven to earth. How many then are on earth now? The same number.

Matthew 7:15

15 Beware of false prophets, which come to you in sheep's clothing, but inwardly they are ravening wolves.

Matthew 8:28

28 And when he was come to the other side into the country of the Gergesenes, there met him two possessed with devils, coming out of the tombs, exceeding fierce, so that no man might pass by that way.

It is the same today and no different. People stopped looking for them because of the deceptions of Satan.

Matthew 8:29

29 And, behold, they cried out, saying, what have we to do with thee,

Jesus, thou Son of God? Art, thou come hither to torment us before the time?

Satan was even working in this verse. We have already seen how Christ is the son of God, and Jesus was the son of Mary. But even the demons know how far they have to travel, and it is short.

Matthew 8:30-31

30 And there was a good way off from them an herd of many swine feeding.

31 So the devils besought him, saying, if thou cast us out, suffer us to go away in the herd of swine.

It is better to have the coat of skin of a pig to be manifested in. Then not to have a coat of skin at all.

I can write a book and tell you what I think, as untold people have done over the years. But it is you, sooner or later, that is going to have to have your relationship with God. I am nothing special; God is the only remarkable thing. I would not be where I am today if God had not called me out of the darkness, I was living in. He has been teaching me ever since. God has been justifying me in this world. And he and only he is my Glory that dwells within me. And every day, he shows me more and more how we are one. And if God is for me, who can stand against me?

2 Corinthians 5:17

17 Therefore, if any man be in Christ, he is a new creature: old things are passed away; behold, all things are become new.

Stand in the Word, my brothers and sisters.

Matthew 7:7-12

7 Ask, and it shall be given you; seek, and ye shall find; knock, and it shall be opened unto you.

8 For every one that asketh receiveth; and he that seeketh findeth; and to him that knocketh it shall be opened.

9 Or what man is there of you, whom if his son ask bread, will he give him a stone?

10 Or if he ask a fish, will he give him a serpent?

11 If ye then, being evil, know how to give good gifts unto your children, how much more shall your "Father" which is in heaven give good things to them that ask him?

12 Therefore all things whatsoever ye would that men should do to you, do ye even so to them: for this is the law and the prophets.

"Some look to the skies to see heaven, the wise find heaven within them." Ray Roberts

Amen

Made in the USA
Columbia, SC
02 December 2024

48215365R00200